BRITISH HISTORY

ENCYCLOPEDIA

From early man to present day

BRITISH HISTORY

ENCYCLOPEDIA

From early man to present day

This is a Parragon Book
This edition published in 2001

Parragon
Queen Street House
4 Queen Street
Bath BA1 1HE, UK

2 4 6 8 1 0 9 7 5 3 1

Produced by Miles Kelly Publishing Ltd
Unit 11, Bardfield Centre, Great Bardfield, Essex CM7 4SL

British Library Cataloguing-in-Publication Data
A catalogue record for this book is available from the British Library

Hardback ISBN: 0-75254-333-4
Paperback ISBN: 0-75254-482-9

Printed in Dubai, U.A.E.

Authors: Nicola Barber and Andy Langley

Project Manager: Sarah Eason

Assistant Designer: Angela Ashton

General Editor: Louisa Somerville

Designer: Branka Surla

Artwork Commissioning: Suzanne Grant

Picture Research: Lesley Cartlidge

Editorial Assistants: Helen Parker and Liz Dalby

Consultant: Clare Robinson

Art Director: Clare Sleven

Editorial Director: Paula Borton

Director: Jim Miles

CONTENTS

THE HISTORY OF BRITAIN 6

EARLY BRITAIN 10

THE MIDDLE AGES 50

TUDORS AND STUARTS 90

THE HISTORY OF BRITAIN

The British Isles lie off the northwest corner of the European mainland. The area that they cover is smaller than that of most European countries, and is well away from the centre of the continent. They are surrounded by sea. The climate is wet and rarely very warm, and the winters can be harsh.

A simple description like that does not sound very promising. Indeed, for many thousands of years the islands were barely inhabited. Most of them were covered with ice. Even a thousand years ago, Britain was still a weak and backward land. Invaders from Italy, Germany, Scandinavia and France had swept over the land, bringing their own languages and customs.

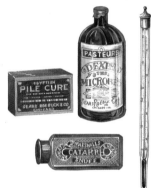

Yet in the last millennium, Britain steadily grew into one of the strongest and most influential countries in world history. The islands were never conquered again. In the 16th century, England became a stronghold of the Protestant version of Christianity. During

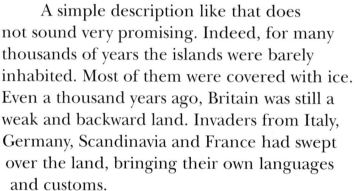

the 17th century, the British people developed a system of government by parliament which was later to be copied in many other countries. The great revolutions in farming and industry that were to take place worldwide, began in Britain in the 18th century. In the 19th century, the development of a massive British Empire brought power and wealth to the nation. And in the 20th century, Britain played a vital part in saving Europe from the threat of Fascism during World War II.

c.2 million BC Mammals begin to colonize the British Isles.

c.500,000 BC First people migrate to Britain from Europe.

c.6500 BC Seas rise, cutting British Isles off from mainland Europe.

c.4500 BC New Stone Age begins; farming peoples arrive from Europe.

c.3000 BC First stone circles erected.

c.2150 BC People learn to make bronze weapons and tools.

c.750 BC Iron Age begins; iron replaces bronze as most useful metal.

c.700 BC Celtic peoples begin to arrive from Europe.

55 BC First Roman landing on south coast of England.

AD 43 Roman invasion of Britain under Emperor Claudius.

AD 401–410 Romans withdraw from Britain; Anglo-Saxon migrants begin to settle.

789 First Viking raids on British coast.

1066 Norman invasion of Britain under William of Normandy.

EARLY BRITAIN

The first part of this book covers a huge period – more than two million years. This is much more than any other section. Chapter Two covers about 500 years, and Chapter Three just 200 years. The last chapter, about modern Britain, deals with less than 100 years.

Why is there such a massive difference? For a start, we know very little about Britain in prehistoric times. Nobody wrote anything down, and all our information comes from fragments of fossil, bone, metal and other relics. From these, historians and scientists have built up a picture of early British life. But the picture is not complete or definite. It is like a giant jigsaw puzzle with most of the pieces missing.

The second reason for covering such an enormous period is that very little happened for most of that two million years. For the first million and a half years, there were probably no human beings in the British Isles. The hills and valleys were roamed by mammals that had crossed over the land "bridge", which joined Britain to mainland Europe at that time.

About half a million years ago, people began to arrive. They were hunters, pursuing the animals that they needed for food. At first, they simply wandered in small groups, sheltering in caves or crude shelters.

They learned skills, such as lighting
fires, cooking food, gathering plants
and making sharp flint tools. The most
important change only occurred about
4,500 years ago. People learned how to
be farmers. They herded livestock and
grew special crops. This meant they could
build more permanent homes, and clear
bigger patches of woodland. With more
food and safer lives, the population of
Britain began to increase.

The First Britons

Half a million years ago, the world was in the grip of an Ice Age. Temperatures everywhere had fallen. In the coldest places – the north and the south – sheets of ice covered land and sea, more than 200 metres thick in places. Only the area near the Equator remained warm.

This was the middle of the most recent Ice Age. There have been many "ice ages" in the world's long history, but each one has contained warmer periods, when part of the ice has thawed. These warmer periods are called "interglacials" and we are living in one now.

At its coldest, the freezing climate brought amazing changes. Most of Britain, except for the extreme south, disappeared beneath the ice. The seas froze over. In fact, so much water had turned to ice that the level of the sea was much lower than it is today. There was dry land connecting Britain with the mainland of Europe.

Across this land "bridge" came people from Europe. They were probably different from us, for they belonged to an earlier type of human,

c.2 million BC Beginning of most recent Ice Age; first mammals probably arrive in Britain.

c.700,000 BC Early human, *homo erectus*, migrates to Europe from Africa.

c.500,000 BC *Homo erectus* crosses land bridge from Europe to Britain.

c.450,000 BC Settlers in southern Britain use hand axes made of flint.

c.230,000 BC New type of human (Neanderthal) begins to displace *homo erectus*.

c.225,000 BC Flint toolmaking a highly developed craft, especially in the Kent area.

c.120,000 BC Temperatures rise, thawing the worst of the glaciation; many more mammals migrate north to Britain.

△ *Large animals such as early elephants were difficult to hunt. Plants and small birds were easier prey. But one elephant might provide enough meat to feed a group of people for a month. To catch these huge creatures, hunters drove them into marshy ground and killed them with stones and spears.*

c.70,000 BC Another period of glaciation begins.

c.30,000 BC First modern humans (*homo sapiens sapiens*) in Britain displace Neanderthals.

c.23,000 BC Last period of most recent Ice Age begins.

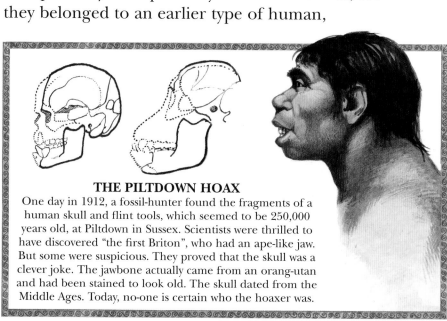

THE PILTDOWN HOAX

One day in 1912, a fossil-hunter found the fragments of a human skull and flint tools, which seemed to be 250,000 years old, at Piltdown in Sussex. Scientists were thrilled to have discovered "the first Briton", who had an ape-like jaw. But some were suspicious. They proved that the skull was a clever joke. The jawbone actually came from an orang-utan and had been stained to look old. The skull dated from the Middle Ages. Today, no-one is certain who the hoaxer was.

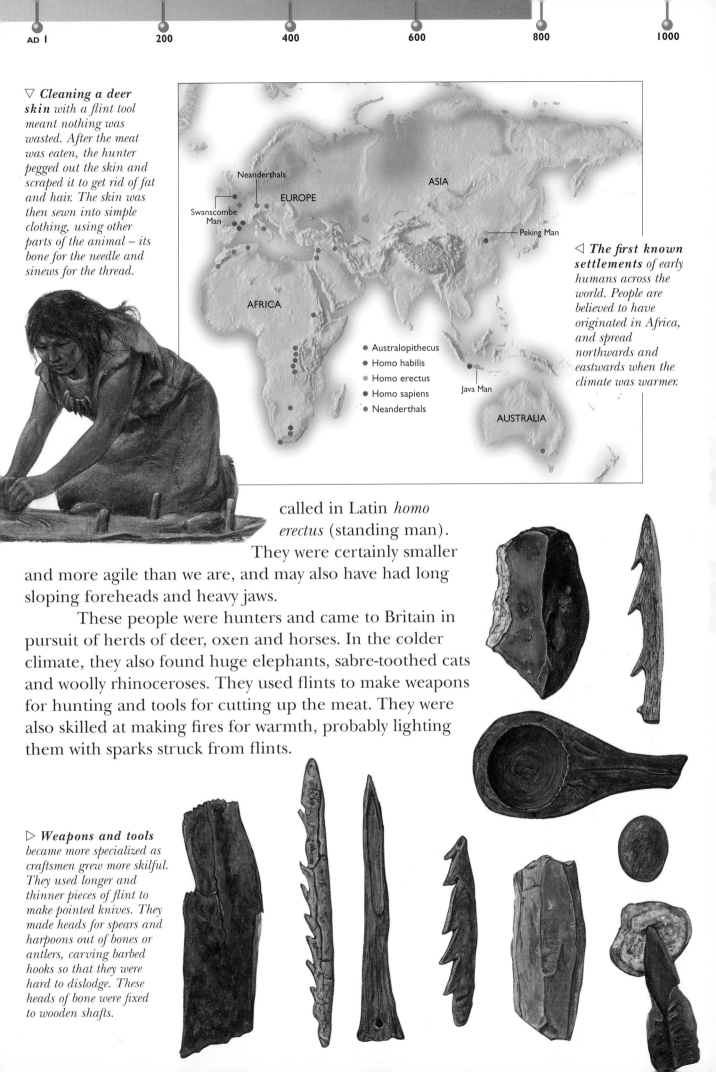

▽ *Cleaning a deer skin with a flint tool meant nothing was wasted. After the meat was eaten, the hunter pegged out the skin and scraped it to get rid of fat and hair. The skin was then sewn into simple clothing, using other parts of the animal – its bone for the needle and sinews for the thread.*

Neanderthals

EUROPE   ASIA

Swanscombe Man

Peking Man

AFRICA

◁ *The first known settlements of early humans across the world. People are believed to have originated in Africa, and spread northwards and eastwards when the climate was warmer.*

- Australopithecus
- Homo habilis
- Homo erectus
- Homo sapiens
- Neanderthals

Java Man

AUSTRALIA

called in Latin *homo erectus* (standing man). They were certainly smaller and more agile than we are, and may also have had long sloping foreheads and heavy jaws.

These people were hunters and came to Britain in pursuit of herds of deer, oxen and horses. In the colder climate, they also found huge elephants, sabre-toothed cats and woolly rhinoceroses. They used flints to make weapons for hunting and tools for cutting up the meat. They were also skilled at making fires for warmth, probably lighting them with sparks struck from flints.

▷ *Weapons and tools became more specialized as craftsmen grew more skilful. They used longer and thinner pieces of flint to make pointed knives. They made heads for spears and harpoons out of bones or antlers, carving barbed hooks so that they were hard to dislodge. These heads of bone were fixed to wooden shafts.*

The Ice Age

c.30,000 BC New cultures reach Britain from Europe; settlers bring new technology, using wood, bone and antler as well as stone.

c.23,000 BC Last glaciation of the most recent Ice Age begins; settlers have reached as far north as Derbyshire (the Creswell Crags).

c.18,000 BC Greatest extent of glaciation; ice covers everything north of the Severn Estuary.

c.16,000 BC Only larger mammals can survive the cold; very few humans remain in Britain.

c.12,000 BC Climate grows slightly warmer; hunters return during the short summer months.

Over thousands of years, the climate slowly changed. After periods of intense cold, temperatures would rise and some of the ice sheet over Britain would thaw. At these times, more hunters would cross the land bridge and settle in the river valleys of the south. Then the great freeze would spread again, forcing people to retreat southwards to warmer regions.

The people, too, were changing. The first arrivals had been replaced by Neanderthals, an early type of modern human beings. Historians gave them the Latin name of *homo sapiens* (wise man). Then, about 30,000 years ago, a race of taller humans began to appear in Britain. These are (confusingly) called *homo sapiens sapiens*, to show that they were more advanced than the Neanderthals. They are our true ancestors.

By this time, people had learned better ways of coping with the chill of winter. Some built simple huts, with frames of animal bones covered with skins. Many also made homes in caves, which sheltered them from the bitter winds and were easier for keeping fires lit.

The last great freeze-up began in about 23,000 BC. Gradually, the climate grew colder again, and the ice sheet crept down from the north. Life for early humans in Britain became slowly harsher. The only ice-free region was the extreme south of England, and this was no more than a soggy wasteland,

△ **Hunting game** *in about 25,000 BC. Our ancestors developed better hunting techniques than the Neanderthals. They made traps for animals, as well as fishing with lines, hooks and harpoons. They may even have used nets and boats. Unable to compete, the Neanderthals probably died out.*

c.10,000 BC Thaw increases, and ice retreats; settlers reach as far north as Morecambe Bay.

c.8000 BC Floods force settlers to move to higher ground, such as the moors of North Yorkshire.

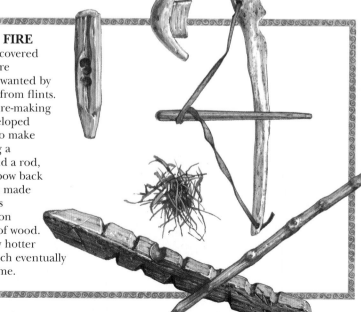

MAKING FIRE
People first discovered how to make fire whenever they wanted by striking sparks from flints. Later, special fire-making tools were developed using friction to make heat. Wrapping a bowstring round a rod, they drew the bow back and forth. This made the rod spin, its point rubbing on another piece of wood. The point grew hotter and hotter, which eventually produced a flame.

▷ **One of the most important early sites** in Britain is Goat's Cave in Paviland, Glamorgan. About 20,000 years ago, a young man was buried here. His corpse was hoisted up into the cave – which is nine metres from the ground on a sheer rock wall. He was covered in red ochre and wore ivory bracelets and a necklace of wolves' teeth. An elephant's skull marked the cave entrance. The skeleton was only discovered as recently as 1823.

where few plants could survive. Animals were scarce, so there was little to eat. Most people moved southwards into warmer mainland Europe to get away from the ice.

In about 12,000 BC temperatures began to rise again very slowly. The ice retreated northwards, and the thawing water drained away into lakes and rivers. The returning hunters were often forced to take refuge in hilltop caves to escape the floods of meltwater. They moved steadily to the north towards what is now Scotland, migrating from the coasts inland.

▽ **Striking a spark.** Humans were the only animals that could make fire. This was important for many reasons. Fires kept people warm through long winter periods and were also used to cook meat. Fire could also scare away dangerous animals or frighten prey, such as deer or mammoths, into boggy ground where they could easily be killed.

◁ **Woolly mammoths** had thick skins to keep them warm in the icy climate. Plant-eating animals such as these were the first to move into new areas, looking for food. They were followed by the flesh-eaters, which fell into two main groups – dogs and cats. The most fearsome cat was the sabre-toothed tiger. Its huge pointed canine teeth were perfectly adapted for stabbing through the thick hide of the mammoth.

15

The Forest Dwellers

By about 8500 BC Britain was almost as warm as it is today. The ice had retreated everywhere, except for the tops of the mountains. The melting water drained down to form rivers, lakes and pools. The sea level rose, so that by 6500 BC the land bridge between southern England and Europe was under water. Britain and Ireland were now islands.

This brought problems for the groups of wandering hunters. They could no longer get back to the European mainland and were forced to settle in Britain. Only a few could build boats strong enough to cross the sea to Ireland. The rising waters also covered many of their best hunting grounds.

▽ *A mask made of deer antlers, with eye holes. People devised better ways of hunting animals. They learned to stalk or ambush their prey. Some hunters disguised themselves with masks like this, and with deer skins, so that they could creep near the animals without being noticed.*

But the thaw made life easier too. The rising temperature and the moisture encouraged plants to grow. Trees began to cover the landscape. Increasing shelter and food attracted many animals, including beaver, red deer and wild boar. The woodland also made a fine home for the growing numbers of British settlers, who by about 6000 BC had spread to most parts of the British Isles. Trees provided unlimited timber for building huts and fuelling fires. There was game to hunt, as well as seeds, fruits and nuts to gather. People on the coast harvested shellfish from the shallow waters and trapped fish in rivers.

ARROWS

Spears and axes were hard to use in thickly wooded areas. By 7000 BC, people were starting to use bows and arrows to hunt game. They were skilful enough to make thin blades of sharp flint for their arrow tips. Hunters also learned that their arrows flew straighter if they had feather flights fixed at the rear end.

▷ *Forest dwellers gathering food. In about 6500 BC, most people in Britain were nomads, wandering the land in search of food. Many moved to higher ground in summer, returning to the shelter of the woods in winter. But in the following centuries they developed into tribal groups, settling in one area and adapting their lifestyles to suit their environment.*

GATHERING FOOD

Wild foods formed an important part of people's diet. Their favourites probably included hazel and pine nuts, tender shoots of birch and willow, and mushrooms. They gathered nuts and seeds in autumn and stored them for the winter. When a patch of "wildwood" was cleared by burning, there was room for young bushes and plants to grow. Their fruits were easier to gather than those of tall forest trees.

c.8500 BC End of the last Ice Age; woodland and lakes begin to spread over southern Britain.

c.7000 BC First settlers move into southern Scotland and northern Ireland; hunters use bows and arrows.

c.6500 BC Sea rises isolating British Isles from Europe.

c.6000 BC Most parts of British Isles now occupied; settlers burn clearings in woodland to encourage green plants.

c.5800 BC Hunting groups begin to develop into tribes with their own territories.

c.5500 BC Hunters on Scottish coast use boats; settlers in southern England live in more permanent huts.

c.4500 BC Woodland covers British Isles, except for extreme north and mountains.

The hunting and gathering of food took up most of people's time. They developed ways to make this easier. By burning areas of woodland, they found that bigger animals such as deer and wild cattle had more space to breed. They discovered that new plants grew in the clearings, which became a better source of fruits and grains to eat. Open country was also suited to building more permanent huts, with sunken floors of beaten earth, and stone hearths.

△ *Trees* in England were mostly hornbeam and lime, in Ireland hazel and elm, and in Scotland and Wales hazel and oak.

Farming Begins

c.4500 BC Arrival of first farming peoples from northern Europe.

c.4400 BC Emmer wheat, barley and other cereal crops are widely grown.

c.4300 BC Woodlands are coppiced (managed) to produce straight, regular wooden poles; in Somerset, poles are used to construct a trackway across the marshy Levels.

c.4100 BC Clay pots made in southern England for storing and cooking food.

c.4000 BC Farmers begin to use ploughs hauled by oxen; clearing of woodland for farming increases; permanent settlements established in Orkney and Shetland islands.

c.3700 BC Farming flourishes in Ireland.

c.3400 BC Causewayed camp constructed at Windmill Hill, Wiltshire, probably as settlement with corrals to keep in livestock, and a market place.

The life of a hunter-gatherer depended every day on what he could find. In the depths of winter there was often little to eat. By 4500 BC, things were getting even harder. As the population of Britain grew, game was being killed in greater numbers. The herds of wild deer and cattle grew fewer and more difficult to find in the dense woodland.

Then new settlers arrived from Europe. They were the first British farmers. The idea of growing crops and keeping livestock had developed in the Near East centuries before, and spread slowly westwards. The new farmers came in boats from northern Europe, carrying seeds of barley and wheat for growing annual crops. They also brought animals to rear for meat, including pigs, cattle and sheep, as well as tame guard dogs.

▷ *Villages*, such as this one at Skara Brae, were built by small communities on the Orkney islands. They built strong, stone-built houses, with roofs of driftwood and thatch. They were sunk slightly below ground to shelter them from the gales.

△ *A fired clay pot. The farming people brought with them the skills to make pots of fired clay. Some were decorated with grooves and spirals, while others were smooth and shaped like bags. Pots like these were used to store grain or milk. Later, special pots were made for religious rituals.*

▷ *An early farming settlement. One-roomed houses were built of mud and timber, and roofed with pieces of turf or with straw thatch. Men and women prepared the cleared land for crops by digging it over with flint or wooden picks. Livestock was fenced into small fields just outside the settlement.*

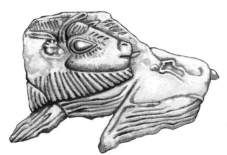

◁ *A carving of a bull made in stone.* A large cattle herd was a symbol of a man's power and wealth. Herders seized areas of land from their neighbours for grazing their animals.

Instead of wandering in search of wild food, they settled in one area and grew their own. They chopped down trees with flint axes. Then they sowed seeds and built fences to enclose their animals. In the autumn, they harvested the crops and butchered most of their livestock, leaving enough to produce young for the next year.

Farming shaped a new way of life in Britain. People now needed to stay where their crops grew and their animals grazed. Men stopped hunting and looked after their herds. Women usually tended the growing cereals. Gradually they gave up their nomadic lives to build permanent homes and storehouses. By 3500 BC there were farming settlements in most parts of Britain. Agriculture also speeded up the destruction of the ancient wildwood. Cattle and sheep chewed on the young shoots, preventing new trees from growing, and so allowing grass to establish itself. More land was cleared for sowing crops. Over the next 3,000 years, nearly half of Britain's woodland disappeared.

SCOTLAND

IRELAND

ENGLAND

WALES

● Windmill Hill and related sites

△ *The main centres settled* by the farming peoples from about 4500 BC onwards. The most suitable areas were in fertile valleys or near supplies of flints and other useful materials.

c.4500 BC The Neolithic (New Stone) Age begins with the arrival of farming peoples from Europe; they introduce more elaborate burial ceremonies.

c.3700–3400 BC Building of earliest long barrows and chambered tombs, such as Wayland's Smithy in Wiltshire, New Grange in County Meath and Pentre Ifan in Dyfed.

c.3500 BC Causewayed camps constructed at Windmill Hill, Wiltshire and Maiden Castle, Dorset; first wooden "henge" built at Stonehenge site in Wiltshire.

c.3300 BC Henge monuments built at Stenness and Brodgar in the Orkneys.

△ *Circles of standing stones may have been used for human sacrifices and fertility rituals. The earliest circles were probably made by setting upright huge stones left behind by melting glaciers at the end of the Ice Age.*

c.3100 BC Corpses buried singly in shaft graves in Yorkshire.

c.3000 BC Early stone circles erected in northern England, including Castlerigg in Cumbria.

c.2900 BC Corpses cremated and their remains buried in small graves beside other monuments in Dorchester and Oxfordshire.

c.2800 BC Complicated burial rituals in use at tombs of West Kennet, Wiltshire.

Tombs and Temples

Once they settled in their farming communities, early Britons learned how to live and work together. The richest among them owned the most cattle and people from the strongest or wealthiest families became leaders of the settlement. Warrior chieftains often led attacks on other groups, seizing their livestock or grain, or taking their grazing land.

But they did not spend all their lives simply farming or fighting. After about 3600 BC they began to build large monuments, some of which took an enormous amount of time and effort. The earliest of these were "camps" on hill tops. Rings of ditches and banks were dug around a large open space, with causeways crossing them.

No-one knows exactly why these camps were made, but they may have been religious centres, where annual ceremonies were held, connected with nearby graves.

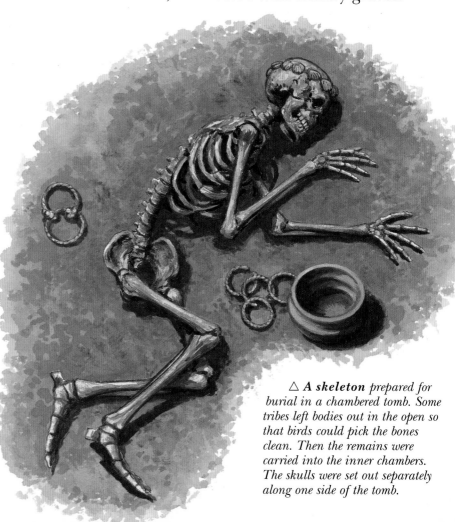

△ *A skeleton prepared for burial in a chambered tomb. Some tribes left bodies out in the open so that birds could pick the bones clean. Then the remains were carried into the inner chambers. The skulls were set out separately along one side of the tomb.*

▷ *Cutaway of the long barrow* at West Kennet in Wiltshire. Over 100 metres long, this is one of the largest barrows in Britain. Inside is a passage with chambers on each side.

GRAVE GOODS

Dead ancestors were honoured by most Neolithic people. Beside the bodies in the tombs, they placed "grave goods" which the dead might need in the next world. These included tools, weapons (such as flint arrow heads), jewellery, pottery and food. The entrances to some tombs were later blocked off with stone slabs, perhaps to prevent robbers ransacking these goods. The tombs often became the centre for elaborate rituals. On special days, such as solstices and equinoxes, people did homage to their dead ancestors. Priests performed these rituals.

At the same time, grand tombs were being built to hold the bodies of chieftains and their families. Earlier peoples had buried their dead in simple graves, but these were the first tombs to be built up into field monuments. Some were rectangular mounds of earth called long barrows. Others, called chambered tombs, had stone spaces inside, with walls and roofs made of big slabs of rock.

Each tomb was the burial place for a family or group over many years. As many as 50 bodies might be buried in one long barrow. Tombs and barrows like these have been found all over the British Isles. Among the most famous are New Grange in Ireland, Belas Knap in Gloucestershire and Maes Howe in the Orkneys.

After about 3400 BC, people began to build larger centres for religious worship. The earliest of these were circles of wooden posts called "henges", set inside round ditches and banks. By 3000 BC, the first circles of standing stones were being erected in Britain.

△ *Grave goods included bronze daggers* (above) and axes, as well as jewellery and other decorative goods.

c.2500 BC The Beaker people migrate westwards from the Rhine and arrive in Britain; coppersmithing skills spread swiftly, notably to southern Ireland.

c.2150 BC Smiths discover how to make bronze alloy from copper and tin.

c.2100 BC Stonehenge becomes a cult site for the Beaker people.

c.1900 BC Flint tools superseded by more malleable bronze.

c.1800 BC Trade in bronze weapons links Britain with Brittany.

c.1700 BC Wessex goldsmiths produce beautiful ornaments to be buried in graves of the wealthy.

c.1600 BC Trade boom in southwest thanks to tin-mining industry.

△ *Bell-shaped earthenware was decorated by the Beaker people by marking it with cords or combs. Some beakers were for burial rituals, and were placed in tombs at the corpses' feet. Beakers were probably also used for drinking a kind of beer, made from fermented barley.*

c.1500 BC Power of Beaker people declines.

c.1450 BC Snowdonia in North Wales becomes the centre of the bronze boom.

c.1150 BC Techniques for making sheet metal reach Britain from Europe.

c.1000 BC Bronze is made stronger and easier to work by mixing it into an alloy with lead.

Bronze Age

In about 2500 BC, a new wave of settlers began arriving on the east coast of Britain from mainland Europe. They are known as the Beaker people because of the bell-shaped decorated pottery cups they used. These people also brought with them a new and important skill – the making of metal tools and weapons.

Stone was still the most widely used material for axe-heads and knife blades. But the Beaker people knew how to make these things out of copper and how to make jewellery and ornaments from gold. They had also developed processes for mining the ore (the rock which contained the metal) and heating it to extract the copper.

Pure copper was too soft to make an effective tool. By about 2150 BC metalworkers were adding tin to make a tough new alloy, or mixture, called bronze. It could be bent or moulded to exact shapes, and honed to give it a sharp cutting edge. At first, metal-workers only used bronze to make small daggers and ornaments. These were not everyday tools, but were placed in tombs as grave goods. As craftsmen grew more skilful over the next 1000 years, bronze replaced stone as the main

▽ *A lunula, or crescent-shaped necklace, fashioned from a single sheet of beaten gold. As coppersmiths and goldsmiths grew more skilful, they could make more daring shapes such as this. Decorative patterns on these ornaments were often copied from pots made by the Beaker people.*

dress pattern

bracelet

▷ *People learned to spin thread and weave woollen cloth during the Bronze Age. Wealthy people began to wear woollen clothes instead of animal skins. Women pinned their hair up tidily with bone pins.*

THE HORSE

The bones of horses have been unearthed in some tombs in southern England, such as West Kennet. People had always hunted herds of wild horses for their meat, but the Beaker people may have been the first to tame them for riding. They were only the size of a small pony, so they could not be used for ploughing or other heavy work.

material for the blades of tools such as axes, spears, arrows and knives.

Britain had large supplies of copper ore in several regions. Tin ore was found only in Devon and Cornwall, and this area became an important centre of trade. Tin miners sent their products by sea all over the British Isles, as well as mainland Europe. In this way a network of trading routes grew up, stretching as far as Spain. By 700 BC Britons were exporting copper, tin and precious metals, as well as animal hides and fleeces. In exchange, they got finished bronze ornaments and tools, and exotic materials such as amber and jet.

▽ *A Bronze Age hut. Most dwellings were still simple, with thatched or brushwood roofs over scooped-out hollows in the ground. But in some areas, more permanent houses were built. One farming settlement on Dartmoor contained over 20 round huts with walls, fireplaces and benches made of granite.*

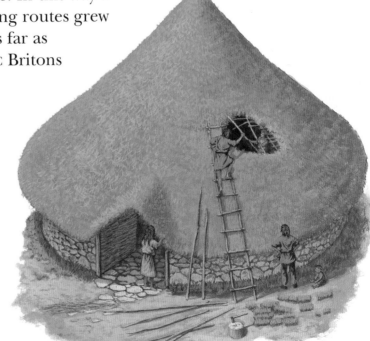

Circles of Stone

c.3300–3200 BC Earliest stone circles built on northwest coast of Britain; also New Grange, County Meath.

c.3100 BC Last long barrows dug; circle at Ballynoe, County Down.

c.3000 BC Circle at Stenness, Orkney.

c.2800 BC First stage of Stonehenge, Wiltshire, made of timber.

c.2600 BC Early copper working; circles at Avebury, Wiltshire.

c.2400 BC Circle at Arbor Low, Derbyshire; also at Merry Maidens, in Cornwall.

c.2200 BC Second stage of Stonehenge; first round barrows appear; erection of Druids' Circle, Gwynedd.

c.2100 BC Third stage of Stonehenge; many smaller circles erected.

△ **Drums carved from chalk**, unearthed at Folkton in Yorkshire. They had been buried next to a child in a round barrow. Among the designs etched on the stone are the face of a goddess (with eyebrows and eyes), pairs of circles and geometric patterns.

c.2000 BC Circle at Callanish, Outer Hebrides.

c.1900 BC Circle at Berrybrae, Grampian.

c.1700 BC Circles at Beaghmore, County Tyrone.

c.1200 BC End of circle-building era.

The greatest of the prehistoric monuments were the circles of standing stones. When the Beaker people arrived in Britain, several stone circles had already been erected. Built from about 3300 BC onwards, they stood in places as far apart as the Lake District, Orkney and southern Ireland.

Over the next millennium, many more circles were completed. By about 1200 BC more than 900 had been built. Some, such as Avebury in Wiltshire, cover a huge area over a kilometre around. Others are much smaller.

The largest circles needed a vast amount of work over a long period of time. Some stones were transported over long distances, probably by boat, and then hauled on sledges by teams of oxen. Hundreds of labourers dug the encircling ditches and the holes for the stones to rest in. The stones had to be shaped and trimmed, then pulled upright with ropes so that they stood firm.

Some circle sites changed greatly over the centuries. The most famous of all, Stonehenge in Wiltshire, went through several different phases. In about 2800 BC a circular ditch and bank were constructed, with sarsen stones to mark the entrance. Six centuries later, Beaker people brought vast "bluestones" from South Wales and

BURIAL URNS

People in northern Britain developed the burial customs of the Beaker people. By about 2200 BC, they were placing their dead in round barrows (circular mounds covered with turf or boulders). The bodies were laid on their sides, bent as if they were asleep. Some were cremated and the ashes placed in special urns (shown here). The urns were closed with flat stones and buried in the round barrows.

◁ *A wooden sceptre* found in Bush Barrow, near Stonehenge. It has a head of rock and is decorated with bone. This probably belonged to one of the powerful chieftains who ruled a kingdom during the Bronze Age. Also in the barrow were three daggers, a shield and an axe. Over his chest was a patterned gold sheet, and at his waist was a golden hook.

SCOTLAND

IRELAND

ENGLAND

WALES

erected two rings, one inside the other. In about 2100 BC, bigger sarsens were set up as a series of "trilithons" – two standing stones with one laid on top. In about 1550 BC, the original bluestones were raised in a circle inside the trilithons.

Nobody knows for certain what these circles were for. They may have been temples where religious rituals took place. Some believe the stones were set out so that people could watch the Sun's changing path and keep track of the seasons.

△ *The major sites of stone circles* and Bronze Age burials that have been rediscovered. Most are concentrated in northeast Scotland, and the northern and southern ends of Ireland.

◁ *Stonehenge as it is today.* Though several of the original trilithons still stand, many stones have fallen down or been taken away over the centuries. The sarsens in the outer ring weigh as much as 25 tonnes each. The smaller bluestones were brought from Wales, over 240 km away.

▽ *Druids* were Celtic priests who worshipped in groves of oak trees. Some people believe that they also held ceremonies in stone circles such as Stonehenge.

25

Iron Age Farmers

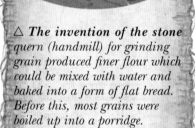

△ *The invention of the stone quern (handmill) for grinding grain produced finer flour which could be mixed with water and baked into a form of flat bread. Before this, most grains were boiled up into a porridge.*

▷ *Harvested grain crops were stored under thatched shelters or in pits. Farmers took out the sheaves when needed and threshed them by beating or using oxen to trample them. This broke up the straw and released the grains from the ears.*

In 750 BC, the population of the British Isles was only about 150,000. However, there were enough people to make a great change to the landscape. England, for example, had once been almost entirely covered with woodland. Now, nearly half of that woodland had disappeared: burned, or felled with axes, to make farmland.

At about the same time, ironworking reached Britain from southern Europe. Smiths learned to extract iron from its ore, and to transform it into weapons and tools. Iron was better than bronze in many ways. It was much tougher and easier to work. Iron ore was also cheaper and more plentiful than copper (the main ingredient of bronze). Britain moved into what is known as the Iron Age. Using axes and picks with iron blades, farmers could clear land more quickly. More important still was the development of the iron-tipped plough. Drawn by a pair of oxen, this could churn up the soil more quickly and deeply than the old wooden plough or bronze hoe. The easiest way to drive a team of oxen was in a straight line. Fields were also ploughed across at right angles, so many Iron Age fields were shaped roughly square.

CHARIOTS

Wheeled carts and chariots were used in the Iron Age. Warriors became very skilful in handling war chariots in battle. A soldier mounted behind the driver and two horses as they raced along enemy lines. He threw spears or shot arrows, then leapt off to fight on foot. Many important chieftains were buried with dismantled war chariots as well as weapons.

Iron Age buildings were clustered together, usually surrounded by their well-fenced arable fields and perhaps an earth bank or timber palisade (fence). Beyond these was the rough grazing for livestock. The main crops were wheat and barley, which were harvested with iron sickles. The grain was either dried (using hot stones) and stored in pits or stacked in huts raised from the ground away from rats. Besides cattle and pigs, farmers were now raising more sheep than ever before, mainly for their wool and milk.

▽ *Specialized metal tools* were being made by smiths for farmers. The bronze "terret" was for attaching the yokes of carts to oxen. The iron reaping-hook with its bone handle was used to cut down grain crops at harvest time.

△ *Inside an Iron Age farmer's hut.* Food was cooked in a metal pot hung over the central fire – the smoke escaped through a hole in the roof directly above. Everything had to be made on the farmstead, including woven cloth, pottery and iron tools.

Celtic Times

c.**500 BC** Increasing number of Celtic peoples migrate to Britain.

c.**400 BC** Climate still warming up, making it possible to grow crops on upland regions.

c.**325 BC** Weapons are increasingly decorated, showing influence of European cultures.

c.**250 BC** Growth in metalworking in southern England; warrior chieftains in Yorkshire buried with dismantled goods including carts or chariots.

c.**175–21 BC** Invasion of southern Britain by Belgic tribes from mainland Europe.

c.**125 BC** Gold coins first used as currency in southeast England.

△ *The round house from an Iron Age farm of about 300 BC. It was reconstructed in Hampshire in the 1970s, using evidence which had been dug up nearby. The experiment showed that Celtic farming methods were very efficient, producing more than enough food to eat.*

c.**100 BC** Growing trade with Rome via her province of Gaul.

c.**90 BC** Introduction of the potter's wheel revolutionizes pottery making.

c.**60 BC** Wine from Italy begins to be imported into southern Britain.

55 BC Julius Caesar makes first Roman landing in Britain.

c.**AD 30** Cunobelinus builds up rich and powerful Celtic kingdom in southeastern Britain.

All through the Iron Age, settlers from mainland Europe continued to flow into the British Isles. As trade increased across the Channel, there was greater contact between Britain and the continent. By about 500 BC, it is clear that a new kind of culture was spreading across lowland Britain. This belonged to a people we now call the Celts.

The Celtic tribes probably came from central Europe and moved outwards into parts of Italy, France and Spain as well as Britain. The Celts were farmers and lived – like Iron Age people – in small village groups in the centre of their arable fields. These groups slowly collected together into larger tribes, living in their own special regions. Each tribe was ruled by a king or queen. There was an "upper class" of warriors (who grew long moustaches) and a "lower class" of slaves and labourers, who did most of the agricultural work.

Celts were also a warlike people. The tribes often quarrelled with each other and fought savage battles. They could be a terrifying sight for the enemy.

△ *The Celts were fine craftsmen, who made splendidly decorated metal weapons and ornaments. This bronze shield was found in the river Thames. It was probably not meant to be used in battle, and may have been an offering to the river god.*

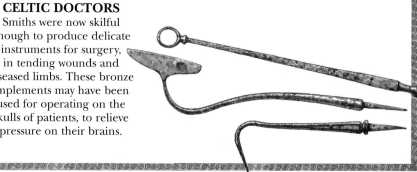

CELTIC DOCTORS

Smiths were now skilful enough to produce delicate instruments for surgery, in tending wounds and diseased limbs. These bronze implements may have been used for operating on the skulls of patients, to relieve pressure on their brains.

Many Celtic warriors were taller than southern Europeans, and many fought naked, their long, fair hair stuck up into spikes whitened with lime. They screamed as they ran into battle, waving their iron swords and blowing horns and trumpets.

      The Celts were proud of their appearance. They kept themselves remarkably clean, using special soaps and perfumes. Their tunics, shirts and cloaks were often colourfully dyed or embroidered, and they loved wearing belts and ornaments of gold and silver. A festival was an excuse for a great feast, where warriors could boast and bards could praise their deeds in songs and poems.

▽ *A Celtic round house was often a large and cleverly made structure. The biggest could be as much as 12 metres high and 13 metres wide. The roof was supported by timber from 200 trees and weighed several tonnes. The walls were made of wattle (split and woven branches) covered in daub (clay, mud or dung mixed with lime and water).*

△ **This gold torque** *is typical of the kind of neck rings that both men and women liked to wear. It was probably made by craftsmen in East Anglia, who also produced beautiful brooches, weapons and mirrors.*

▷ **The shape of a horse** *was made by a local tribe on the downs at Uffington. It was made by stripping away the turf to expose the white chalk beneath. The White Horse is 110 metres long and 40 metres high.*

29

Religions and Ritual

The Celts were ruled by kings and queens, but there was another class which was almost as powerful. These were the priests, or Druids. They were in charge of religious rituals, and settled arguments between tribes or individuals. They set the times for the annual festivals that marked vital moments in the farming year, such as ploughing or harvest. They were also teachers, in charge of educating the sons of tribal leaders.

To become a Druid, you had to be born as part of the warrior class. You were chosen by a vote among your tribe, though sometimes candidates had to fight each other to decide who joined the priesthood. Then came the training, which might last as long as 20 years. Druids had many privileges. They did not have to take part in wars, yet they shared plunder gained in battle. They also had great influence on the decisions made by their rulers.

The main job of the Druids was to organize religious activities. The Celts believed in many gods and goddesses, as well as spirits and sacred animals and birds. These magical

△ This relief tells the story of a Celtic myth. The Druid on the far left is performing a human sacrifice to please the gods. The Celtic religion was full of myths and legends. Each tribe had many different customs and gods, with their own stories. The Druids were the only people who knew the myths, together with the correct spells and chants.

▽ This bronze cup shows a horse and the heads of gods in relief. Celtic craftsmen developed many new skills, copied from the techniques used in Greece and the Near East. They liked to decorate everything they made, from iron and bronze shields and swords to pottery, mirrors and coins.

◁ A stone cross from Saxon times, intricately carved using Celtic designs. The cross is, of course, a symbol of the Christian faith, which swept away most Celtic religion during late Roman times. But this cross still uses Celtic symbols, showing that traces of the old religion lived on for many centuries.

30

creatures controlled every part of a person's life. Among them were Sucellos, the sky god, with a hammer that caused lightning, and Nodens, who made clouds and rain. Others had no names, but lived in springs, woods and other places.

The Druids were the link between the supernatural world and the ordinary human one. They were able to predict what would happen in the future, by interpreting the flight of birds and other natural happenings. They also tried to please the gods by giving them sacrifices. Humans as well as animals were killed in religious rituals. Sometimes, the sacrifices were placed inside giant baskets made of wicker and burned to death. Druids claimed that they could also tell the future by watching the death struggles of the victims.

THE HORSE GODDESS

The goddess with a horse depicted by this statuette was called "Epona". Her name comes from the Celtic word *epos*, meaning "horse". There were several horse-goddesses in Celtic mythology, including Rhiannon, the Great Queen. Horses figure in many other legends, from Pegasus the Winged Horse of Greek legend to Sleipnir, the eight-legged horse ridden by Odin, chief god of Norse mythology.

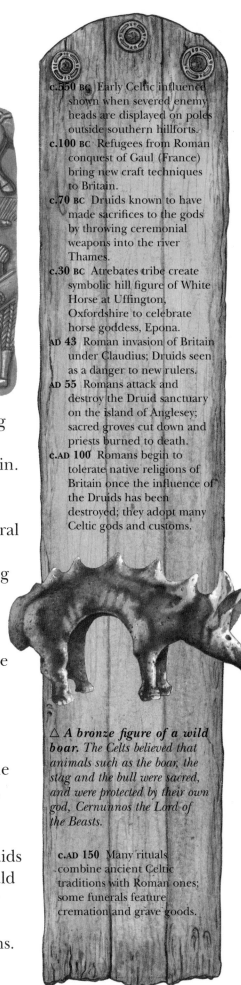

c.550 BC Early Celtic influence shown when severed enemy heads are displayed on poles outside southern hillforts.

c.100 BC Refugees from Roman conquest of Gaul (France) bring new craft techniques to Britain.

c.70 BC Druids known to have made sacrifices to the gods by throwing ceremonial weapons into the river Thames.

c.30 BC Atrebates tribe create symbolic hill figure of White Horse at Uffington, Oxfordshire to celebrate horse goddess, Epona.

AD 43 Roman invasion of Britain under Claudius; Druids seen as a danger to new rulers.

AD 55 Romans attack and destroy the Druid sanctuary on the island of Anglesey; sacred groves cut down and priests burned to death.

c.AD 100 Romans begin to tolerate native religions of Britain once the influence of the Druids has been destroyed; they adopt many Celtic gods and customs.

△ *A bronze figure of a wild boar. The Celts believed that animals such as the boar, the stag and the bull were sacred, and were protected by their own god, Cernunnos the Lord of the Beasts.*

c.AD 150 Many rituals combine ancient Celtic traditions with Roman ones; some funerals feature cremation and grave goods.

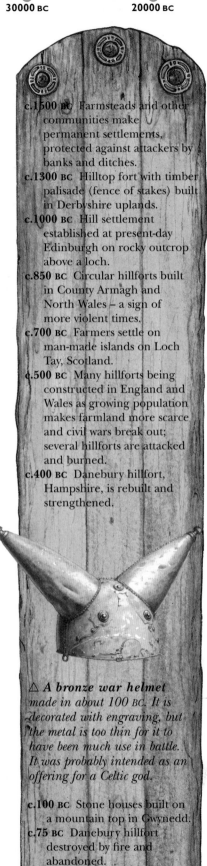

△ *A bronze war helmet made in about 100 BC. It is decorated with engraving, but the metal is too thin for it to have been much use in battle. It was probably intended as an offering for a Celtic god.*

Celts and Hillforts

Britons had been building forts on hilltops since before 1500 BC. These were places of refuge, which were difficult for an enemy to attack. Ringed with ditches and banks, they gave a good view of the land all around. Cattle and food stores could be kept inside, as well as supplies of weapons.

The earliest forts were probably farmsteads or villages with simple wooden stockades (barriers made of stakes) around them, to keep out wild animals or human raiders. Then people began to choose sites on higher ground, which were easier to defend. As Britain's population grew, so did the threat of attack from other tribes. People needed strongholds to retreat to in dangerous times.

They dug ditches around the summit of a hill and heaped the earth into banks. Then they erected double stockades of timber and filled between them with rammed soil and rubble. Sentries could patrol along the top. Some large hillforts, such as Maiden Castle, in Dorset, had several rings of ditches and stockades.

Most hillfort sites were uneven. The ditches and ramparts had to follow the contours of the hills they were

built on. A few had slopes on each side, making them almost perfect strongholds. Other forts were built on narrow cliff headlands which jutted out into the sea, so that an enemy could only approach along the narrow neck.

These hillforts gradually changed from being emergency places of safety into more permanent settlements. By about 100 BC, the larger ones had grown into towns, their streets lined with timber huts and grain stores. They became the headquarters for the local tribe and centres of trade.

SCOTLAND

IRELAND

ENGLAND

WALES

◻ Hill forts
◼ Smaller defended sites

◁ *A Celtic war trumpet, or carynx. It consists of a long metal tube, which broadens out into a large horn end shaped with the head of a sacred animal. The trumpet was held upright when it was being blown. The Celts rushed into battle to the blare of instruments like this, as well as their own yells and screams. They often fought without armour, and painted their bodies in bright colours. They attacked with slings and stones, spears and long swords, and defended themselves with metal helmets and shields made of wood and leather.*

△ **The major sites of hillforts** in Celtic Britain. By the time the Romans first settled in Britain in 55 BC, there were nearly 1,400 hillforts in England and Wales alone, and over 400 in Scotland.

△ **A Celtic hillfort.** The gateway is protected by a small earthwork at the front, and by timber gatehouses on either side. The palisaded (fenced) walls round the settlement are built on top of earth banks. Inside, there are huts of wood and mud – some for living in, others for storing food or weapons. The tribal meeting hall is at the centre.

Roman Invasion

55 BC Julius Caesar's first raid on southeast England.

54 BC Second Roman landing; Kentish tribes defeated.

AD 40 Roman emperor Caligula calls off invasion of Britain when his troops mutiny.

AD 42 Death of Cunobelinus, most powerful British leader.

AD 43 Major Roman invasion of Britain; Emperor Claudius visits the island.

AD 44 Claudius celebrates the invasion of Britain with a triumphal procession in Rome.

AD 47 Roman armies reach Devon and Cornwall in the west.

AD 51 Caratacus, last major leader of British resistance, is captured in Wales.

△ *Julius Caesar became one of Rome's three leaders in 60 BC. He conquered Gaul (France) in a brilliant campaign, then raided Britain. Back in Rome, he ousted his colleagues and made himself dictator, but was assassinated five years later.*

AD 60 Revolt of the Iceni tribe, led by Queen Boudicca, is suppressed.

AD 77 Agricola subdues Welsh tribes.

AD 84 Agricola defeats Caledonian tribes in Scotland.

In 55 BC a fleet of 80 Roman ships landed on the coast of Kent. This was the first raid across the English Channel by Julius Caesar, the Roman leader in Gaul. But it was short-lived. The invaders were beaten back by storms and by resistance from local tribes. The next year Caesar returned with 800 ships. This time he defeated the Kentish tribes, who agreed to give him hostages and pay a yearly tribute (sum of money). Soon Caesar had more urgent business and returned to Gaul.

It was not until almost a century later that the Romans made a serious attempt to conquer Britain. The Emperor Claudius wanted to secure trading links with the island. He also needed an easy victory to boost his standing in Rome. So in AD 43 a force of 40,000 Roman troops landed in Kent. They defeated the local leader Caratacus, who fled westwards. Claudius arrived to lead his army into Colchester, where ten tribal chiefs surrendered to him. Even the king of the Orkney islands, far to the north, sent a promise of loyalty.

The invaders now spread out to establish their control over lowland Britain. One legion marched to the southwest, where they dislodged the local tribes from their strongholds. Two legions went north, establishing a series of forts. By AD 61 Roman rule reached the river Humber in the north and the Severn in the west. The advance went on for the next 20 years. Under their governor, Agricola, Roman troops subdued Wales and northern England.

▷ **The Roman army** *is shown in this carving defeating a German tribe. It was a ruthless and well-trained fighting machine. Few could match the Romans' discipline and battle tactics. Staying in close formation, they walked towards the enemy and flung iron spears. Then, still in a straight line, they drew their short swords and closed in, stabbing and slashing as they moved.*

Then they penetrated into Scotland, defeating the Caledonian tribes in the Grampian Hills in AD 84. Britain was now the Roman Empire's newest province.

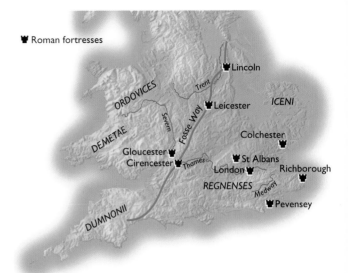

▽ Roman fortresses

△ **The major strongholds** built by the Romans by about AD 100 are shown on this map. At this time they controlled most of southern Britain. The names of the most powerful Celtic tribal areas are shown in capital letters.

△ **Boudicca,** leader of the Iceni in East Anglia, rebelled against brutal treatment by the invaders. Her army destroyed Colchester, St Albans and London before it was crushed by the Romans. More than 80,000 Britons were killed.

▷ **The Roman footsoldier's sword** was a short, double-edged stabbing knife called a "gladius". It was sheathed in a wooden or leather scabbard which hung from a belt round his waist or shoulder. This sword, with its decorated scabbard and handle, would probably have belonged to an officer.

35

Edge of the Empire

Britain lay at a corner of the enormous Roman Empire, and more than 1,200 kilometres from Rome itself. A treacherous sea cut it off from mainland Europe. Many British tribes, such as the Caledonians and Brigantes of the north, threatened rebellion. How did the Romans control this remote province?

The answer was the army. Roman soldiers were the strongest, best-armed and best-trained in the world. After the invasion, there were over 50,000 troops in Britain – nearly 10 percent of the Roman army. Most of these were in the highland areas of the north and west, where peace was harder to maintain.

The soldiers were stationed in fortresses. The largest of these were built at key points such as Chester, York and Caerleon. There were also dozens of smaller bases, most of them spaced one day's march apart. Between the fortresses the Romans built a network of stone-covered roads, so that armies could travel swiftly across country.

87 Romans give up attempt to subdue the Scottish Highlands and withdraw south.

105 Romans withdraw from Scottish Lowlands.

118 Revolt by the Brigantes in northern England.

c.120 Major road-building programme begins.

△ *Roman legionaries' sandals were usually made of heavy leather with iron studs in the soles. They also used leather for making aprons, straps for their armour, shields and tents. Each fort had its own tannery for curing leather from cattle hides.*

122 Building work begins on Hadrian's Wall.

c.125 Britons join Roman army.

140 An advance north: work begins on the Antonine Wall.

c.150 Britain and Ireland included in world map compiled by the Greek geographer Ptolemy.

163 Romans withdraw from Antonine Wall.

208 Emperor Septimius Severus divides Britain into two provinces.

c.217 Most of Britain now peaceful.

◁ *A Roman centurion commanded a "century" of about 80 foot soldiers. Centurions wore plumed helmets and specially coloured cloaks. The century was the army's basic unit: a group of six centuries made a cohort, and ten cohorts made a legion. There were up to 30 legions in the whole army.*

▷ *Hadrian's Wall. In AD 122, the Emperor Hadrian ordered a wall to be built from the Solway Firth to the North Sea, to separate the rebellious Brigantes from the northern tribes. In spite of their early victories, the Romans never conquered Scotland or the far north.*

They also organized Britain to make it easier to rule. They divided the land into regions, each one based on a tribal area. Much of the day-to-day governing of the regions and tax collecting was left to local chieftains. So the chieftains kept most of their power – but only if they remained loyal to Rome.

△ **Soldiers patrolled the wall** *night and day, watching both sides for enemy movements. Summer might be warm, but woollen cloaks and leggings were needed for the cold, wet winters.*

▽ **The map shows** *Hadrian's Wall stretching from the Solway Firth to the North Sea. The army headquarters were at Carlisle.*

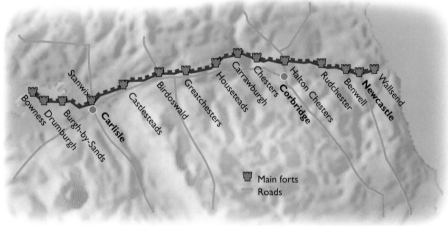

Bowness
Drumburgh
Burgh-by-Sands
Stanwix
Carlisle
Castlesteads
Birdoswald
Greatchesters
Houseteads
Carrawburgh
Chesters
Corbridge
Halton Chesters
Rudchester
Benwell
Newcastle
Wallsend

Main forts
Roads

△ **Remains of Hadrian's Wall.** *It took eight years to complete and stretched for 117 km. There were fortified milecastles (gateways) every mile, with two lookout towers between each milecastle.*

Roman Towns

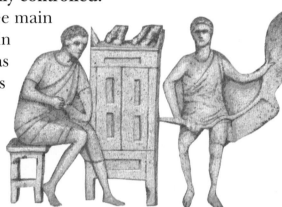

When the Romans arrived, nearly everyone in Britain still lived in the countryside. The Romans began to establish towns, which were an important part of their system for maintaining peace. Throughout the empire, they imposed the same system, moving people from their hillforts to settlements on the plains. In a town, people could be encouraged to live a more "Roman" way of life and could be more easily controlled.

There were three main types of Roman towns in Britain. The colonia was only for Roman citizens who had full rights under Roman law. Next was the municipium, or free town, where only the

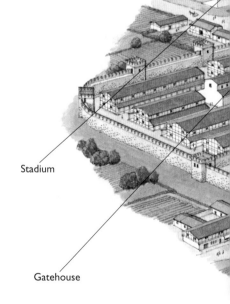

△ *Roman carpenters and other craftsmen* had their workshops around the town's forum or in the narrow back streets. Most people (except slaves) worked only about six hours a day, from sunrise to noon.

Stadium

Gatehouse

△ *Most women wore a tunic* of wool or linen which reached down to the ankles. Only the rich could afford silk or cotton clothes. Women wore their hair piled high on their head in plaits and ringlets.

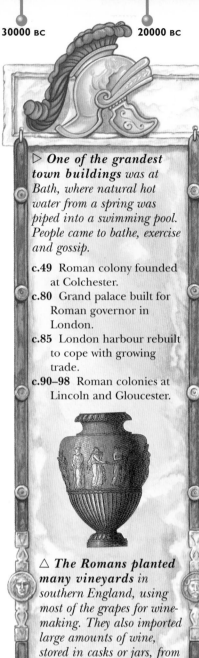

▷ *One of the grandest town buildings* was at Bath, where natural hot water from a spring was piped into a swimming pool. People came to bathe, exercise and gossip.

c.49 Roman colony founded at Colchester.

c.80 Grand palace built for Roman governor in London.

c.85 London harbour rebuilt to cope with growing trade.

c.90–98 Roman colonies at Lincoln and Gloucester.

△ *The Romans planted many vineyards* in southern England, using most of the grapes for wine-making. They also imported large amounts of wine, stored in casks or jars, from Italy, Spain and France.

c.100 Legionary fort at Caerleon rebuilt in stone.

c.110 Stone amphitheatre built at Cirencester.

c.156 Carmarthen redeveloped as a new town with grid system.

c.195 London's city wall completed.

212 Emperor Caracalla grants Roman citizenship to most of Empire, including Britain.

c.217–270 Period of peace in which many towns are rebuilt in stone.

296 Britain divided into four provinces, with capitals at London, Cirencester, York and Lincoln.

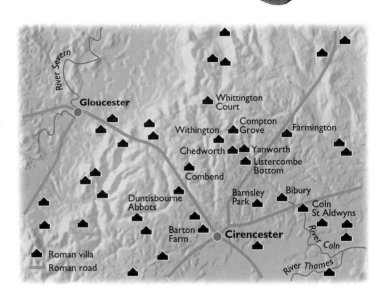

ruling families were accepted as citizens. At the bottom was the civitas town, or capital of a tribal region, where no one had citizen's rights. By about AD 200, there were dozens of thriving towns in southern Britain.

Many of the bigger towns were laid out in a grid pattern. At the centre was an open space called the forum. This had colonnades on three sides, behind which were shops, workshops and offices. On the fourth side stood the basilica, which contained the council chamber and the law courts. The forum's central space was used as a market-place.

Roman builders took care to keep towns as healthy as possible. Pipes brought in clean water from lakes and rivers, while drains and sewers carried away dirty water. Most towns had at least one public bath.

△ *The Cotswold region* of southern England was a popular area for villa-building. Most were working farms, built near roads or rivers along which produce could be taken to market.

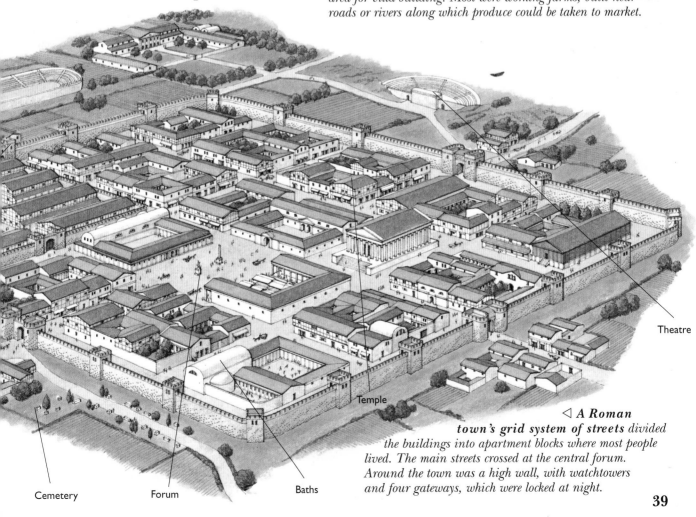

Theatre

Temple

Cemetery   Forum   Baths

◁ *A Roman town's grid system of streets* divided the buildings into apartment blocks where most people lived. The main streets crossed at the central forum. Around the town was a high wall, with watchtowers and four gateways, which were locked at night.

39

Life in Roman Britain

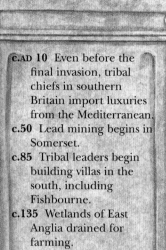

c.AD 10 Even before the final invasion, tribal chiefs in southern Britain import luxuries from the Mediterranean.

c.50 Lead mining begins in Somerset.

c.85 Tribal leaders begin building villas in the south, including Fishbourne.

c.135 Wetlands of East Anglia drained for farming.

c.150 Romans make farming more efficient and increase harvests.

c.160 Over 40 iron-smelting sites at work in Sussex.

c.300 Pottery works flourish in Oxfordshire and East Anglia.

△ **Luxury tableware and ornaments** *in precious metals were produced by smiths from their city workshops. Gold was mined in Wales and silver was extracted from lead deposits in Somerset and Derbyshire.*

c.320 British woollen textiles are popular on the continent.

359 Surplus British grain shipped to Gaul to feed Roman troops.

c.370 New boom in building country villas.

By AD 300, southern Britain was booming. "Britain is a most wealthy island", wrote one Roman visitor. For the first time in their history, Britons used metal coins to buy and sell goods.

Farming had expanded, as the Romans ordered vast new areas to be ploughed for growing crops. Well-organized factories, such as those in East Anglia and Oxfordshire, were producing large amounts of pottery. British woollen coats and rugs were very popular in Gaul. Gold, lead and silver were being mined in Wales and the west, and the iron industry was growing rapidly. Foundries have been found in the centres of towns such as Silchester in Hampshire.

There was plenty of work for people in these industries, as well as for house builders, road engineers, woodmen, who cut timber for fuel and charcoal-making, and carters or bargemen (who transported the goods). There was also a much greater variety of food to eat. Farmers had been raising grain, cattle and pigs for several centuries, but the Romans introduced many new crops, including apples, grapes, onions and cabbages. Olive oil and wine were imported from Gaul and Spain. British chieftains and powerful Romans lived very comfortably in grand palaces in the countryside, usually within a short ride of a major town. Besides these luxury buildings,

◁ **Roman legionaries** *are shown in this fresco (wall painting). They were the frontline of the army and were backed up by auxiliary troops. Britons were encouraged to join the auxiliary army and were granted citizenship.*

there were hundreds of villas built in the Roman style. Each villa was surrounded by an estate, with farmland and workshops for ironworking and pottery. But poorer country people lived in simple timber roundhouses, just as they had before the Romans came.

Meanwhile, in Hibernia (Ireland) life had scarcely changed. The Romans had never tried to conquer the island. As a result, the Irish tribal system remained as strong as ever.

△ **Mosaic patterns and pictures** *were made by craftsmen to decorate the walls or floors of fine houses. They used thousands of tiny cubes of coloured stone, clay or glass. Several preserved mosaics can be seen today.*

ROMAN SEWING KIT

All clothes had to be sewn by hand, using needles and a thimble made of bone or iron. The thread was usually linen, made from flax or wool. (Cotton, from Asia, was still scarce and costly.) The fibres were spun into yarn, which was then woven into cloth. Spinning and weaving were part of the daily work of the women of a household.

▽ **Women wore little jewellery**, *following the fashion in Rome. Simple necklaces and bracelets were worn with rings and brooches of bronze, but earrings were thought to be very vulgar and uncivilized.*

▽ **A villa** *was both a farm and a place to live. It had comfortable living-quarters for the owner and his family. On one side, the bedrooms opened onto a pillared veranda facing the private garden. On the other side was the courtyard, surrounded by farm buildings.*

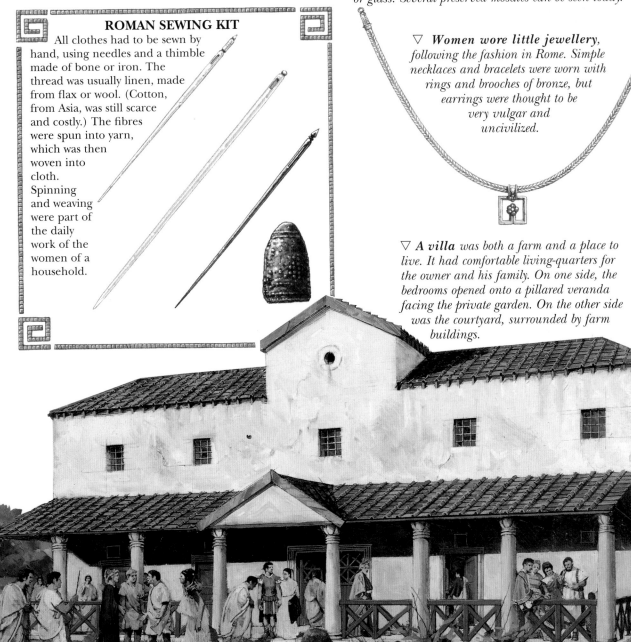

c.280 Chain of forts built on south coast to guard against Saxon raiders.

312 Emperor Constantine recognizes Christianity as a legal religion.

321 Constantine makes Sunday a day of rest throughout Empire.

367 Hadrian's Wall overrun by alliance of Picts, Scots and Saxons.

391 Christianity becomes the official religion of the Roman Empire.

395 Roman Empire divided into two parts: West and East.

c.400 Irish settle on Britain's west coast.

△ *A stone cross. Christianity possibly reached far northern Britain in about AD 200 and slowly spread southwards. Christians were often persecuted, but the later discovery of stone crosses and other symbols suggests that they must have continued to worship in private.*

401 Roman troops begin withdrawal from Britain to defend their homeland.

c.408 Saxon invasion of Britain.

410 Emperor Honorius tells Britons to defend themselves: the city of Rome is sacked by Visigoths.

Gods and Goddesses

The Romans had no single religion. Traditionally, they believed in a group of gods and goddesses, ruled by Jupiter, who took care of every part of their lives. Later, they worshipped their emperors, who proclaimed themselves to be gods as well!

In Britain, the Romans did not try to stamp out the old beliefs of the Celts. The only exception were the Druids of North Wales. The Romans saw them as a threat, and disliked their custom of human sacrifice. In AD 60, they sacked the Druid stronghold on Anglesey.

The Romans brought their own kinds of worship. They built temples for their gods, with altars where they sometimes sacrificed animals. Their homes also had small shrines, where families placed gifts for the household gods. By about AD 200, they had adopted several Celtic gods, such as Sulis the water goddess and Nodens the god of health.

Now, however, another powerful religion was taking hold: Christianity. At first, the Roman emperors banned the new faith, because Christians only believed in one God, and refused to worship the old gods. But in 325 Christianity became the official religion of the Roman Empire.

△ *Vesta was goddess of fire and the hearth. She was worshipped in nearly every Roman home and a symbolic fire was kept lit in her special temple in Rome through out the year.*

◁ *This earthenware plate shows the heads of Roman gods and goddesses. Among the most important of these were Jupiter the sky god, Juno the goddess of birth, Mars the god of war and Venus the goddess of love. The Romans also adopted gods from the East, such as Bacchus.*

End of Empire

By AD 300, the vast Roman Empire was in trouble. Large numbers of Huns, Goths and Vandals from northeast Europe were on the move. They threatened the borders of Rome's provinces and the imperial army was not strong enough to defend them properly. In Rome there were food shortages and civil war.

The Romans decided to abandon their most remote provinces first. Despite the profits from British trade, the cost of keeping a large garrison on the island was very high. There were frequent attacks from the north. In 367, an alliance of Picts, Scots and other tribes ravaged much of northern Britain. At the same time, Saxon pirates from Germany raided the southeast coast, and Irish tribes attacked in the west.

To meet these dangers, the Romans sent fresh troops and built new forts. But in 401, Roman troops were called home to defend northern Italy. By 407 almost the entire army had left the island. When the Britons begged the Emperor Honorius for help against their enemies, he refused. Roman rule in Britain was at an end.

△ **Roman legionaries** on the march. Troops in Britain felt cut off from Rome and in 383 elected their own emperor, Magnus Maximus. He weakened the island's garrison by taking an army to invade Italy, and was killed.

△ **This cavalry parade helmet** from Ribchester in Lancashire probably belonged to a Sarmatian horseman, a member of an army of 5,000 brought by the Romans from the Danube region. By AD 200, the Romans were enlisting many foreign soldiers from the countries within their empire.

◁ **These stones pillars** are from a temple at Carrawburgh on Hadrian's Wall. It was founded in AD 205 for the worship of Mithras, the Persian god of light and truth. The temples were often built underground, to look like caves.

43

Anglo-Saxons

c.409 Roman soldiers and officials leave Britain.

c.420 Saxon settlers land on East Anglian coast.

c.430 Vortigern hires German mercenaries to defend Britain against other invaders.

c.450 Scots from Ireland establish Dalriada, a colony on Scottish west coast.

c.491 Saxons gain control of south coast.

c.500 Britons win rare victory against Saxons at Mount Badon.

577 Saxon victory at Dyrham, Gloucestershire, pushes remaining Britons back into Wales and Cornwall.

c.625 Lavish burial of Radwald at Sutton Hoo.

632 Kings of Mercia and Gwynedd unite to defeat Northumbria.

△ *Arthur's sword. The heroic Arthur may be just a legend, although an Arthur is mentioned in a poem (c.600) as a leader who defeated the Saxons in about 500. After he had been mortally wounded in battle, his sword is said to have been thrown into a lake and caught by a hand that rose from the water.*

672 Egfrith of Northumbria defeats the Picts in Scotland.

736 Ethelbald of Mercia proclaims himself King of all Saxon kingdoms.

757–796 Offa rules Mercia and builds dyke between his kingdom and Wales.

As the Romans left Britain in about AD 407, power fell into the hands of invaders. From Ireland came the Scots, who established colonies on what is now the west coast of Scotland. From the far north came the Picts. But the strongest and most successful groups came from northwest Europe, mainly Denmark and northern Germany.

These were the Angles, Saxons and Jutes – now known as the Anglo-Saxons. Their own lands had become overcrowded and they were seeking new places to live. Some conquered territory by force, but others arrived peacefully. At first, they settled in the south and east of Britain, but by about AD 600 they occupied most of what is today England (or Angle-land).

The remaining Celtic Britons had struggled to keep their homes. They won several victories over the Anglo-Saxons. In one, at Mount Badon in southwest England in about 500, they may have been led by a king called Arthur. But in the end they were forced to retreat into Wales, Cornwall and Cumbria. Some even emigrated to Gaul (to the part that is now called Brittany).

△ *A Saxon pot. By AD 700, the Saxons had established new trading ports, notably Southampton on the south coast, with a population of 5,000. Cargo boats from mainland Europe brought in luxury goods made in silver and gold, and earthenware pots, exchanging them for farming produce, lead and woollen cloth.*

The Saxon settlements merged and grew into kingdoms ruled by their leading warriors. The most powerful of these kingdoms were Kent, East Anglia, Sussex (meaning "South Saxons"), Wessex ("West Saxons"), Mercia ("people of the Marches") and Northumbria. They frequently fought with each other to gain more land. By 627, King Edwin of Northumbria was strong enough to be called Bretwalda, or "Ruler of Britain". But fifty years later the Northumbrians were defeated by the Mercians and in 757 the greatest of the early Bretwaldas came to the throne of Mercia. This was Offa, who was to become the first proper English king, treating other kingdoms as his provinces. He ordered the building of an earthwork (called Offa's Dyke) from the river Severn to the river Dee, to keep Welsh raiders out of Mercia. He devised new laws and encouraged trade with Europe.

△ *This is a map of the Saxon kingdoms* in about AD 700. In the far north, present-day Scotland was occupied by the Celtic Picts and Scots. Bernicia and Deira were later absorbed into the much larger kingdom of Northumbria. Britons were now confined to Wales and Cornwall, while much of southern Britain had been settled by Saxons.

◁ *This warrior's iron helmet* was reconstructed, using fragments found at Sutton Hoo, Suffolk. It is part of a magnificent hoard of grave goods buried with King Radwald of East Anglia in about 625. His body, with a collection of silver, bronze and gold items, was placed in a full-size wooden ship which was then buried whole beneath a massive earth barrow.

▷ *A soldier's shield.* Soldiers of high rank, such as kings, had special servants to carry their shields in battle. They also wore shirts of chain mail and were the only ones to use swords. The swords were of iron, with grips of wood covered in horn or leather. Ordinary footsoldiers fought with clubs, axes or short stabbing spears.

Life in Saxon Times

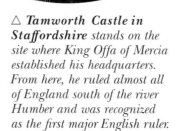

c.450 St Patrick begins his conversion of the Irish to Christianity.

563 St Columba founds monastery on island of Iona, off Scotland.

597 Augustine lands in Kent on Christian mission from Rome.

c.600 King Athelbert of Kent baptized as a Christian.

c.695 Southampton established as major trading port.

c.725 *Beowulf*, the greatest surviving poem of the age, is written.

731 Bede writes his *History of the English Church and People*.

c.750 London grows to become largest town and busiest port in Britain.

c.800 Completion of the *Book of Kells* in Leinster, Ireland.

▽ *Bede, the greatest scholar of the age,* spent most of his life in the monastery at Jarrow, Northumbria, where he died in 735. His writings are a valuable source of information about life in Saxon times.

△ *Tamworth Castle in Staffordshire stands on the site where King Offa of Mercia established his headquarters. From here, he ruled almost all of England south of the river Humber and was recognized as the first major English ruler.*

Even after the arrival of the Saxons, there were few people in the British Isles. By 800, the combined populations of Great Britain and Ireland was little more than one million.

The Anglo-Saxon kings rewarded their most important followers called thanes, or lords, by giving them land. Each thane then rented out land to churls (farmers), who paid him by working his land and giving him some of their crops. Thanes and churls owned slaves, who did all the worst jobs.

The settlers preferred to live in the river valleys, where the soil was richer and there was plenty of water. Most churls rented an area called a hide – a piece of land big enough to produce food for one family. Even so, they had to work hard to survive. First of all, the land had to be cleared.

Farmers cut down woodland to make pasture for cattle and sheep, or to plough for crops. There was a yearly routine of sowing, weeding, harvesting and threshing grain crops (mainly wheat, oats and barley). The churls built themselves simple storehouses and workshops of timber and thatch. Each family lived and slept in its own hall, which had a hearth in the centre.

Houses were often grouped together and fenced to keep out raiders. People made everything they needed, such as cloth, clay pots and ironwork, and preserved food for the winter. As well as homes, there were monasteries where Christian monks lived. The Saxon invasion had driven most Christians west into Wales and Ireland, but from the 500s, missionaries worked to convert the Saxons.

△ *This Saxon arch* is part of a church. They were the most important buildings in Saxon Britain, so they were often made of stone. This means that they survived while timber houses rotted away. In the 600s, Italian masons were hired to build churches. This rounded arch shows the influence of Roman architecture.

CHIEFTAIN AND FOLLOWERS
Saxon society had a strict hierarchy. At the bottom were the slaves, who had few rights or property. Above them were the freemen – churls and the more powerful thanes. Freemen were loyal to a chieftain or local king, who could call on them to raise troops to fight for him. The bond of loyalty to a king was central to a Saxon warrior's life.

◁ *A Saxon family.* Starvation was always a threat in Saxon times. Bad weather might ruin the farmer's crops, disease kill his animals, or raiders steal his produce. It was vital that enough grain, beans and other vegetables were safely stored.

47

Viking Invasions

In the year 789, the Saxons of northern England had a shock. Three longships from Denmark appeared on the coast. From them poured Vikings, eager to steal, butcher and burn. Over the next decades these raids grew bigger and more widespread. Even the monastery at Lindisfarne in Northumbria was sacked in 793. Fleets of up to 350 ships brought terror and destruction.

But the Vikings were not just looking for easy plunder. They were also searching out new land for settlement and new outlets for trade. By 850 they had established a series of bases running from the Orkney and Shetland Islands down the east coast as far as the Thames. By 870 they had overrun East Anglia, Mercia and Yorkshire, and controlled the Irish coastline.

The Viking spread westwards was halted by King Alfred of Wessex. In 878, he defeated the Danes at Edington in Wiltshire and forced them to agree to a treaty. This limited their settlement to the area north of a line from Chester to London – the Danelaw. The Danes were defeated, but not for long. A century later they re-conquered much of the island and in 1017 their monarch, Cnut, became the king of England as well.

Ring

Sword

Shield

▽ *Thor's hammer amulet.*
Thor, god of thunder and war, was a Viking god. His hammer represented a thunderbolt.

◁ *Viking warriors* came not only from Denmark but also from Norway and Sweden. They were well-organized soldiers and sailors whose fleets crossed the Atlantic to Iceland, Greenland and even landed in North America. Their armies marched through Europe as far as Spain and Asia.

VIKING LONGSHIP

The longship was a perfect form of transport for short raiding trips. Though up to 25 metres long, it was only 2 metres wide. Slim and strongly built of timber, it slid easily through the waves powered by a big square sail or long oars. A longship could carry between 40 and 60 men. There was no deck or keel, so the boat rocked wildly in stormy seas. For this reason, most raids were in spring and summer, and the boats hauled up on shore for winter.

△ **Major Viking raids on Britain** began in 789. The first to attempt a conquest was the Great Army, which invaded Northumbria, East Anglia and Mercia in 865.

▷ **Viking brooch.** *Large, round brooches that fastened with a pin were made*

▽ **A Saxon and Viking in battle.** *More assaults began at the end of the 900s. King Ethelred tried to pay them off with Danegeld (money) but they kept returning. In 1013, the Danish king Sweyn Forkbeard led a full-scale invasion and Ethelred fled to France.*

789 The *Anglo-Saxon Chronicle* reports first Viking raid on English coast.
793 Vikings loot monastery at Lindisfarne.
806 Devastating raid on Iona, in which 68 monks and laymen are killed, and the abbey burned.
c.837 Viking fleets sail up the rivers Boyne and Liffey, Ireland.
841 Vikings establish base at Dublin and dominate Irish sea shipping.
865 Scandinavian "Great Army" overruns East Anglia.
878 Alfred defeats the Danes at Edington and forces surrender; treaty agreed at Wedmore, Somerset.
902 Danes expelled from Dublin.
c.943 Much of Wales united under Hywel Dda "the Good".
c.991 Major new Viking attacks on Britain.
1017 Cnut accepted as king of all England.

△ **A chieftain or leader's helmet** *and armour were made of metal. Other Viking warriors were protected by cone-shaped helmets and body armour made of leather, sometimes reinforced with bones. The Vikings fought mainly with broad axes (which they swung with both hands), two-edged swords and short, stabbing spears.*

49

1066 Duke William of Normandy defeats English army at Hastings and is crowned king.

1086 *Domesday Book* compiled.

1169 English conquest of Ireland begins.

1173 King William 'the Lion' of Scotland invades northern England.

1189–91 King Richard I of England joins Third Crusade in Palestine.

1215 King John forced to sign *Magna Carta* by barons and church leaders.

1240 Death of Llywelyn the Great, who had united most of North Wales.

1265 Simon de Montfort, leader of rebellious barons, defeated and killed at Evesham.

1277 King Edward I begins conquest of Wales.

1296 Edward I invades Scotland.

1314 Robert Bruce defeats English army at Bannockburn.

1337 Beginning of the Hundred Years' War with France.

1348 First major outbreak of Black Death in Britain.

1381 The "Peasants' Revolt" crushed.

1400 Rebellion of Welsh leader Owain Glyn Dwr against English rule.

1419–20 English conquest of Normandy.

1455 Civil war (Wars of the Roses) begins between families of York and Lancaster.

1477 William Caxton produces first printed book in Britain.

1485 Death in battle of King Richard III ends the Wars of the Roses: Henry Tudor takes the throne.

THE MIDDLE AGES

The Middle Ages in Britain cover a huge period. They take us from the shock of the Norman Conquest, which began in 1066, to the devastating Black Death of 1348, the Hundred Years' War with France and the Wars of the Roses, which finally ended in 1485.

During this time, Britain grew from a chaos of warring districts into a collection of much larger kingdoms. After his invasion, King William of Normandy established firm control over most of England. A century later, the Normans conquered Ireland. Meanwhile, a series of strong monarchs united much of Scotland. In the 1200s, central government in England, Scotland and Ireland was made stronger by the development of national parliaments to make laws and raise taxes.

England became the dominant country in medieval Britain. Her monarchs conquered Wales, though their repeated attempts to take control of Scotland and Ireland met with failure. They also launched a long and costly war to capture the throne of France.

For the vast majority of Britons, life changed very little. Over 90 percent of

people lived and worked in the countryside, struggling to grow enough food to eat. Towns were very small and travel between them slow and difficult. Trade only began to grow in the 1330s, when the wool industry developed.

However, the Middle Ages also saw the first great period of British architecture. Kings and noblemen built massive stone castles as centres of power. The Christian Church grew stronger, too, and the landscape was dotted with splendid cathedrals, abbeys and parish churches. Many of these buildings can still be seen today.

Norman Conquest

When King Edward "the Confessor" died in January 1066, he was childless. Who was going to be the new English monarch? There were two candidates – Duke William of Normandy, and Harold, the son of the Earl of Wessex. William claimed that the throne had been promised to him by Edward. But the Witan, or royal council, did not want a foreign ruler and recognized Harold as the new king instead.

Harold's first problem lay in the north, where a Norwegian army had landed and seized York. He marched swiftly northwards and smashed the invaders at Stamford Bridge. Almost immediately, he got news of another, even bigger, threat: Duke William's army had landed at Pevensey on the south coast.

Turning his weary troops around, Harold hurried to face the Normans at Hastings. The battle was even at first, with the English lines standing firm on a hilltop. Then William's footsoldiers pretended to retreat and the defenders rushed down after them.

▷ **The Norman army land** on Pevensey beach in Sussex. The Normans were partly Viking – the descendants of Norsemen who had settled in northern France in 911. They were tough and ambitious soldiers, with highly trained cavalry and skilled archers allowing them to attack at long range. After 1066, the Normans controlled territory in southern Italy, Sicily and Malta as well as Britain. Their empire survived for over a century.

This was fatal. The Norman cavalry closed in on both sides and butchered the English, and Harold himself was killed.

After his victory William captured the ports of Romney and Dover, then advanced towards London. At Berkhamsted he was met by the last remaining English leaders, who surrendered and promised loyalty to him. William the Conqueror was crowned on Christmas Day 1066 as king of England, in Westminster Abbey.

△ **The Bayeux tapestry** was made, probably in England, after the conquest. It was paid for by William's half-brother. The embroidered linen strip, 69 metres long, tells the story of the invasion, from Harold's visit to William in 1064 to his defeat at Hastings.

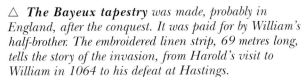

Castles
Route taken by William in 1066

Newcastle
Durham
WASTE
York
Nottingham
Norwich
The Border Castles
Worcester
Cambridge
Oxford
London
Canterbury
Deal
Salisbury
Lewes
Dover
Bramber
Hastings
Exeter

△ **The map shows England and Wales** after the Norman invasion. The major castles throughout the land served as bases for imposing control or conquering the surrounding areas.

1035 Death of Cnut; collapse of Scandinavian Empire.
1042 Edward the Confessor becomes king.
1051 Edward rumoured to have promised the English throne to William of Normandy.
1064 Harold Godwinson visits Normandy; Normans claim he promised loyalty to William.

▽ **King William I** was born in 1027. He became duke of Normandy when he was only seven years old. As king of England, he was intelligent and fair. He died after falling from his horse in 1087.

1065 Harold's brother, Tostig Earl of Northumberland, expelled by rebels.
1066 Death of Edward the Confessor; William of Normandy claims the throne; William's army lands at Pevensey; William defeats Harold at the Battle of Hastings and is crowned king of England on Christmas Day.
1067–70 Normans crush rebellions in the north of England.
1077 Completion of the Bayeux tapestry.
1087 Death of William I; his son William II "William Rufus" becomes king.

Norman Rule

1067 Normans extend rule into Welsh borders after crushing revolt by Welsh and Mercian nobles.

1068 Programme of castle-building under way, with castles at London, Hastings, Dover and Winchester; violent disturbances in York, Warwick and Exeter.

△ **At least 500 castles** *were spread throughout England and Wales by 1100. Stone castles, with a tower or keep at the centre, were much more expensive than timber, but were far stronger.*

1069 Northern England laid waste in revenge for revolts.

1070 William boosts control of the Church by appointing Norman abbot at Canterbury and two Roman cardinals.

1071 Hereward the Wake, English rebel leader in the Fens, captured.

1072 King Malcolm of the Scots pays homage to William.

1075 Major revolt crushed in Herefordshire.

1078 Building of White Tower, part of eventual Tower of London, begins.

1079 Rebellion in Normandy by William's son, Robert Curthose.

1085 Normans impose heavy tax on landowners to raise army against threat of Danish invasion.

1086 Launch of Domesday survey.

"The king set a heavy tribute [tax] on poor folk, though he still let his men harry [harrass] all that they went over." This entry from the *Anglo-Saxon Chronicle* for 1067 shows that William was ruthless in exerting power over his new kingdom.

His army of no more than 10,000 men was faced with a hostile British population of over two million. The early years of his reign saw major rebellions against the Normans in areas as far apart as Kent, the West Country, Wales, northern England and the Fens of East Anglia. These were put down with harshness.

The most famous resistance to William came in the Fens. In 1070 a band of outlaws led by Hereward the Wake ("the Watchful") made a stand on the Isle of Ely.

▽ **The style of dress** *worn by ladies of the Norman ruling class had developed from long simple tunics. These dresses had very wide sleeves and were laced closely on the upper part of the body. Men wore shorter tunics, with breeches or tight leggings beneath. Most clothes at this time were made of linen or woollen cloth: only the most wealthy could afford to wear cotton or silk.*

DOMESDAY BOOK

In January 1086, William launched a remarkable survey of England. He sent commissioners to almost every area to collect details about the size and value of landholdings, who held them, and what livestock they kept. The king's aim was to find out how much tax he could draw from different regions. But the Domesday survey also gives an amazingly thorough picture of life in over 13,000 settlements. It shows that farmland covered about 65 percent of the country, but woodland only about 15 percent.

△ *Most people in England were villeins (villagers), who held small areas of land, or they were humbler cottars, who had even less. They served the local lord by working his land. The lord himself was granted the land by the king, in return for promising to raise troops when needed. This system, called feudalism, was made stricter during Norman times.*

They beat off fierce attacks by the Normans, but were eventually betrayed by local monks. Hereward himself escaped and was never captured.

William's first step was to build a series of castles at key points, to guard important roads, ports, river crossings and towns. Based in each castle were Norman troops, who patrolled the area. These early castles had to be erected quickly, so they were made of timber and sited on top of an earth mound, surrounded by a ditch and a bank. Later castles were built of stone.

The king also rewarded his followers by giving them important positions in the Church, and land seized from the owners. This meant that he would have loyal barons to govern England in his place whenever he returned to Normandy. By 1086, the Domesday survey showed that only two English noblemen were still major landholders.

The Norman barons formed a brand-new ruling class, which spoke French and had French customs. French replaced English as the main language at court and in matters of law, and French words were absorbed into English speech. The influence was permanent; today thousands of common words, such as parliament, royal, city, soldier and prince have French origins.

SCOTLAND

Areas of uncertainty

1080s

1070

1071

1070-80

WALES

1068-70   London

1067-8

△ *Norman rule was gradually extended north and west over England between 1066 and 1087. William divided up the conquered land among his supporters.*

△ *Normans playing an early form of cricket. One man wields a curved stave called a "cric", an Anglo-Saxon word meaning "shepherd's crook". The ball is wood or leather. The word umpire comes from the Norman French "non-pair", meaning "odd man out".*

55

Plot and Civil War

△ *These four Norman kings ruled England between 1066 and 1154. At the top are William the Conqueror (left) and his second son William II. Below are his third son Henry I (left) and grandson Stephen.*

William I had ruled England and Normandy together. But after he died in 1087, the lands found themselves with two different rulers. The new king of England was William II, the Conqueror's second son, known as "Rufus". The new duke of Normandy was his eldest son Robert.

King William was immediately faced with a challenge. In 1088, several powerful barons united behind Robert, who claimed the English throne. This rebellion failed, but it marked the start of a long struggle between the brothers. When William Rufus was killed in a hunting accident in 1100, a third brother entered the fray. This was Henry, who had himself crowned King Henry I of England only three days later. Now he had to fight against Robert. The war ended in 1106, when Henry defeated Robert at Tinchebray in Normandy.

Soon a new crisis loomed. In 1120, the king's only legitimate son, Prince William, was drowned. Who was to take the English throne after Henry I? He was forced to recognize his daughter Matilda as his heir.

▷ *A Norman knight's sword was his main weapon. It was large and double edged, with a heavy pommel (knob) to balance the weight of the blade. Knights also carried shields and lances, and fought on horseback. Their bodies were protected by mail coats, and their heads by mail hoods and iron helmets with noseguards.*

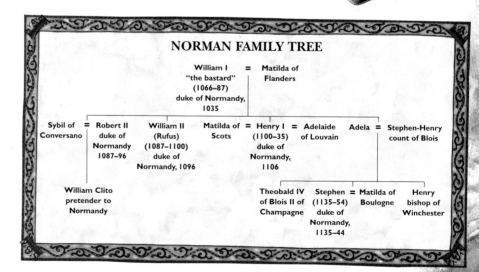

NORMAN FAMILY TREE

		William I "the bastard" (1066–87) duke of Normandy, 1035	=	Matilda of Flanders		
Sybil of Conversano = Robert II duke of Normandy 1087–96		William II (Rufus) (1087–1100) duke of Normandy, 1096	Matilda of Scots = Henry I (1100–35) duke of Normandy, 1106	= Adelaide of Louvain	Adela =	Stephen-Henry count of Blois
William Clito pretender to Normandy			Theobald IV of Blois II of Champagne	Stephen (1135–54) = Matilda of duke of Boulogne Normandy, 1135–44		Henry bishop of Winchester

Henry died in 1135. Before Matilda could reach England from her home in France, another claimant grabbed the throne. This was Stephen, Henry I's nephew, who was crowned the same year. Matilda invaded England in 1139 and by 1141 had defeated Stephen and imprisoned him. Though Matilda's campaign failed and he was freed, Stephen had lost much of his power. He agreed that her son Henry of Anjou should be his heir. Stephen died in 1154 and a new line of French kings came to England's throne – the Plantagenets.

▽ *The map shows sites* in the struggle between King Stephen and the Empress Matilda. She eventually abandoned her claim to the throne in 1148.

York
Lincoln
Shrewsbury
Norwich
Worcester
Hereford   Winchcombe   Cambridge
Radcot Bridge   Oxford
Malmesbury   Faringdon
Bristol   Marlborough
Dunster   Devizes   Wherwell
Castle Carey   Wilton
Wareham   Corfe Castle

◆ Main civil war battle sites

◁ *King William I* ruled wisely but with firm control. After his death, feuding between his sons Robert, William and Henry brought chaos and civil war.

▽ *"The White Ship"* founders off the Normandy coast. King Henry I's son, Prince William, set sail from Barfleur for England in November 1120. A drunken helmsman steered the ship onto a submerged rock. The "White Ship" sank, drowning over 300 people including the young prince.

Scotland United

The Normans never tried to conquer the Scots people. When they took power in England, Scotland was still divided into small provinces, which did not pose a threat. Nor was the land rich enough to attract invaders. Besides, the centre of English power was far to the south, making a full-scale invasion expensive and difficult.

In the 1100s, Scotland remained mostly at peace. It also grew more united under a succession of strong and wise kings. They extended the kingdom northwards from the south and east. In 1266, the Western Isles were added.

However, Norman influence on Scotland was very strong. In 1112, the Scots king Alexander invited Norman knights to settle in his country. This was a clever way to show friendship and avoid full-scale war. When his brother David became king in 1124 he also encouraged Norman barons by granting them estates in southern Scotland.

The arrival of the Normans brought feudalism to Scotland. King David gave land in return for an oath of

1057 Malcolm III kills Macbeth and becomes king.

1070 Malcolm makes link with England by marrying Margaret, sister of Edgar, who is heir to the English throne.

1072 Malcolm attempts to invade Northumbria, but is forced to submit to William I.

1074 Malcolm begins to fortify city of Edinburgh.

1091 William II forces Malcolm to submit again after crushing his invasion of Northumbria.

1112 King Alexander invites Norman barons to settle in Scotland.

1121 First royal burgh founded in Scotland at Berwick-upon-Tweed.

1124 David I becomes king; grants land to more Norman knights, including Robert de Brus (Bruce).

1139 Treaty with England allows Scots to retain conquered area south of the border.

1149–57 Scots seize Northumbria.

1153 Death of David I: his 12-year-old grandson Malcolm becomes king.

1160 Malcolm IV subdues Argyll, Dumfries and Galloway.

1165 Death of Malcolm; William I becomes king.

1173–74 William invades northern England and is taken prisoner; he is released after signing treaty and handing over castles and lands.

1176 Pope allows Scottish Church to remain independent of England.

1214 Death of William I.

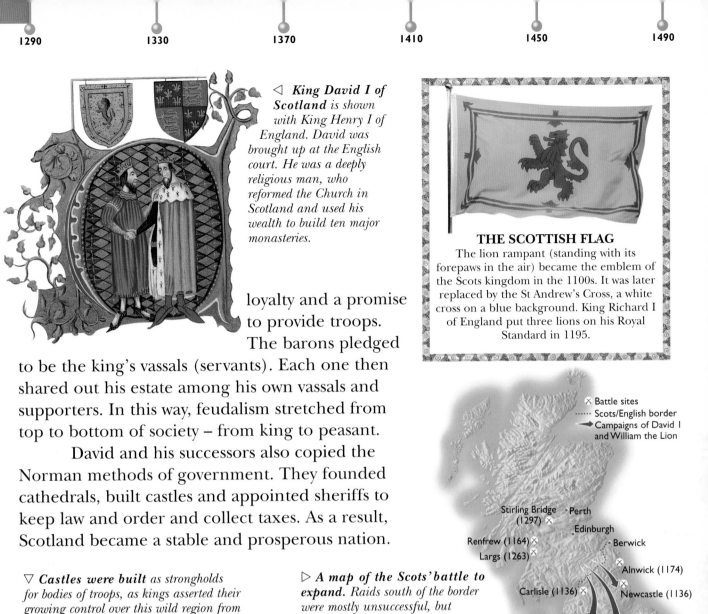

◁ **King David I of Scotland** is shown with King Henry I of England. David was brought up at the English court. He was a deeply religious man, who reformed the Church in Scotland and used his wealth to build ten major monasteries.

THE SCOTTISH FLAG
The lion rampant (standing with its forepaws in the air) became the emblem of the Scots kingdom in the 1100s. It was later replaced by the St Andrew's Cross, a white cross on a blue background. King Richard I of England put three lions on his Royal Standard in 1195.

loyalty and a promise to provide troops. The barons pledged to be the king's vassals (servants). Each one then shared out his estate among his own vassals and supporters. In this way, feudalism stretched from top to bottom of society – from king to peasant.

David and his successors also copied the Norman methods of government. They founded cathedrals, built castles and appointed sheriffs to keep law and order and collect taxes. As a result, Scotland became a stable and prosperous nation.

▽ **Castles were built** as strongholds for bodies of troops, as kings asserted their growing control over this wild region from King David I onwards. Good building stone was hard to find, so these castles were often simple in design.

▷ **A map of the Scots' battle to expand.** Raids south of the border were mostly unsuccessful, but victories against Norway (at Largs) and England (at Stirling) strengthened the Scots kingdom.

✕ Battle sites
····· Scots/English border
→ Campaigns of David I and William the Lion

Stirling Bridge (1297) ✕
Perth
Edinburgh
Renfrew (1164) ✕
Largs (1263) ✕
Berwick
Alnwick (1174) ✕
Carlisle (1136) ✕
Newcastle (1136) ✕
Northallerton 'Battle of the Standard' (1138) ✕

Plantagenets

Henry Plantagenet was not just king of England. He was also duke of Normandy and count of Anjou. Through his wife Eleanor he was duke of Aquitaine. This made him the most rich and powerful ruler in France, and brought him many rivals and enemies.

In the British Isles, Henry II quickly established firm control after the chaos and civil war of Stephen's reign. In 1157, he forced Malcolm IV of Scotland to give back the territory he had seized in northern England. He tore down the "adulterine" castles, which the barons had built without royal permission. He reformed the legal system, introducing trial by jury and circuit courts.

Henry also conquered Ireland. The Normans had left the Irish chieftains to fight amongst themselves. But in 1166 the king of Leinster asked Henry for help against his enemies. A band of knights was sent to recover his lands and soon began to build themselves a kingdom in the southeast. Alarmed at their power, Henry gathered a large army and seized Dublin, forcing the Irish kings to submit to him.

Strong and energetic as he was, Henry made some disastrous mistakes. He quarrelled with his wife, Eleanor of Aquitaine, who urged his sons to turn against him. When he died in France in 1189, he was at war with his third son, Richard. It was Richard who took his place on the English throne.

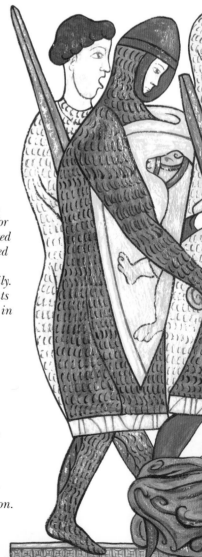

▷ **Thomas Becket** was promoted by his friend Henry II to be archbishop of Canterbury in 1162. But Henry was enraged when Becket opposed many of his reforms for the Church. The Archbishop was forced to flee to France, but foolishly returned in 1170. "Will no one rid me of this turbulent priest?" asked Henry angrily. Eager to impress the king, four knights rode to Canterbury and killed Becket in the cathedral.

◁ **Henry II is crowned king.** The new king was to spend well over half of his reign outside Britain, governing his lands in France. His Angevin (meaning "from Anjou") Empire was a flourishing centre of learning, art, music and poetry. The English court was crude by comparison.

◁ **The extent of the Angevin Empire** in about 1200. It stretched from the east coast of Ireland down to Gascony on the border between France and Spain.

SCOTLAND
ULSTER
ONNAUGHT
IRELAND MEATH
Dublin●
LEINSTER
LINSTER
Principality of North Wales
ENGLAND
London ●
NORMANDY ● Paris
BRITTANY
MAINE ● Orleans
ANJOU
POITOU
AQUITAINE
GASCONY
BEARN

△ **Canterbury Cathedral.** Soon after Thomas Becket's death, people claimed to have seen miracles performed at his tomb in the cathedral. It became a holy shrine visited by many pilgrims. Thomas Becket was made a saint by the pope in 1173.

1154 Accession of Henry II, first Plantagenet king of England.
1165 Henry makes peace with Welsh princes after his military expedition fails.
1166 Dermot MacMurrough, king of Leinster, is exiled in England and asks Henry for help.
1170 Thomas Becket murdered in Canterbury Cathedral.
1171 Henry II takes an army to invade eastern Ireland.
1173 Rebellion by Henry's three eldest sons; Queen Eleanor is imprisoned.
1183 Last of the Irish High Kings gives up his throne.
1189 Death of Henry II: his third son Richard becomes king.

△ **The broom plant** was the symbol of the Plantagenets, whose name comes from the plant's Latin name: "Planta Genista". Henry II's father, Geoffrey of Anjou, is said to have worn a sprig in his cap. The term "Plantagenets" was not used until 1450, when they no longer ruled Britain.

1190–94 Richard absent on Crusade; his return delayed by capture in Germany.
1194 Richard returns to France after stay in England of less than three months.
1199 Death of Richard I; his brother John becomes king.

61

Medieval Britain

Britain in the High Middle Ages was a dangerous place. In England, the three centuries between 1189 and 1485 saw countless uprisings, attempted invasions, civil wars and riots. Several kings met violent ends, including Edward II, Richard II and Richard III.

In Wales, people lived in fear of conquest by the English. In Ireland, the chieftains fought against each other and against the might of the Normans. Even Scotland, the most peaceful region, faced threats from Scandinavian and Irish raiders and, in the end, invasion by the English.

Violence was not the only danger. For most people, getting enough to eat was the biggest difficulty. By 1300, the population of the British Isles had increased to five million. Farmers, using methods which had hardly changed since Roman times, could not grow sufficient food for everyone. The resulting famine killed nearly 15 percent of the population by 1318.

The problem of famine was solved by something far worse – disease. Plague (now known as the Black Death) reached southern England from Europe in 1348 and Scotland and Ireland a year later. This time almost half of the British population was wiped out. However, this meant that there were fewer mouths to feed, and food became more plentiful.

△ *A procession of penitents* during the Black Death. *Many people believed that the plague was God's punishment for human wickedness. They walked in religious processions, praying for forgiveness. Some even whipped themselves to show their penitence. Death was regarded as a way of making all people equal, for it came to rich and poor alike.*

▽ ***Market-day*** *in a medieval town. Most big towns held a weekly market. Merchants, pedlars and craftsmen set up their stalls. Villagers sold the cheese, vegetables and eggs they could spare. Drovers brought in cattle and other livestock. There might be acrobats, jugglers or even a dancing bear to entertain the crowds.*

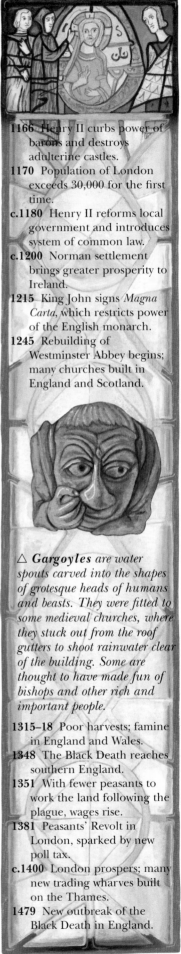

FEUDAL SYSTEM

After Saxon times, feudalism grew more complicated. Kings rewarded their nobles with fiefs (grants) of land, in return for military service. The nobles rented fields to peasant-farmers, also in exchange for service. After about 1300 the system declined as towns grew, people began to pay rent in cash, and kings hired professional soldiers to fight wars.

Despite the dangers, life slowly improved for many people during the Middle Ages. Slave labour began to die out after the Norman Conquest. Reforms to the legal system allowed free men to seek justice at local courts, with trial by jury. Trade with Europe increased. By about 1400, cargo ships travelled regularly as far as the eastern Mediterranean and the Baltic.

Towns grew bigger. Guilds (trade organizations) of craftsmen controlled city affairs and brought in greater wealth.

▷ *Religious texts had been illustrated by monks and scribes since Saxon times. They were decorated with a great variety of patterns and pictures, painted in bright colours. Some parts of the manuscripts (such as the capital letters at the head of each page) were delicately picked out in gold leaf. When properly polished, the gold still shines as brightly as it did eight hundred or more years ago. These illustrated religious texts provide us with valuable evidence of everyday life in the Middle Ages.*

1166 Henry II curbs power of barons and destroys adulterine castles.
1170 Population of London exceeds 30,000 for the first time.
c.1180 Henry II reforms local government and introduces system of common law.
c.1200 Norman settlement brings greater prosperity to Ireland.
1215 King John signs *Magna Carta*, which restricts power of the English monarch.
1245 Rebuilding of Westminster Abbey begins; many churches built in England and Scotland.

△ *Gargoyles are water spouts carved into the shapes of grotesque heads of humans and beasts. They were fitted to some medieval churches, where they stuck out from the roof gutters to shoot rainwater clear of the building. Some are thought to have made fun of bishops and other rich and important people.*

1315–18 Poor harvests; famine in England and Wales.
1348 The Black Death reaches southern England.
1351 With fewer peasants to work the land following the plague, wages rise.
1381 Peasants' Revolt in London, sparked by new poll tax.
c.1400 London prospers; many new trading wharves built on the Thames.
1479 New outbreak of the Black Death in England.

Farming the Land

△▷ *Two peasant-farmers at work. One digs a trench for plants. The other harvests wheat with a sickle. Work had to go on from dawn until dusk whenever the weather allowed it.*

As the population grew between 1100 and 1300, more food was needed. Nearly all of this had to be grown at home; very little was imported from abroad. To increase the harvest, more land than ever before had to be cleared for farming. Woodland was destroyed, marshes and fens drained and livestock put to graze on moorland.

Most peasant-farmers in England lived on a manor – the estate organized around a lord's residence. It usually contained a village, the central house or castle, a church and surrounding farmland. The lord of the manor and his officials governed the community, making sure that rents were paid and services performed.

There were three or four large arable fields around the village. These were divided into strips and shared out among the families. The peasants often helped each other to plough and harvest their strips, but did the rest of their fieldwork separately. Besides this, they were also bound to take their turn at working on the lord's own demesne (private land) as part of their feudal duty.

In summer, villagers drove out their cattle and sheep to graze on the unfenced common land around the arable fields. In autumn, the lord allowed them to loose their pigs in his woodland to feed on acorns and beechnuts. This food was vital, for there was only enough food for a few animals in winter. The rest were slaughtered and their meat was preserved by smoking or salting, so it would keep for several months.

◁▷ *A pair of farming tools.* The saw was useful for pruning hedges and fruit trees. The long-handled scythe was used for mowing grass in the village's hay-meadow. Everyone helped with the hay harvest in midsummer. Straw and hay were important materials – not only for animal feed in winter, but also for thatching roofs and stuffing mattresses.

▽ *A typical medieval village* in the English Midlands. Cottages and workshops were built of timber and thatch. Only the church and the lord's house were of stone. Peasants knew little about crop rotation or manuring the land. In their "three-course" system, they grew crops on a field for two years, then left it fallow (unploughed) for one year so that it regained some fertility.

△ *Peasants* usually had a very hard life. Those at the bottom of the scale (the serfs) owned nothing – not even their clothes or animals. Serfs were not allowed to leave the manor without permission. There were only two ways for a serf to gain his freedom: by marrying a "free" peasant, or by saving money to buy a piece of land. However, few achieved this. Poor food and unending work meant that the average peasant in 1300 would not live past the age of 25.

65

Monastic Life

▽ *The ruins of Fountains Abbey in Yorkshire. The community was founded here in 1132. By the end of the Middle Ages, it had become one of the grandest Cistercian abbeys in England.*

400–500 First monasteries in British Isles established in Ireland.

598 First monastic community in England, under St Augustine, at Canterbury.

c.1066 About 35 male houses and 10 nunneries in Britain.

1093 Durham Cathedral begun.

1128 First Cistercian monastery in Britain established in Surrey.

1136 First Cistercian monastery in Scotland founded at Melrose; by 1160, there are over 50 Cistercian houses in Britain.

△ *Important manuscripts were kept in monastery libraries. A scribe would have spent much of his day sitting at his sloping desk, copying out Latin texts such as this one.*

The Church was at the centre of medieval life. Catholicism was the only religion in Britain and few people questioned it. Even the poorest peasant went to mass every Sunday, where he was told that he would go to Heaven if he followed Christ's teachings. If not, he would go to Hell.

The Church had power – not just over people's minds, but over scholarship, the production of books and schooling. It raised its own tithes (taxes) from villagers and townspeople, made its own laws and owned huge areas of land. Church leaders sat on the king's council.

Since early Saxon times, groups of Christians had lived in communities where they could work and pray together. When the Normans arrived, there were already about 45 monasteries (for men) and nunneries (for women) throughout Britain.

Once a monk entered a monastery and took his vows, he was expected to spend the rest of his life there. The daily routine was busy and unchanging. Starting at about two o'clock in the morning,

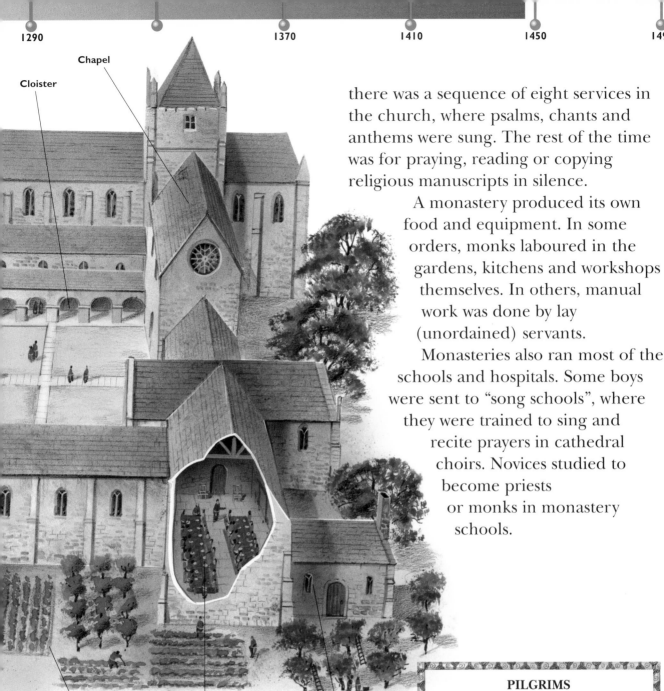

Chapel

Cloister

there was a sequence of eight services in the church, where psalms, chants and anthems were sung. The rest of the time was for praying, reading or copying religious manuscripts in silence.

A monastery produced its own food and equipment. In some orders, monks laboured in the gardens, kitchens and workshops themselves. In others, manual work was done by lay (unordained) servants.

Monasteries also ran most of the schools and hospitals. Some boys were sent to "song schools", where they were trained to sing and recite prayers in cathedral choirs. Novices studied to become priests or monks in monastery schools.

Herb and vegetable garden

Refectory

Kitchens

◁ A child is taken to a monastery by his parents. Some monks were given to the order as babies, and knew nothing of life outside. But usually novice (new) monks lived in a monastery for a year before they took their holy vows of poverty, chastity and obedience to the leaders of the order. Then they shaved the crowns of their heads.

△ In the private world of a monastery, one side is taken up with the large abbey church, where the eight daily services are performed. On the other three sides are living and eating quarters, and important buildings such as the chapter house, where meetings are held. At the centre is an open space, surrounded by a covered walkway called the cloister, where the monks work and read. Monasteries were usually sited near a stream to provide drinking water and power for a mill.

PILGRIMS

Since the 4th century, Christians had gone on pilgrimage to visit holy places and the shrines of saints. In spite of the hardships and the dangers of robbers on the road, bands of pilgrims travelled long distances. The most popular shrines in Britain included Canterbury, where the bones of Thomas Becket were kept, Durham and St David's in West Wales.

67

Castles

If a king or chieftain wanted to keep control of an area of land, he needed soldiers and a fortified base for them to live in. From here, they could patrol the district for about 16 km around – the distance they could ride out and back in a day.

There had been hilltop forts in Britain since Iron Age times, but the Norman kings deliberately built a chain of castles to impose order on their conquered land, and to guard important sites. These castles developed from timber towers on earth mounds to massive stone keeps surrounded by curtain walls.

By the 1300s, more than 1,500 castles dotted the countryside of Britain and Ireland. They were now so strongly built that only a long siege could force their garrisons to surrender. They had water-filled moats, two sets of curtain walls, strong gates and portcullises. From the towers archers could shoot at anyone below the walls, or drop stones or burning pitch.

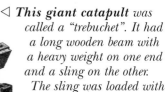

1066–86 Early Norman castle-building; 50 are recorded in Domesday Book.

c.1100 Keeps built of stone become the main castle stronghold.

1215 King John lays siege to Rochester; his miners cause a wall to collapse and the castle is taken.

c.1280 Edward I begins building castles in Wales, including Caernarvon and Harlech.

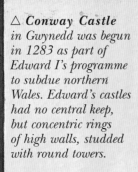

△ *Conway Castle in Gwynedd was begun in 1283 as part of Edward I's programme to subdue northern Wales. Edward's castles had no central keep, but concentric rings of high walls, studded with round towers.*

1297 Gunpowder first used in siege warfare, by Edward I against Stirling Castle.

c.1370 Small guns being used to defend castles.

1464 Use of big guns signals the end of the castle's effectiveness.

◁ *This giant catapult was called a "trebuchet". It had a long wooden beam with a heavy weight on one end and a sling on the other. The sling was loaded with a stone and then released. Weapons such as this were put together at the site of the siege and were hard to move. Other weapons included balls of flaming oil, severed heads and the rotting bodies of animals.*

Baron's bedroom

Great hall

Kitchen and store rooms

▽ *Jesters*, acrobats, musicians or jugglers might entertain the lord of the castle and his guests at supper. Sometimes a knight would sing songs about love and brave deeds.

◁ *The keep* was the castle's central stronghold. It was a tall tower with thick stone walls. The single entrance, through the gatehouse, could be reached only when the gate and portcullis were open and the drawbridge let down over the moat.

CASTLE LIFE

By about 1200, a castle was really a fortified home for a king or lord. He lived there with his wife, children and servants for at least part of the year. The lord and his family were the only people to have a private room, called a solar. Everyone else slept in the castle's great hall.

An attacking army had plenty of special weapons too. Giant siege machines hurled stones to shatter the walls. Battering rams thudded at the timber gates. Miners dug tunnels beneath the walls, then lit fires. As the props burned, the tunnel fell in, making the wall above collapse. Attackers could also climb over the walls using tall scaling ladders. The best weapon was starvation. A besieging army could stop food supplies from going into a castle, and could also dam up or poison the water supply.

Knights and Chivalry

c.500 Heavy mounted Frankish soldiers become successful in western Europe.

c.1000 Beginnings of feudal system, in which knights serve local lord and are in turn served by serf class.

1066 Norman knights lead conquest of southern Britain

▷ *This shield shows the sign of a lion rampant. Shields in the 1300s were usually made of wood and covered with leather. Later shields were specially shaped for jousting, with a curved edge to rest the lance on.*

c.1100 Knights wear more extensive mail armour, covering arms and legs as well as the body.

c.1150 5,000 knights recorded in Britain.

c.1300 The number has declined to about 2,500 knights; many families do not take up knighthood due to the expense of armour and so on.

c.1300 Knights' armour strengthened with steel plates covering the limbs.

1314 Scots' triumph at Bannockburn is a significant reverse for mounted knights; their spearmen halt charges by English cavalry.

c.1400 Knights begin to wear full suits of plate armour.

1415 British longbowmen destroy mounted knights at Agincourt.

c.1450 Only a few hundred knights now recorded.

c.1550 Plate armour reaches its decorative peak, but armoured knights are already obsolete, thanks to developments in warfare, especially firearms.

When William I swept into Britain in 1066, his army was headed by mounted horsemen. Norman knights used the fighting methods of the Frankish warriors who had dominated warfare in Europe for three centuries. The knight had many advantages over the poor footsoldier. He could move faster on horseback, and was better protected with his coat of mail.

By about 1300, the descendants of these knights had become part of Britain's ruling class, numbering around 2,500. They had to promise to serve the king in battle, in return for grants of land. Only boys who were born into this noble class were usually trained as knights.

A knight's career began at about the age of seven, when he was sent to live in a lord's household. Here he was taught good manners, how to ride and even how to sing ballads. At 14 he became a squire, working as a servant for another knight. He learned all the fighting skills, from wrestling and archery to swordplay and putting on armour.

At last, aged about 21, the squire became a full knight. He was "dubbed" kneeling before the king, his father, or his master, who tapped his neck with a sword. He made the vows of chivalry – promises to protect the weak and poor, and to punish evildoers.

△ *A knight and his lady might live on the produce of their land or manor. They lived in castles or fortified manor houses and their land was worked by peasants who owed them service. The lord's wife, the lady of the manor, ran the kitchens and living quarters and was responsible for the house when the knight was away.*

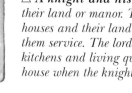

Helmet

Visor

Backplate

Breastplate

Gauntlet

Cuisse

Greave

Sabaton

Finally, he was presented with spurs, a sword and – sometimes – a full suit of armour.

Some knights had their own lands to look after in times of peace. Others hired themselves out to fight for someone else. A knight in full armour was hard to recognize in battle. In the 1100s they began to display their own special signs, called arms, on their shield or armour.

◁ *This suit of armour* is made of metal plates fixed together with rivets, or with leather straps. This allowed the knight to move about quite freely. Underneath, he wears a tunic of mail or a padded jerkin.

CHIVALRY
There was more to knighthood than fighting. Knights were expected to follow a strict code of conduct, called chivalry. This demanded not only courage and fighting skill, but loyalty, generosity and courtesy (good manners – especially towards women).

▽ *These two knights are* meeting at a joust. The joust, when knights tried to knock each other off their horses, was often part of a tournament. Tournaments began by 1000 as a practice for battle. They might also include a tourney (a mock fight between teams of knights) and combat on foot.

71

Crusades

c.660 Arab Muslims conquer much of the Near and Middle East, including Palestine; Christian pilgrims are allowed to visit sacred sites.

c.1050 Seljuk Turks invade the Near East and make access for pilgrims harder.

1095 Pope calls on Christians to recapture Holy Land.

1096 First Crusade: Jerusalem retaken.

1147 Second Crusade: Christians defeated and forced to retreat.

1187 Muslims under Saladin take Jerusalem again.

1189–91 Third Crusade: Christians fail to recapture Jerusalem.

1202–54 Four more Crusades to Holy Land achieve little.

1271 Prince Edward joins Eighth Crusade in Palestine.

1272 Edward forced to return home on death of his father, Henry III.

1291 European interest in Crusades begins to fade.

△ *Saladin, Sultan of Egypt and Syria, was the greatest of the Muslim leaders, not only defeating the Crusaders, but ruling wisely and efficiently.*

▷ *Turkish cavalrymen wore much lighter armour than the Crusader knights. They had light mail coats, pointed metal helmets and small round shields. They fired volleys of arrows from the saddle.*

King Richard I of England preferred fighting for his religion overseas to governing his kingdom. For three years after his coronation in 1189, he was not even in Europe. He was leading a Crusader army against Muslim forces in Palestine.

The Crusades had begun as a noble idea nearly a century before. In about 1000, the Seljuk Turks (who were Muslims) had advanced from their homeland in Central Asia and conquered a large area of the Byzantine Empire in Asia Minor. This included the city of Jerusalem and other places in Palestine which Christians believed were important holy sites.

The Byzantine Emperor had begged for help from the Christian monarchs of Europe. The pope supported him by promising that God would forgive the sins of those who took part in this Holy War. So in 1096 the armies of the First Crusade set off to drive the Seljuks out of the Holy Land. At first they were successful. Jerusalem was recaptured, and a Christian army was left to guard it.

But the Second Crusade of 1146 was a disaster, and by 1189 the Muslim forces, led by Saladin, had taken Jerusalem once again. King Richard swiftly gathered soldiers for a Third Crusade. The Christian army – English, French and German troops – landed in Palestine in 1191.

With Richard at their head, the Crusaders quickly captured the town of Acre. However, they failed to retake

▷ *Transport ships* carried Crusaders and
their equipment. Knights had to pay large
sums of money for the transport and provisions
for their horses, servants and pack animals.
To raise this, they might levy a tax from
people who lived on their lands or sell part
of their estate.

▽ *A Crusader knight* (top)
and a Muslim warrior do battle.
Crusaders found the climate of
Palestine unbearably hot.
Many soon copied the
Turks, wearing loose airy
surcoats over their mail
armour and protecting
their heads from the
strong sun.

Jerusalem. Their leaders quarrelled amongst
themselves, and Richard was left behind to
make a treaty with Saladin. The Muslims kept
Jerusalem, but allowed visits from Christian
pilgrims. There were to be five more crusades
against the spread of Islam, most of which
ended in failure. One, in 1204, even brought
disaster when the crusading army turned on
the Byzantine Emperor, sacking his
capital, Constantinople.

▽ *A Crusader castle.* The
Crusaders took over Muslim castles,
or built new ones, to defend the
states they had conquered.
Several of these castles were
on ideal sites, protected on
two or three sides by
water or sheer
rock cliffs.

Kings and Parliament

After the death of Henry II, England became an even more difficult place to govern. The new king, Richard I, spent most of his reign in France or on crusade. He made sure that leading barons and churchmen kept strict control while he was away, but they could not prevent a rebellion by his brother John in 1194. Nor could the barons prevent the French king Philip from seizing part of Normandy.

Things quickly grew worse after Richard's death in 1199. John was the new ruler of England and the Angevin Empire. The barons in Anjou did not like this: they wanted John's young nephew, Arthur, as king. But in 1203 Arthur mysteriously disappeared, and many suspected that John had murdered him.

King Philip of France took the opportunity to invade Anjou and Normandy, and soon John had scarcely any empire left. He scurried back to the safety of England and tried to prepare an army to regain his lands. But this meant raising taxes, which made him very unpopular. Then in 1214 came yet another defeat in France.

The English barons had had enough. They rebelled against the king and seized London. In June 1215 they forced John to accept the terms set out in the *Magna Carta*, meaning "Great Charter". In it, he agreed to respect the rights of the Church and nobles, and to set up a committee of elected men to safeguard the law.

John died a year later without acting on any of these conditions. The new king, Henry III, was only nine years old, and the country was governed by a council until 1232. Henry was a quiet, religious man who was happier building palaces and churches than dealing with the growing

△ *King John's great seal* on "Magna Carta". The barons set up a tent in a meadow called Runnymede by the Thames in Surrey. The king arrived and the Archbishop of Canterbury read out the articles of "Magna Carta". King John did not "sign" the charter, but set his mark, or seal, in wax which was attached to it.

△ *"Magna Carta"* contained 63 clauses, most of which were aimed at protecting the feudal rights of the barons and churchmen. Among the most important demands is that the king should allow justice for everyone, and should not imprison anyone without a legal process. John later ignored the charter, but in 1225 Henry III confirmed it as a bill of his subjects' rights and it became a vital part of English law.

◁ *King Henry III* *made only weak attempts to win back the lost parts of the Angevin Empire, and renounced them altogether in the Treaty of Paris in 1259. He also angered the English barons by having many French relatives as his friends and close advisers.*

discontent among his barons.

In 1264 this exploded into civil war. The barons, led by Simon de Montfort, wanted to restrict the king's power, and demanded that he must consult a council of noblemen three times a year.

They defeated Henry at Lewes and imprisoned him. In 1265, de Montfort called together the promised council, consisting not just of barons, but also of men who were elected from the shires and cities. This was the first time that an English parliament had represented anyone other than noblemen. But it did not last long. Within a few months, de Montfort had been defeated and Henry had restored royal power.

▷ *Simon de Montfort* *was born in France. He married Henry III's sister and governed Gascony for him until 1252. But he turned against the king and led the rebellious barons who published the provisions of Oxford in 1258 (demanding that the king should govern through a council). After defeating Henry, de Montfort became virtual ruler of England and summoned the first representative English parliament in 1265.*

1189   Richard I becomes king of England.
1193   Richard imprisoned in Germany; John tries to seize power in England, but later flees to France.
1199   Death of Richard; John is crowned king.
1203   John's nephew Arthur disappears.
1203–04   Philip of France conquers Anjou and Normandy.
1214   John's allies defeated at Bouvines in France; most land on continent lost to French.
1215   Civil war in England; barons force John to put seal to *Magna Carta.*
1216   Louis of France invades England (leaves 1217).

△ *The House of Commons.* *In Saxon times the king had been advised by a witan (council) of the most powerful men in the realm: noblemen and churchmen. These became known as parliaments (discussions). Only in 1265 were the first community representatives, or "commons", invited to parliament.*

1216–32   England ruled by council.
1258   Barons seize power.
1264   Henry captured at Battle of Lewes.
1265   De Montfort calls enlarged parliament; de Montfort killed.
1272   Death of Henry III; Edward I becomes king.

Ireland

1171 Henry takes army to Ireland and receives homage from the King of Leinster.

1198 Death of the Ruaidri of Connacht, last of the Irish High Kings.

c.1200 English settlers introduce advanced methods of farming in eastern Ireland.

1204 King John imposes English laws concerning property and inheritance on Irish.

1243 Henry III sends out commissioners to extend English landholdings.

1264 First recorded meeting of the Irish Parliament.

1315 Invasion by Scots, led by Edward Bruce.

1318 Bruce killed in battle at Faughart near Dundalk.

1348 The Black Death reaches Ireland.

1366 The Statutes of Kilkenny, an attempt to keep separate the English and Irish cultures.

1394 Richard II's army re-conquers Leinster.

1399 Richard's second expedition to Ireland cut short by rebellion at home.

The Normans had first landed in Ireland in 1169. Two years later, King Henry II led a major expedition here and received vows of loyalty from the king of Leinster. He seized Dublin, and the Irish kings submitted to his rule, agreeing to pay him tribute (taxes). By 1183, the last of the High Kings had been forced to give up his throne. Henry made his son, Prince John, Lord of Ireland.

Over the next century, the invaders gradually established themselves, seizing land from Irish chieftains and settling in many areas, from Ulster in the north to Leinster in the south. By 1300, the English controlled most of Ireland and imposed English systems of law and local government. The settlers began to intermarry with the native Irish. New cathedrals, parish churches and castles were built. Trade and farming flourished. There was a demand for imported luxuries. (So much wine was consumed that in 1278 a new wine tax was introduced.) Ireland had its own parliament, which first met in 1264.

Many Irish chieftains had managed to avoid being drawn into the feudal system. In remote areas the Gaelic language and traditions scarcely changed. Then in 1315 a Scottish army landed in County Antrim, invited by a local chieftain who wanted to expel the English. The Scots were led by Edward Bruce, brother of King Robert. Within a year they had invaded Meath and Edward had been crowned King of Ireland.

△ **Castle Hall in Dublin** was the centre of English rule for over 700 years. The city of Dublin was founded by the Vikings in about 850 and given its Gaelic name, which means "black pool". Norman soldiers captured Dublin in 1170 and built the castle.

▷ **As the Norman settlers** intermarried with the Irish and took on Irish language and customs, their loyalty to the English decreased. Ulster, in the northeast, was invaded by the Scots in 1315, and by the 1400s English control dwindled to the "Pale" in the southeast.

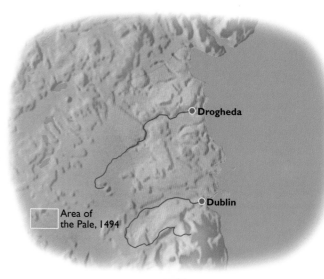

Drogheda

Dublin

Area of the Pale, 1494

STRONGBOW

Richard de Clare, nicknamed "Strongbow", was one of the Norman knights sent to Ireland in the 1160s to help the king of Leinster. He married the king's daughter and in 1171, inherited the king's lands, becoming Lord of Leinster and ruler of Dublin. At this point, Henry II grew alarmed at de Clare's growing power. He gathered a large army and landed in Ireland. De Clare was too wise to offer battle, and swore loyalty to Henry instead. He was allowed to keep his lands.

Bruce was defeated and killed in 1318, but by then much of Ireland was in ruins. Many had died in the bloody warfare, and many more starved as towns were burned and crops destroyed. English power, centred in Dublin, was badly weakened, and Irish leaders had regained control of much of Antrim, Ulster and County Down. Some hired Scottish mercenaries called gallowglasses to fight for them.

The English kings Edward III and Richard II tried to re-establish their grip on Ireland. In 1366, the Statutes of Kilkenny became law, forbidding English settlers from using the native Irish language and customs. They were banned from marrying Irish people or even selling them horses!

In 1399, Richard II landed an army in County Waterford, but with little success. By the early 1400s, English power in Ireland had shrunk to a small area around Dublin. This was called the Pale, and had to be defended with castles, beacons and ditches.

△ *A celtic harp*, similar to the famous harp of Brian Boru. Brian was king of Munster in about 1000, and became Irish High King after conquering most of southern Ireland. He died – victorious – at the Battle of Clontarf in 1014 against the Viking ruler of Dublin. The O'Brien families of Ireland take their name from his.

▽ *The rich farmland of central Ireland.* The Norman settlers brought better farming methods, so that by the 1250s surplus food was being exported abroad. But the Scots' invasion of 1315–18 wiped out large areas of crops and led to famine.

◁ *An Irish footsoldier.* From the late 13th century, Irish armies were strengthened by gallowglasses hired from Scotland. These heavily armed infantrymen got their name from the Gaelic "galloglaigh", meaning "foreign soldier".

The Conquest of Wales

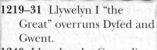

1219–31 Llywelyn I "the Great" overruns Dyfed and Gwent.

1240 Llywelyn the Great dies.

1256–57 Llywelyn II "the Last" controls most of Wales.

1257 Treaty of Montgomery; Henry III acknowledges Llywelyn prince of Wales.

1277 Edward I invades Gwynedd; English forces invade the south; Llywelyn keeps some lands.

1282 Edward begins new castle-building programme.

1283 Llywelyn rebels, is captured and executed horribly.

1284 Statute of Wales; newly conquered lands are divided into shires.

1301 Prince Edward, son of Edward I, given title of prince of Wales.

▷ *The seal of Owain Glyn Dwr, the last leader of an independent Wales. After an argument, Henry IV took his lands. In 1400 Welsh supporters proclaimed him prince of Wales. He led an uprising against English rule.*

▽ *Modern replicas of Owain Glyn Dwr's sword, shield and crown. By 1405 Glyn Dwr ruled much of Wales, but his revolt was eventually crushed.*

William I had not attempted to conquer Wales. The mountains of the north were difficult for cavalry to fight in. But during Norman times several barons had seized land in the south. They built castles in the Welsh borders with England.

The Welsh were members of different groups who fought each other as well as the Normans. In about 1215 Llywelyn the Great united Wales. He drove the English out of Gwynedd and destroyed Carmarthen Castle.

After Llywelyn's death, the Welsh again began to quarrel. The armies of Henry III regained much territory in the south. A new leader took charge: Llywelyn's grandson, Llywelyn the Last. By 1257 he had overrun most of the north-east and centre of Wales. Henry was forced to give him the brand-new title of prince of Wales. However, the new king, Edward I, wanted Wales under control. In 1277, he attacked Llywelyn's stronghold in Gwynedd and forced him to surrender. Wales was now ruled by an English king. Edward built a chain of castles in north Wales. He divided the country into shires and encouraged English people to settle.

◁ *The coronation of Edward I. Unlike his father, he was an ambitious soldier, who wanted to rule all of Britain. He also reformed England's government and called the first parliament to represent the whole country.*

Beaumaris　Conway　Ruddlan　Flint

Caernarfon

Ruthin

Harlech

Pool

Aberystwyth

Castles besieged by Welsh rebels

Builth

Cardigan

Haverford　Carmarthen

Swansea

Caerphilly　Newport

Cardiff

△ *The map shows the Welsh castles besieged by Owain Glyn Dwr's supporters. They began by attacking the far northern strongholds in 1400, moving south to take Harlech and Aberystwyth in 1404.*

◁ *The mountainous country of North Wales was well suited to the guerrilla tactics of Welsh tribesmen. But the building of massive castles in the 1280s allowed the English to station permanent garrisons of troops to assert control.*

THE WELSH FLAG

The modern Welsh flag features the red dragon of Cadwallader, prince of Gwynedd. The dragon has been the symbol of Wales for over 1,000 years. The white and green areas represent the colours of Prince Llywelyn the Great.

Wallace and Bruce

△ *According to legend, a spider was watched by Robert Bruce, in hiding after a defeat. As it tried to swing from one beam to another, he was encouraged by its determination and went on to win his next battle.*

For most of the 1200s, Scotland was a strong and stable country. The Scots were ruled by the Canmore dynasty of kings, who extended control into Argyll and Caithness and drove the Norwegians out of the Western Isles. In 1251 King Alexander III forged a link with England when he married Margaret, daughter of Henry III.

Disaster soon struck. Alexander died in 1286, the last male of the Canmore line. The only heir was his infant granddaughter Margaret, who also died, while travelling across the sea to her new realm in 1290. Suddenly, Scotland was adrift without a clear leader.

The Scots asked Edward I of England to decide who should be their new king. He chose John Balliol, a relative of David I, hoping that he would help in an English takeover of Scotland. Balliol, however, rebelled against him and in 1296 Edward invaded and Balliol surrendered.

It seemed that Scotland was about to fall. The only resistance came from William Wallace, who won a victory over the English at Stirling in 1297. A year later he, too, had been defeated.

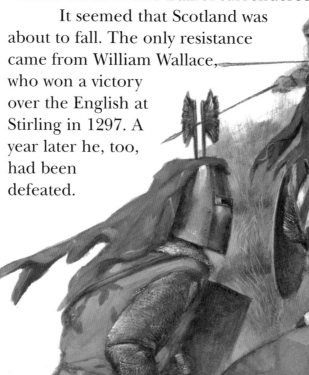

In 1305 he was captured and killed. Edward began to gain control of southern Scotland.

Two events saved the country. One was the death of Edward I in 1307: his successor, Edward II, was weaker and a poor military leader. The other was the rise of Robert Bruce, who seized the throne in 1306. He was supported by many Scots, who hated the English occupation. Things at first were desperate. Robert was twice defeated by the English, but in 1314 his army routed Edward's troops at Bannockburn, near Stirling. Robert went on to capture Berwick Castle and raided northern England. Edward's grip on Scotland was broken. In 1328 his son, Edward III, recognized Robert as king.

△ **Robert Bruce in armour**. Robert's grandfather had claimed the Scottish throne in 1290, but had been passed over for John Balliol. Robert himself seized the throne in 1306 after the murder of a rival baron, John Comyn. He went on to recapture most castles held by the English in Scotland.

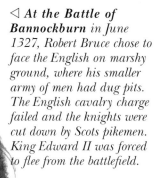

▷ **A Scottish hero**, Robert Bruce died in 1329 having secured Scots independence. England under the warlike Edward III invaded Scotland several times in the years until 1357, when peace was made.

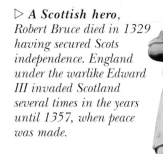

◁ **At the Battle of Bannockburn** in June 1327, Robert Bruce chose to face the English on marshy ground, where his smaller army of men had dug pits. The English cavalry charge failed and the knights were cut down by Scots pikemen. King Edward II was forced to flee from the battlefield.

81

1298 Edward I's war against France ends, having cost £750,000 in four years; this was partly paid for by a wool tax of £2 per sack.

1304–11 Nearly 40,000 sacks of wool exported each year.

1315–17 Food shortages lead to famine and riots in Bristol, Wales and Lancashire.

c.1336 England's population reaches 7 million; famines increase hardship.

1348 Black Death reaches England and spreads to Scotland and Ireland within months; one third of the population is killed.

c.1350 Wages for farmworkers rise, while prices fall. There are over 1,000 markets active in England and Wales.

1377 Edward III raises "poll tax" – fourpence (about 1.5p) from all except beggars.

△ **Merchants** extended their businesses as the economy grew and more goods were produced. They built warehouses and hired cargo ships. Land carriers brought goods along a network of trading routes which linked the cities of Europe and the Near East. Ships brought silks and precious metals from the Mediterranean, returning with British coal, wool and timber.

1381 Peasants' Revolt against the poll tax.

c.1400 Rise of wealthy trade guilds in London; up to 40 wool ships leave the port for Europe every day.

Towns and Trade

The 14th century was full of disasters. The population grew rapidly, but farmers could not grow enough food to keep up with the increase. Many people starved, especially when bad weather destroyed crops and disease killed livestock during the famine of 1315–17. Then came the Black Death, which wiped out a third of Britain's population between 1348 and 1351. After this, kings raised crippling taxes to pay for the long and futile war against France.

Each of these disasters had a powerful effect on trade. The vast majority of people were peasants, who made their living from the land. After the Black Death there were barely enough people to grow crops and tend animals. Many refused to do feudal work on their lords' land. On some manors, peasants were allowed to pay their rent in cash, rather than in goods and labour.

Landowners began to look for an easier way of farming. The solution was simple: sheep. Huge flocks of sheep could be kept on grassland, which needed no ploughing or harvesting. Their fleeces could be sold for a large profit. By 1400 there were as many as 18 million sheep in England alone.

The wool, woven into cloth, became England's most important product. Huge amounts of cloth were exported to northern Europe and Spain. Wool merchants grew very rich, and

TALLY STICKS

During the 13th century, deals between two traders were recorded with tally sticks. The amount owed was marked on the stick with notches – thick ones for pounds, thinner ones for shillings and thinnest of all for pennies. Then the stick was split in two, and each trader kept half. The amount of the debt could be checked by putting the two halves together again, so that they "tallied". When the debt was paid off, the whole stick might be kept as a record. By the 14th century business methods were more complicated, and merchants used paper bills instead. The amount of paperwork grew rapidly and tally sticks were no longer used. Clerks and scribes were employed to write out bills of sale, contracts, orders and other documents. The merchant sealed them with wax seals.

weaving centres, such as Leeds, Halifax and Bury St Edmunds, quickly developed into thriving new towns.

British ports grew rapidly as well. Ships from Bristol took cloth to southern France. Venetian and Genoese traders came to Southampton, bringing spices, dried fruits and silks from the East, as well as wine and oil from the Mediterranean. London was the most important city in the land. It was the chief port and trading centre, and had the biggest population.

▽ *A medieval wine jug.* On market and fair days, many people came to the towns to buy and sell goods. They also came to have a good time in the taverns, drinking cheap ale, cider or wine. Ale had to be tasted by an "ale-conner" before it could be sold.

△ *Jesters entertain* at a grand feast, while minstrels play in the gallery overlooking the Great Hall. The most important guests sat at the high table on the raised dais with the lord. They probably had padded seats, while others sat on hard benches at the side tables. The dishes were carried in from the kitchens by a procession of servants.

▽ *Carpenters at work cutting planks.* Anyone who wanted to learn a trade such as carpentry or masonry had to pay a sum of money to become an apprentice in a guild. For up to seven years, he was taught all about the craft by a guild master. Then he would be qualified as a journeyman and could work for a daily wage. Many guilds grew very wealthy. They used their funds to look after members who became ill or poor. They also built splendid guild halls for their meetings and their masters wore grand and expensive livery (uniforms).

Black Death

△ A red cross marks the doorway of a plague house to warn others not to enter. At the time, nobody knew why the disease spread, or how it could be cured. The infection was in fact carried by the fleas which lived on black rats and transferred to humans. Most people died within three days.

In June 1348 a fleet of Gascon ships from Bordeaux sailed into the Dorset port of Melcombe Regis. The ships carried wine – and bubonic plague. This deadly disease had already swept across Europe from the plains of Asia, killing millions in its path.

The plague, or Black Death as it was later called, spread with terrifying speed. From Dorset, it raged across Britain. The first sign was a black swelling in the armpit or the groin, oozing blood. Death was almost certain and very quick but agonizing. A doctor might catch the disease from a patient and die in minutes. Peasants dropped dead in the fields.

So many perished that the graveyards were soon full and corpses had to be buried in fields. Within a year, about one third of the population of England and Wales had died. By 1350 the Black Death had reached all of Scotland except the far north. Ireland had also been ravaged.

This was the greatest disaster in British history. The population plunged from about

five million to three million. It kept falling, as the plague broke out again several times. Whole villages were abandoned and some towns were almost deserted. By 1450, there were barely two and a half million people left in England and Wales.

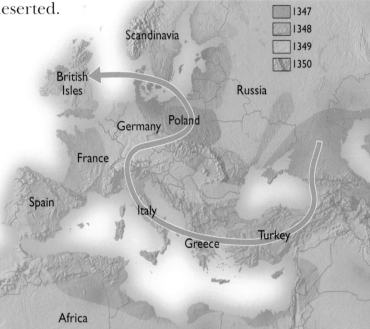

▽ *From East Asia, the plague swept into the north and west of Europe.*

▽ *Families bury their dead in a crowded graveyard. In many places the sick died too fast for the living to bury them. People were afraid of being infected by the corpses, and left them in the street, to be collected. When coffins ran short, bodies were carried on planks and dumped in mass graves.*

▽ *Medieval towns made ideal places for disease to spread. The streets were filthy, with open gutters in the middle where townsfolk threw all their waste. In the crowded houses, people rarely had clean water for washing.*

△ *An image of Death rides on a cart full of dead plague victims. Many people saw the Black Death as a punishment from God for their sins. They believed that it marked the end of the world. Doctors were unable to find any cure. Priests were often too frightened to go out*

Hundred Years' War

The Hundred Years' War actually lasted from 1337 to 1453. It covered the reigns of five English kings, each of whom tried in vain to gain control of France.

The conflict began with the death of Charles IV of France, who left no male heir. Edward III of England claimed the throne because he was grandson of an earlier French king. Also England ruled Gascony in France and the French were trying to seize power there. France angered Edward by supporting the Scots in their struggle against England and by interfering with England's wool trade in Flanders.

The first stage of the war lasted until 1360. Edward defeated the French in two battles, at Crécy and Poitiers. He also captured King John of France and seized Calais. After this Edward agreed to give up his claim to the French throne, in return for rights over Gascony, Calais and other territory. War broke out again in 1369.

▷ **Light mail** or padded leather jerkins were worn by foot soldiers and bowmen. By the 1400s, many knights sported full suits of plate armour. These were light enough to run in.

1328 Charles IV dies leaving no male heir.
1337 Philip of France seizes Gascony; Edward III claims French throne and declares war.
1346 English win Battle of Crécy.
1347 Calais falls to Edward III after long siege.
1356 English win Battle of Poitiers; French king captured.
1360 Treaty of Bretigny brings brief peace.
1369 War resumes; England lose territory.
1375 One-year truce agreed at Bruges.
1377 Richard II becomes king.
1399 Richard II deposed and murdered; Henry IV becomes king.
1413 Death of Henry IV: his son Henry V becomes king.
1415 Henry defeats French at Agincourt.
1419 Henry captures Rouen after long siege and seizes Normandy.
1420 Treaty of Troyes; Henry is heir to French throne.
1422 Death of Henry V; Henry VI becomes king at only 9 months old.
1429 Joan of Arc leads French to defeat English.
1451 French capture Bordeaux and Bayonne.
1453 English driven out of Gascony; end of the war.

▷ **King Henry VI** came to the throne as a baby and did not take power until 1437. He was a poor king, being too gentle and weak-willed to hold onto England's territories in France.

△ **England's famous Black Knight** was one of many to fight in the 100 years war.

JOAN OF ARC
Believing that God had called her to save France, this peasant girl inspired the French army to rescue Orléans. She then led troops to Rheims so that France's new king could be crowned. Tragically, Joan fell into the hands of the English, who tried and burned her as a witch.

This time Edward lost much of what he had gained before. When Henry V became king in 1413 the next phase of war began. Henry's victory at Agincourt led to his ruling much of northern France. But by the 1430s these gains were being swept away by the French army, inspired by Joan of Arc. By 1453, England had lost all except for Calais.

⊗ Sluis (1340)

Calais (1347)

⊗ Agincourt (1415)
⊗ Crécy (1346)

Harfleur (1415)

⊗ Rouen (1419)
⊗ Rouen (1449)

Formigny (1450)

⊗ Melun (1420)

⊗ Patay (1429)
⊗ Orléans (1428)

⊗ Poitiers (1346)

⊗ La Rochelle (1415)

⊗ Auberoche (1356)

Bordeaux (1453)   ⊗ Bergerac (1450)

⊗ French victories
⊗ English victories

▷ **This map shows** sites the major battles of the Hundred Years' War. The English victories came mostly in the early stages.

◁ **A Welsh longbowman** at the Battle of Agincourt. The power and rapid shooting of the longbow (up to ten arrows per minute) made it a devastating weapon. At Agincourt, these archers shattered the French cavalry charge and opened the way for victory over a bigger force by a small English army.

▷ **French troops** besiege the port of Cherbourg. The English surrendered the town in 1450, losing their last stronghold in Normandy. France's success at the end of the war was due to her reformed army, which was well paid and properly trained. The English army was poorly paid by comparison: the cost of the long conflict had been crippling.

Wars of the Roses

**War with France ended in 1453. Soon a
series of civil wars began in England which
lasted until 1485. These were fought between
rival branches of the Plantagenets, the Houses of
York (whose symbol was the white rose) and of
Lancaster (their symbol was the red rose). Henry VI was
from the Lancastrian branch. He was a weak ruler who
suffered fits of madness.**

While Henry was ill, his brother Richard
governed as Protector. But when the king
recovered, Richard was dismissed. With an army of
supporters, Richard defeated the royal army at St Alban's in
1455 and became Protector again. Henry's wife, Margaret, was
determined to get rid of the Yorkist threat. In 1460, her
Lancastrian army defeated the Yorkists at Wakefield, and the
duke of York was killed. His son, Edward of
York, took on the cause and had himself
proclaimed King Edward IV of England in
1461. He went on to crush Margaret's

1453 King Henry VI insane;
York appointed Protector.

1455 King recovers; York
dismissed, but defeats
Lancastrians at St Albans.

1460 Lancastrians defeat and
kill Duke of York at
Wakefield.

△ *Elizabeth Woodville*
(above right) *was Edward
IV's queen. When he died,
Richard of Gloucester said
that her children were
illegitimate. Edward V and
his brother were probably
then murdered.*

1461 Edward of York defeats
Lancastrians; deposes
Henry.

1470 Lancastrians and Yorkist
rebels restore Henry to
the throne; Edward flees.

1471 Edward returns and
takes throne; Henry
murdered.

1483 Edward V becomes
king under Protector,
Richard of Gloucester,
who seizes throne.

1485 Henry Tudor defeats
and kills Richard III at
Bosworth; becomes
Henry VII.

△ *This gold sovereign*
*celebrates the marriage of
Henry Tudor and
Elizabeth, daughter of
Edward IV. This
wedding united the
Houses of York
and Lancaster*

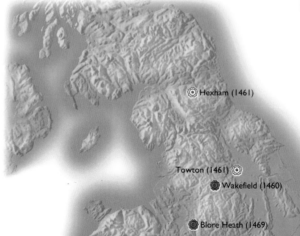

◎ Hexham (1461)

Towton (1461) ◎
● Wakefield (1460)

■ Blore Heath (1469)

Bosworth Field (1485) ◎   ◎ Stamford (1470)
◎ Mortimer's Cross (1461)
                    ● Northampton (1460)
    ◎ Tewksbury (1471)

St Albans (1455) ◎
St Albans (1461) ●

◎ Yorkist victory
● Lancastrian victory

△ *The map shows the principle
battles of the Wars of the Roses of
1455–85, which ended with the
decisive struggle at Bosworth Field.*

forces and depose Henry. In 1469
Margaret forced Edward to flee
and Henry became king again.
Edward returned in 1471 and
reclaimed his throne. He ruled
until his death in 1483, when
war broke out again. The king's
son, Edward V, was only 12 years
old, so his uncle Richard became
Protector. Richard locked Edward
in the Tower of London. He had
himself crowned King Richard III.
The last Lancastrian claimant,
Henry Tudor, defeated Richard
at the Battle of Bosworth in 1485.

HENRY VI

King Henry VI's weak
and indecisive reign was
marked by periods of
mental illness when he
had to be looked after like
a child. It came to a halt
altogether in 1465 when
he was captured by the
Yorkists and imprisoned
in the Tower of London.
He was freed in 1470 and
restored to the throne,
but was too ill to rule.
When his only heir, the
prince of Wales, was killed
in battle, Henry's
supporters melted away.
He was murdered in 1471.

▽ **Henry Tudor,** *the new king,
kneels after the battle at Bosworth.
Several of the king's supporters
changed sides, helping Henry to
victory. Richard was killed as he
fought on foot.*

TUDORS AND STUARTS

1485 Tudor Age begins; Henry VII becomes King of England after Battle of Bosworth.

1534 Henry VIII's Act of Supremacy marks the start of the English Reformation.

1536 England united with Wales.

1588 Attempted invasion thwarted by defeat of Spanish Armada.

1599 Globe Theatre in London opens, with William Shakespeare as chief playwright.

1603 Stuart Age begins; James I succeeds Elizabeth I.

1607 First successful colony established in North America.

1613 British trading station opens in Surat, India.

1642–8 Civil War in England and Scotland.

1649 Execution of Charles I.

1660 Monarchy restored in England.

1688 William of Orange invades England and replaces James II.

1690 William defeats Irish and French at the Boyne.

1707 Act of Union joins England, Wales and Scotland.

1714 Death of Queen Anne ends Stuart Age.

The age of the Tudor and Stuart monarchs lies at the heart of British history. Within just over two hundred years, there were staggering changes, which mean that Britain was established as a major and growing power in the western world.

In 1485, when Henry VII seized the throne, the British Isles were still emerging from the Middle Ages. Scotland, Ireland, Wales and England were still separate nations. They were looked on as poor and uncivilized countries in a remote corner of Europe. The vast majority of British people lived in the countryside, working on the land, and were very poor. There were few big towns, and little organized industry.

By 1714, when Queen Anne died, the picture was vastly different. There was a United Kingdom of Great Britain after the Union of Scotland with England and Wales in 1707. Two great European powers, France and Spain, had been defeated and the British navy ruled the oceans. Britain was the most successful trading nation in Europe, with the beginnings of an empire which stretched from North America to the coast of India. The Age of

DIEU·ET MON·DROIT

Industry was beginning, and people were starting to migrate from the land to the developing factory towns.

In between, crucial influences had been at work. The Renaissance had reached Britain from southern Europe, producing some of the greatest writers, musicians and artists in history. The Reformation had brought religious divisions. And the power of parliament had increased hugely, following the shocks of the Civil War.

The Age of the Tudors

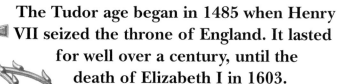

1485 Richard III defeated and killed at Bosworth; Henry VII becomes first Tudor monarch.

1509 Death of Henry VII; his son Henry VIII is king.

1512 Scotland and France at war with England.

1533 Henry divorces Catherine and marries Anne Boleyn; English Reformation begins.

1536 Dissolution of the monasteries.

1547 Henry VIII dies; his nine year-old son Edward VI becomes king; English victory over Scotland at Pinkie.

1553 Death of Edward VI; his sister Mary becomes queen.

1555 Mary begins persecution of Protestants.

1558 Death of Mary; her sister Elizabeth I becomes queen.

1564 Birth of William Shakespeare.

△ *Tudor Britain saw a boom in new building, from great palaces to humbler town houses. Many of these smaller dwellings were half-timbered, with wooden frames, clay or brick walls and thatched roofs.*

1585 War begins between England and Spain.

1587 Execution of Mary, Queen of Scots.

1588 Defeat of Spanish Armada.

1603 Death of Elizabeth I; James VI of Scotland becomes King James I of England.

The Tudor age began in 1485 when Henry VII seized the throne of England. It lasted for well over a century, until the death of Elizabeth I in 1603. During this time, Britain was a more stable and peaceful place than it had ever been. There were rebellions, and minor wars between England, Scotland and France. But the turmoil that had been experienced during the fifteenth century, with its civil wars and exhausting struggle against the French, was over for good.

For many, Britain became a more prosperous place. Industry and farming expanded, and there was an explosion in overseas trade. British explorers and merchants opened up new sea routes across the Atlantic and Indian Oceans. The boldest of them all, Francis Drake, became the first man to lead an expedition right round the world.

The Tudor age also saw England growing much stronger than her neighbours. Wales was formally placed under English rule by Henry VIII. His armies also inflicted severe defeats on Scotland, in spite of French support for the Scots. The crowns of Scotland and England were united in 1603. By that time, too, Ireland was controlled by England.

TUDOR COSTUME

Clothes were a means of displaying your wealth. Rich women could afford clothing made of fine wool, linen or silk. They wore padded skirts held up with loops. Over these went bodices and colourful floor-length gowns. These might have all sorts of fashionable features – puffed sleeves, high collars or starched ruffs around the neck. Silk stockings were a great luxury. Middle-class women wore knitted woollen stockings, and white aprons to protect their gowns.

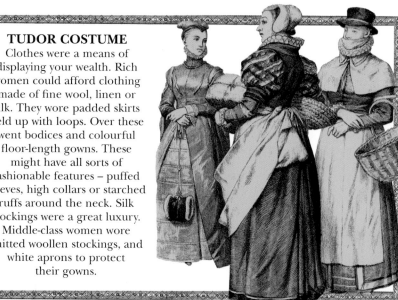

△ **Henry VII's coat of arms.** *At the centre is a shield quartered with lions (representing England) and feathers (representing Wales). On the left stands the dragon symbol of York and on the right, the symbol of Lancaster. The French motto means "God and My Right".*

△ **King Henry VII** *married Elizabeth of York. By marrying Elizabeth, he united the warring Houses of York and Lancaster. Henry's most important task was to found a dynasty and leave a strong son to succeed him. But his eldest child Arthur tragically died of disease in 1502, and Arthur's ten-year-old brother Henry became heir to the throne.*

However, the most far-reaching change was to divide Britain from parts of Europe. The Reformation separated the English Church from the control of the Roman Catholic Church. This caused conflict with Catholic nations such as Spain, but it also spurred a feeling of independence. Britain's growing sense of itself as a nation was reflected in many ways, from the plays of William Shakespeare to the victory over the Armada – a fleet sent by Philip II of Spain to invade Britain.

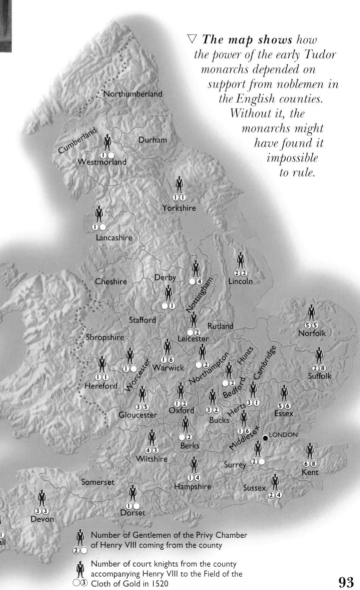

▽ **The map shows** *how the power of the early Tudor monarchs depended on support from noblemen in the English counties. Without it, the monarchs might have found it impossible to rule.*

Number of Gentlemen of the Privy Chamber of Henry VIII coming from the county

Number of court knights from the county accompanying Henry VIII to the Field of the Cloth of Gold in 1520

Henry VIII

King Henry VII was a clever ruler. He kept control of his nobles by offering them important offices or land in exchange for their support. He chose advisers who were shrewd and loyal. He acted swiftly to get rid of any rivals to the throne, having the Yorkist Earl of Warwick put to death in 1499.

Just as importantly, Henry made the monarchy rich again. He raised rents, forced nobles to pay heavy fines and increased taxes. His grasping ways made him unpopular. One historian of the time wrote: "he began to treat his people with more harshness and severity, in order that they remained more thoroughly in obedience to him".

It is not surprising that when Henry VII died in 1509, there was general rejoicing. The new king Henry VIII seemed very different from his father. Tall, handsome and full of energy, he looked like a hero. He loved hunting and was a fine athlete and swordsman. Henry spoke four languages, played music and sang well, and wrote ballads. He had a large appetite and was also immensely fond of both food and drink.

△ *Every inch a king. Henry VIII in his thirties was still strong and athletic. He spent many hours practising single combat or jousting in full armour, and was a fine marksman with the bow. However, though he led his army in France, he did not take part in any battles.*

Yet Henry only became king by accident. His elder brother Arthur had been heir to the throne, but he had died young. So Prince Henry took Arthur's place, and married his widow, the Spanish princess Catherine of Aragon.

Henry was determined to win glory in war. In 1513, he led an army to France. The expedition wasted a lot of money and gained little. Meanwhile another English army stopped an

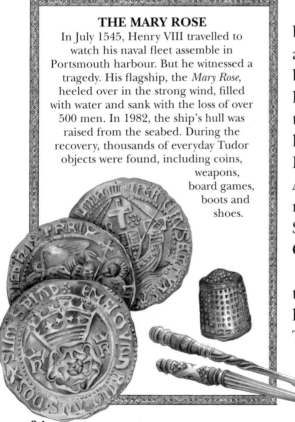

THE MARY ROSE
In July 1545, Henry VIII travelled to watch his naval fleet assemble in Portsmouth harbour. But he witnessed a tragedy. His flagship, the *Mary Rose*, heeled over in the strong wind, filled with water and sank with the loss of over 500 men. In 1982, the ship's hull was raised from the seabed. During the recovery, thousands of everyday Tudor objects were found, including coins, weapons, board games, boots and shoes.

▽ *A "lira da braccio", an early kind of violin. Music was one of Henry's greatest loves. He composed several songs, played the organ and the lute, and sang to his own accompaniment. He even sang with the choirs in his royal chapels.*

invasion by the Scots at the Battle of Flodden. Bored by the daily running of government, Henry left most of this work to his powerful and ambitious Lord Chancellor, Thomas Wolsey. The king preferred to spend his time hunting, jousting and playing music.

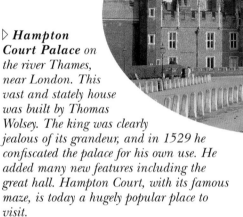

▷ **Hampton Court Palace** on the river Thames, near London. This vast and stately house was built by Thomas Wolsey. The king was clearly jealous of its grandeur, and in 1529 he confiscated the palace for his own use. He added many new features including the great hall. Hampton Court, with its famous maze, is today a hugely popular place to visit.

1486 Henry VII marries Elizabeth of York.
1487 Rebellion of Lambert Simnel crushed by royal forces.
1491 Prince Henry born, second son of Henry VII.
1497 Perkin Warbeck, pretender to the English throne, captured after attempt at revolt.
1501 Death of Prince Arthur; Prince Henry becomes heir to the throne.
1509 Henry VIII takes the throne on the death of his father; marries Catherine of Aragon.
1512–13 War against France; Henry leads troops to Calais.
1513 Scots heavily defeated at Battle of Flodden.
1515 Thomas Wolsey becomes Lord Chancellor.
1520 Henry meets King Francis of France at the "Field of the Cloth of Gold".
1522–25 War with France again.

△ **A royal hunt**, pictured on a Tudor tapestry. It shows deer being chased by hounds. Henry VIII was a keen huntsman and an expert rider. He sometimes stationed up to ten horses along the line of his day's hunting and rode one after the other, leaving them all exhausted.

95

Henry's Six Wives

1501 Henry's brother Arthur dies, leaving Catherine of Aragon a widow.

1509 Henry becomes king and marries Catherine, with special dispensation from the Pope.

1511 First son born, but dies two months later.

1513–14 Two sons die after birth; a third is still-born.

1516 Birth of Princess Mary.

1526 Henry falls in love with Anne Boleyn.

1527 Henry requests the Pope to annul his marriage; papal court set up in London to decide the question.

△ *An executioner's axe. Henry sentenced to death many who opposed him. Sir Thomas More, one of the king's chancellors, and John Fisher, Bishop of Rochester were beheaded in 1535.*

1529 Henry dismisses Wolsey.

1531 Henry declares himself Supreme Head of the English Church.

1533 Henry divorces Catherine and marries Anne Boleyn; birth of Princess Elizabeth.

1536 Henry divorces Anne and has her executed, marries Jane Seymour.

1537 Birth of Prince Edward; death of Jane.

1539–40 Henry marries and divorces Anne of Cleves; marries Catherine Howard.

1542 Catherine Howard executed.

1543 Henry marries Catherine Parr.

Henry VIII was blessed with palaces, wealth and immense power. He was good-looking and highly talented. He had married a clever and able wife. But there was still one thing he desperately wanted – a son to become king after him.

Catherine of Aragon had given birth to a son, who died. Between 1513 and 1514, three more sons were born, but none survived. In 1516, Catherine produced a girl, who was christened Mary. Henry was a religious man, and he came to believe that God was punishing him. The Bible stated that a man should not marry his brother's wife. Catherine had been Prince Arthur's widow, and the Pope had had to give permission for her to marry Henry.

Here was one answer to the king's problem: his marriage was sinful. In 1526 another answer appeared. Henry fell in love with Anne Boleyn, who had recently come to his court. But Anne would not become his mistress. She wanted Henry to divorce Catherine and marry her. Then she could bear him a son. The king ordered his Chancellor, Thomas Wolsey, to arrange for the Pope to reverse his decision and end the marriage. Months slipped by without a judgement, for the Pope disapproved of the divorce. Henry blamed Wolsey for the delay and in 1529 he sacked him.

Henry began to ignore the Pope's authority. In 1532, he forced priests to recognise him as Head of the English Church. A year later, he appointed a new

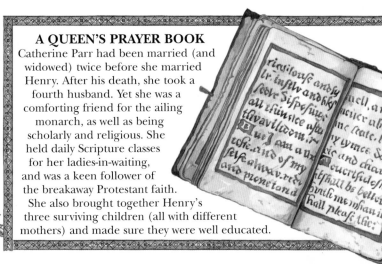

A QUEEN'S PRAYER BOOK
Catherine Parr had been married (and widowed) twice before she married Henry. After his death, she took a fourth husband. Yet she was a comforting friend for the ailing monarch, as well as being scholarly and religious. She held daily Scripture classes for her ladies-in-waiting, and was a keen follower of the breakaway Protestant faith. She also brought together Henry's three surviving children (all with different mothers) and made sure they were well educated.

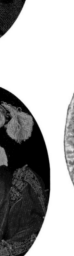

The six wives of Henry VIII.
At the top (from left to right) *are*
Catherine of Aragon, whom he divorced,
Anne Boleyn, who was beheaded, and Jane
Seymour, who died soon after giving birth.
At the bottom (from left to right) *are*
Catherine Howard, who was also
beheaded, Anne of Cleves, whom
Henry quickly divorced, and
Catherine Parr, who survived
the king.

ANNE BOLEYN

An Italian visitor wrote that
Anne Boleyn was "not one of
the handsomest women in
the world", with a long neck,
dark skin and wide jaw.
However, she captivated the
king with her eyes "which are
black and beautiful", her wit
and her strong personality.

ROMAN CATHOLICS

Until the reign of Henry VIII, nearly
everyone in England was baptized and
brought up in the Church of Rome. They
were surrounded by colourful images and
rituals of Catholicism. Catholics prayed
regularly, using their rosary beads as
counters. Many went on pilgrimages to
important shrines, such as Canterbury.
They believed that these journeys would
bring them forgiveness for their sins.

Archbishop, Thomas Cranmer, who granted him a
divorce from Catherine. He and Anne were secretly
married, and Anne was crowned queen. She gave
birth to a girl, Princess Elizabeth, in September 1533.
No sons came, and by 1536 Henry wanted to be rid of
Anne. She was accused of adultery, divorced and
beheaded. Only days later, the king married Jane
Seymour. She also produced a male heir for Henry –
Prince Edward. Soon after Edward's birth Jane died
of fever. Henry now had a son at last, but no wife.

Henry was to marry three more times. In 1539
he agreed to marry a German princess, Anne of
Cleves, before he met her. This would give him a
useful ally in Europe. But he found Anne dull and
quickly divorced her. Next was Catherine Howard,
who became queen in 1540 and was beheaded for
adultery in 1542. A year later, Henry married
Catherine Parr, who looked after his children and
nursed him through his final illness.

The English Reformation

When the Pope would not allow Henry VIII to divorce Catherine of Aragon, Henry decided that he would defy the Pope, and take charge of the English Church himself. This would gain him a divorce, extra power and wealth.

In 1532, he called Parliament and pushed through a series of statutes which cut England off from Rome. One stopped the payment of special taxes to the Pope. Another declared that the king was "Supreme Head of the English Church and Clergy". The Treason Act of 1534 threatened a death sentence on anyone who denied Henry's power over the Church. These measures had a lot of support. The Catholic clergy were already very unpopular in Britain. People resented the huge wealth of the Church. There were hundreds of monasteries, nunneries and other religious houses throughout Britain. In 1536 Parliament passed an act to "dissolve", or close down, many of the

1532 Henry calls Parliament; Act of Submission forces Church assemblies to get royal approval for new religious laws; Act of Annates stops payment of taxes to Rome.

1533 Act of Appeals forbids people from asking Rome to settle disputes; Thomas Cromwell is chief minister.

1534 Act of Supremacy declares English king to be head of the Church; Succession Act bars Catherine's daughter (Mary) from succeeding to the throne; Treason Act outlaws denial of king's supremacy.

1535 First English translation of the *Bible* (begun by William Tyndale) completed by Miles Coverdale; Thomas Cromwell, Henry's Vicar General, assesses wealth of religious houses.

1536 Dissolution of the smaller monasteries.

1538 Every parish church forced to buy a copy of *English Bible*.

1539 Dissolution of larger religious houses begins.

▽ *Thomas Cromwell's men* destroy a monastery in 1539. Treasures were seized, statues smashed, paintings defaced, books burned and stained glass windows broken. This sacking, plus the sale of Church lands and property, gained Henry about £1.5 million.

△ *Before the Reformation, few English people could read the Bible. It was in Latin, and English translations were banned – an act supported by Thomas More. Henry VIII permitted a translation, and the first English Prayer Book followed in 1549.*

smaller communities. Later, the larger ones were dissolved as well. Their treasures were plundered and most of the wealth was seized by the monarch.

The dissolution of the monasteries turned many ordinary people against Henry. Noblemen in Lincolnshire and northern England used this discontent to start a rebellion, which spread across the country. The rebels demanded an end to the destruction of the religious houses and a return to rule by the Pope. Over 30,000 people took part in a "Pilgrimage of Grace" in Yorkshire. The uprisings ended peacefully, but Henry took revenge by executing nearly 250 of the leaders.

PROTESTANTISM
French-born John Calvin was a leader of the Reformation in Europe. His ideas greatly influenced Protestants in Britain. Calvin believed that faith in God was more important than good works.

◁ *Martin Luther was a German priest who became unhappy with the Church's corruption. In 1517, he protested against some Catholic practices. This sparked the Reformation, which led to the founding of several independent, or Protestant, churches.*

◁ *A gold cross that survived the dissolution. Nearly everything of value was taken away from the monasteries, including lead from the roofs and ornaments such as this. They were then melted down for their metal and jewels.*

Scotland and the Tudors

During the first half of the Tudor period, Scotland was still independent and thriving. Scottish kings were determined not to come under English control. They turned for help to England's most powerful rivals – the French. The alliance between Scotland and France was renewed in 1512.

A year later, war broke out between England and France. The Scottish king, James IV, seized the chance to help his ally and invaded northern England. Near the village of Flodden in Northumberland, the Scots were cut to pieces by a smaller English force, and James was killed.

After this there was peace for a while. The new king, James V, was horrified by Henry's split with Rome, and tried to prevent the same thing happening in Scotland. He passed laws to ensure obedience to the Pope. This pleased his allies in France, a Catholic country.

Peace came to an end in 1542. The ageing Henry VIII was now very fat and could scarcely walk. All the same, he planned one last attempt to conquer France. First he had to stop the Scots attacking him from the rear.

MARY STUART
Mary, Queen of Scots, had a strong claim to the English throne. Henry VIII had been her great-uncle. When she married the French dauphin Francis in 1558, she posed an even greater threat to the English monarch.

▽ **Rival positions at the Battle of Pinkie in 1547.**
The Scottish army, weakened by battle, was easily defeated by the English.

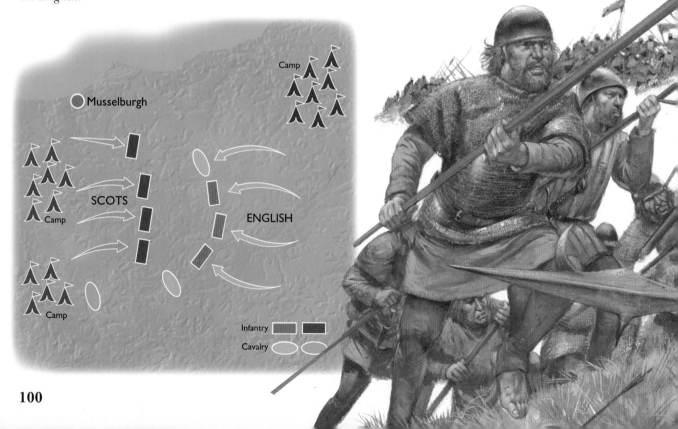

Musselburgh

Camp

Camp

SCOTS

ENGLISH

Camp

Infantry

Cavalry

His army defeated the Scots at Solway Moss. After Henry's death in 1547, the Scottish army was once again battered to defeat at Pinkie, in Lothian.

By this time James V was also dead. Scotland's new monarch was his infant daughter, Mary. When she grew up, she strengthened the ties between Scotland and France by marrying the dauphin, heir to the French throne. But he died in 1560, and Mary returned to Scotland. She found that things had changed. The Protestant faith had grown very popular, and she could not keep control. Mary, Queen of Scots, was forced to give up her throne in 1567 and take refuge in England.

▽ **At Flodden,** the Scottish troops charged downhill armed with long pikes. They were easily outfought by the English, who had shorter and more handy "halberds" which could smash through armour. The English killed anyone they caught. The Scots lost 10,000 men, including King James himself.

△ **Tartan cloth** had been worn by the Scots since at least the 13th century. There was a different pattern of stripes for each district or clan. At this time, a single length of tartan plaid was worn over the shoulder and held at the waist with a belt.

1513 King James IV killed at Flodden; his heir is 18-month-old James V.

1537 James marries Madeleine of France.

1541 James uses Scots Parliament to protect the authority of the Pope.

1542 English army defeats Scots at Solway Moss, Cumberland; death of James V, whose heir is the week-old Mary (later Mary, Queen of Scots).

1543–49 English attacks on southern Scotland.

1547 English victory at Battle of Pinkie.

1558 Mary marries Francis, heir to the French throne.

1560 The "Reformation Parliament" scraps papal authority and bans the Mass; death of Francis.

1561 Mary returns to Scotland.

1567–68 Mary flees to England; her son James VI (later James I of England) becomes yet another infant king.

△ **Pikes, axes and swords** were some of the battle weapons used at Flodden. Training was sorely lacking among the Scots and, despite their enthusiasm, probably lead to their defeat.

Edward VI and Mary

1547 Death of Henry VIII; Edward VI becomes king, under the Protectorate of the Duke of Somerset.

1548 King's council orders all religious images to be destroyed.

1549 *Book of Common Prayer* authorized by parliament; riots in Devon, Cornwall and East Anglia in protest at rising prices and high rents.

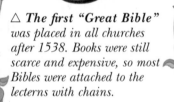

△ *The first "Great Bible" was placed in all churches after 1538. Books were still scarce and expensive, so most Bibles were attached to the lecterns with chains.*

1550 Somerset replaced by Duke of Northumberland.

1551 Mary refuses to accept new Protestant services; holds Catholic Mass.

1553 Death of Edward VI; Lady Jane Grey reigns for nine days before being ousted by Mary Tudor.

1554 Reunion with Rome; Mary marries Philip of Spain; rebellion in Kent led by Sir Thomas Wyatt.

1555 Persecution of Protestants begins; two Protestant bishops burned at the stake.

1556 Thomas Cranmer, once Archbishop of Canterbury, burned.

1557 England joins Spain in war against France.

1558 England forced to surrender Calais to the French; death of Mary; Elizabeth becomes queen.

Henry VIII died in 1547. He was hugely fat and in great pain from ulcers. His long reign had ended sadly, with the terrible waste of men and money in his last expedition to France. As he lay dying, the old king had written his will. He stated that his children Edward, Mary and Elizabeth should succeed him. Within the next 11 years, they all came to the throne.

The new king, Edward, was only nine years old, so England and Wales were governed by a "Protector", the Duke of Somerset. But Somerset was a poor leader. His rule led to riots in the western counties, and conflict between powerful nobles. In 1550 he was replaced by the Duke of Northumberland.

Meanwhile, the English Reformation was gathering pace. More religious houses were dissolved, and their treasures seized by the Crown. The first English Prayer Book became the official text for religious services. Edward VI was a keen Protestant, and hated his sister Mary, who remained Catholic. He made a will declaring that the next monarch should be Jane Grey, relative of the Tudors.

PHILIP OF SPAIN
Philip became King of Spain in 1556 and was also, briefly, the only Spanish King of England whilst he was married to Queen Mary. After her death, he also offered to marry the new Queen, Elizabeth I, but she refused.

▷ *Mary Tudor had a tragic and loveless upbringing. She was separated from her mother, rejected and declared a bastard by her father, and scorned by her brother. Even marriage to Philip of Spain brought little relief, for he abandoned her shortly afterwards.*

When the teenage king died in 1553, there was almost civil war. Jane ruled for just nine days before Mary displaced her and condemned her to death.

It soon became clear that Mary was determined to reverse the Reformation and stamp out the Protestant faith in England. Her aim was to reunite the English Church with Rome. In 1554 the Pope sent a cardinal to London to restore his power. Parliament repealed (cancelled) the religious laws of Edward's reign. And about 270 leading Protestants were condemned to death and burnt at the stake.

Mary made herself even more unpopular by marrying her cousin Philip, the heir to the throne of Spain. Philip became joint ruler, so now England was allied with a leading Catholic power. There was an uprising in Kent, and England was forced to join Spain in war against France. During this, the French captured Calais, the last English stronghold in Europe.

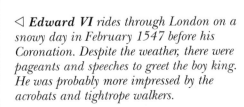

◁ *Edward VI rides through London on a snowy day in February 1547 before his Coronation. Despite the weather, there were pageants and speeches to greet the boy king. He was probably more impressed by the acrobats and tightrope walkers.*

PROTESTANT MARTYRS
Condemned Protestants suffered a nasty death during Mary's reign. They were tied to stakes and surrounded with bundles of firewood, which were then lit. At least 275 people met this slow and agonizing end. These victims were later commemorated by the Protestant writer John Foxe, whose *Book of Martyrs* contained many grisly pictures and descriptions. It was a huge bestseller during Elizabeth's reign, and helped to exaggerate Mary's brutality.

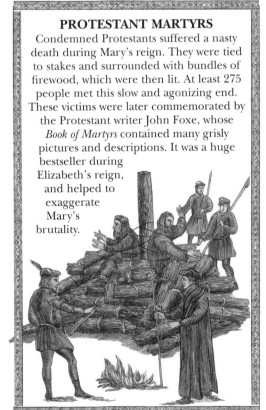

Elizabeth I

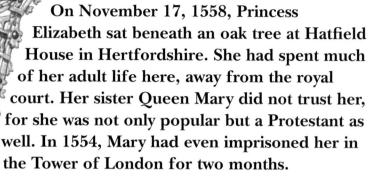

1533 Elizabeth born in Greenwich Palace, London, to Henry VIII and Anne Boleyn.

1536 Anne Boleyn beheaded.

1554 Elizabeth arrested on Mary's orders and accused of involvement with rebellions; she is held in the Tower and released after two months.

1558 Death of Mary; Elizabeth becomes the new queen.

1559 Laws confirming the Protestant faith in England; Elizabeth rejects offer of marriage from son of Holy Roman Emperor.

△ *Sir Walter Raleigh* *was a talented poet, soldier and explorer. He was one of Elizabeth's favourites in court, and had many rivals. He fell from favour when the queen discovered that he had secretly married one of her maids.*

1562 Elizabeth nearly dies of smallpox; parliament urges her to marry.

1569 Anti-Protestant rebellion in northern England.

1570 Pope excommunicates Elizabeth.

1571 Ridolfi Plot to assassinate Elizabeth discovered.

1572 Treaty signed between England and France.

On November 17, 1558, Princess Elizabeth sat beneath an oak tree at Hatfield House in Hertfordshire. She had spent much of her adult life here, away from the royal court. Her sister Queen Mary did not trust her, for she was not only popular but a Protestant as well. In 1554, Mary had even imprisoned her in the Tower of London for two months.

But now news arrived that Mary was dead and Elizabeth was the new queen. She travelled to London, where she was crowned eight weeks later. It was a time of great uncertainty. Many people feared that a young female monarch would not be strong enough to rule the country. There were two major problems to be solved at once: religion and marriage.

Mary's attempt to turn England back into a Catholic country had caused turmoil.

△ *Elizabethan ladies of fashion. Clothes for the wealthy grew more ornate throughout Elizabeth's reign. Both sexes wore clothes which were padded, quilted, embroidered or stiffened with whalebone. The sleeves on women's dresses were separate and tied or pinned to the bodice, with padded pieces to disguise the join.*

◁ *Dozens of grand houses were built in Elizabeth's time. Some, like the one shown here, retained features of the old fortified castle such as the moat – though this was for decoration rather than defence. Others were huge palaces or "prodigy houses", with many windows, and interiors adorned with tapestries, carvings and stone staircases.*

THE ROYAL COAT OF ARMS

Queen Elizabeth's coat of arms showed a shield quartered with the lions of England and the feathers of Wales. Above was a helmet and crest, and around it was a French motto which means "Evil Be To Him Who Thinks Evil". Underneath was another motto in Latin, which means "Always the Same". The supporters on either side were the lion symbol of England and the dragon symbol of Wales. Henry VIII's Parliament had passed the Acts of Union between 1536 and 1543, bringing Wales officially under English rule. It also became a Protestant country, and a Welsh translation of the New Testament first appeared in 1567.

▷ *Portraits of Elizabeth I were painted to stress her power and grandeur. They were not meant to be accurate likenesses. Here, she wears a sumptuous costume and jewels. Her left hand touches the globe, as a symbol of her subjects' explorations and conquests. Portraits also had to flatter her, of course. Those she did not like were destroyed.*

In 1559, Elizabeth framed new religious laws with the help of her chief minister, William Cecil. These established England as a Protestant country. The queen became Supreme Governor (rather than Head) of the Church, and priests had to use the *English Prayer Book*.

The problem of Elizabeth's marriage was never settled. Many kings and princes were keen to marry her, and her ministers wanted her to produce an heir to the throne. But Elizabeth realized that a foreign husband would make her unpopular and lessen her own power.

England now needed friends abroad. After the queen's new Protestant laws, many Catholic countries became enemies. The Pope "excommunicated" Elizabeth, cutting her off from the Catholic Church and declaring that she had no right to rule. But the queen found an ally in the French. In 1572 England and France made a treaty promising to help each other if they were attacked by another power.

Mary, Queen of Scots

Many Catholics in England and Europe wanted to get rid of Elizabeth I, and they had an ideal candidate to put in her place – her cousin Mary Stuart. Mary had a strong claim to the English throne, being a great-grand-daughter of Henry VII. She was a Catholic. She was already queen of Scotland and, unlike Elizabeth, she had given birth to an heir (James VI).

However, Mary was a poor ruler. By 1561, Scotland had become a largely Protestant nation, and the Catholic queen found it hard to keep control of her churchmen and nobles. Needing a husband to support her, she married Lord Darnley in 1565. This was a disaster. Mary soon hated her new husband, and grew close to her secretary, David Rizzio. In 1566, Darnley and his followers stabbed Rizzio to death.

Less than a year later, Darnley himself was killed when a massive explosion wrecked the house where he was sleeping. Many people suspected Mary of plotting his murder with her new lover, the Earl of Bothwell. When the queen married Bothwell, her subjects rose in revolt. She was forced to abandon her throne and flee south to England.

Elizabeth was not pleased to see her. Mary was a dangerous rival, and for the next 20 years Elizabeth kept her imprisoned in a series of remote country houses. But this did not stop her being the centre of several

△ *The Tower of London was not just a prison and the most important fortress in the land, but a centre for royal meetings and ceremonies. Elizabeth had been confined here during her sister Mary's reign. At her own coronation, Elizabeth's first act was to enter the Tower once again.*

1542 The infant Mary becomes queen of Scotland on the death of her father, James V.

1560 King of France, Mary's husband, dies.

1561 Mary returns to rule Scotland.

1565 Mary marries Lord Darnley, who is declared king of Scotland.

1566 Darnley and followers murder Mary's secretary, David Rizzio.

1567 Darnley killed in house explosion; Mary marries Bothwell.

1568 Mary defeated by rebels and forced to flee to England.

1569–71 Mary detained in Tutbury Castle; Catholic plots against Elizabeth, involving the Duke of Norfolk, aimed at rescuing Mary.

1583 Throckmorton Plot uncovered.

1586 Mary implicated in Babington Plot; she is tried and found guilty of treason.

1587 Mary executed at Fotheringhay Castle.

MARY AND LORD DARNLEY

When Mary married Lord Darnley in July 1565, they ruled as king and queen of Scotland. It seemed a perfect match. They were both young, handsome and Catholic. They were cousins and great-grand-children of Henry VII, giving them strong claims to the English throne. But Darnley was spoilt and vain. The Scots people disliked his arrogance and bullying.

△ **Mary Stuart**
became queen of Scotland at only six days old. She spent most of her childhood in France, where her first husband ruled and she was queen. At his death, she was still only eighteen, and returned to Scotland. Her son James was to become king of England and Scotland after Elizabeth's death.

Catholic plots. In 1569 some northern noblemen marched south with an army to rescue Mary. They were put to flight by royal troops. In 1571 another plot (known as the Ridolfi Plot) was uncovered. Elizabeth was shocked to find that one of the ringleaders was the Duke of Norfolk, a trusted adviser. Norfolk was beheaded in 1572.

Still the danger grew. In 1583 government spies arrested Francis Throckmorton, who told them (after torture) of a French plan to rescue Mary. In 1586 an even more alarming plot was discovered. Anthony Babington, a wealthy Catholic, had arranged for Elizabeth to be murdered and for a joint Spanish and French army to invade England. This time, there was clear evidence that Mary was involved. She was found guilty of treason and beheaded in 1587.

◁ **Mary was beheaded**
in the great hall at Fotheringhay in front of 300 people. She went to the block clothed in a black dress, which she took off to reveal a bright red petticoat. Her little dog trotted in, hidden under her skirts. The executioner needed three strokes of the axe to remove her head completely.

△ **Mary and Darnley** *were married in Holyrood Palace, Edinburgh. It had once been a monastery, but had been converted into a royal residence at the beginning of the century. It was also the scene of the fatal stabbing of Mary's secretary David Rizzio.*

◁ **Elizabeth's seal on Mary's death warrant.**
She took a long time to sign because she was unwilling to execute someone who was not just of royal blood but her own cousin. Elizabeth also realized that Mary's death might give Catholic plotters overseas a better excuse to assassinate her.

107

Life in Elizabethan Britain

1558 Thousands perish in epidemic of influenza and famine caused by bad harvests.

1559 Protestants, led by John Knox, occupy Edinburgh.

1560 Scotland breaks with Rome and becomes formally Protestant.

1563 New laws fix hours of work for labourers.

1565 Sweet potatoes brought to England from the New World.

1572 New Poor Law gives parishes the duty of providing for poor and old people.

1574 Scots pass law to control wandering beggars.

1580 Longleat House in Wiltshire completed.

△ *The gardens of great Tudor houses* were laid out neatly and regularly, to show how order had been created out of chaos. Paths and hedges were sometimes made into intricate patterns, such as the complex shapes of "knot" gardens or mazes.

1587 Burghley House in Lincolnshire completed.

1588 First complete Welsh translation of the *Bible*.

1589 First flushing lavatory built by Sir John Harington.

1596 Food riots in Kent; protesters against land enclosures march from Oxfordshire to London.

At the beginning of the Tudor Age, Britain's population increased for the first time since the Black Death. That growth continued (in spite of outbreaks of famine and disease) through Elizabeth's reign. By 1603 the population of England and Wales, for example, had risen from 3 million to 4.25 million.

More people meant greater demand for food and goods. Industry began to prosper and more land was cultivated to grow crops. But this was not good for everyone. As farmland became more valuable, landowners enclosed more fields for their sheep to graze. Villagers had less space to grow crops and feed their own animals. Rents and prices rose, too – much faster than workers' wages. The old manorial system of the Middle Ages had broken down by the 1570s, leaving many labourers without jobs or land. This caused a massive increase in begging. Parliament passed a series of Poor Laws to try to deal with them. In 1572, each parish was made responsible for providing jobs for the poor.

◁ *Rich people* liked to show off their wealth by wearing bright and exotic clothes. But members of the growing merchant class dressed more quietly. Their clothes were less colourful, but still made of the best quality materials such as velvet and satin. For everyday use a merchant's wife might wear a wool or linen gown covered by an apron, and a hat of linen or fur outdoors.

Meanwhile, merchants, sheep farmers and other members of the new "middle class" could spend their wealth on a greater variety of clothes, furniture and food. The rich built magnificent houses, which were much cosier places than the grim old castles.

▷ **Meals,** *for most people, consisted mainly of bread, soup and boiled meat. Rich people could afford luxuries such as sugar, wine, spices and bread made from white flour.*

▽ **Town houses** *were built with a timber frame covered with bricks and plaster, and roofed with clay tiles. Servants slept in the attic. The family living room and bedrooms were on the first floor, and the kitchen and storerooms on the ground floor.*

ELIZABETHAN MUSIC

The Elizabethans loved making music, from the simple tunes of wandering ballad singers and village fiddlers to the great choral works of the new Anglican Church. Children from wealthy families were taught to sing and play instruments such as the lute, the flute or the virginals (an early kind of piano). Especially popular was the singing of madrigals – songs for two or more voices singing separate melodies. Most great households employed groups of musicians to entertain them.

109

Life in Towns

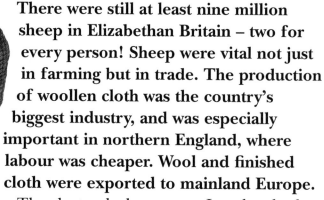

1550s Rise in exports of coal through Swansea; decline of Antwerp as major wool-trading port; London expands.

1560s Immigrants from Flanders bring new weaving technology to southeast England.

1561 Henry VIII's "base" English coinage is replaced by coins worth their weight in silver.

1565 Steel first produced from iron in Kent.

1579 First Scottish silk factory opens in Perth; the import of English cloth banned.

1582 New water supply system for London, using pumps on the River Thames.

△ *Cock-fighting* had been a popular town sport since Roman times. Spectators put bets on fights between gamecocks wearing metal or bone spurs on their legs. Fights took place on a raised platform in a special round "cockpit".

1592–7 Disastrous fall in value of wages compared with prices.

1598 Annual shipping of coal from Newcastle to London rises to 163,000 tonnes.

1600 Price of food has risen by about five times in 100 years.

There were still at least nine million sheep in Elizabethan Britain – two for every person! Sheep were vital not just in farming but in trade. The production of woollen cloth was the country's biggest industry, and was especially important in northern England, where labour was cheaper. Wool and finished cloth were exported to mainland Europe.

Thanks to cloth exports, London had become one of the greatest ports and trading centres in the continent. Cargo ships carried many other British products abroad, including coal, copper, salt and gunpowder. Steel as well as iron was made in the newly developed blast furnaces. By 1600, workshops were turning out everything from paper and glassware to sailcloth and cannons.

London, Britain's biggest town, had a population of over 200,000 in 1600. It was overcrowded, noisy and smelly. One visitor described the city as

"the filthiest in the world". Outbreaks of plague were frequent, especially in the hot summers. Queen Elizabeth feared that London would grow so large that it would become a focus of riots. She tried to limit the number of new buildings and inhabitants.

Over 90 percent of Britons still lived in the countryside and depended on townspeople to buy their produce. Town merchants also needed the country people to buy their goods. A barrier to trade was the state of the roads, which were little better than muddy tracks. Traders sent their cargo by river or sea whenever they could.

◁ **Coins** were made of pure gold or silver in early Tudor times. But Henry VIII debased (spoiled) the coinage by mixing it with base metals such as lead. In 1561, Elizabeth restored coins to their proper purity.

WORKING CLOTHES

Ordinary people could not afford to copy the fantastic and colourful costume of the wealthy. They wore clothes which were more comfortable and practical, though very drab. Men wore a loose-fitting shirt and breeches of coarse woollen cloth. Women wore a kirtle (dress) and apron of the same material, which were usually coloured brown or blue with simple vegetable dyes. These would rarely get washed, and in winter underclothes were never removed at all. Outer garments, hats and boots were made of leather.

▽ **The streets of an Elizabethan town** would be crowded with street stalls, shoppers, carts carrying goods, horsemen and country people bringing in their goods to sell. Shops of craftsmen such as cobblers and metalworkers were on the ground floor of houses. Each workshop or inn had its own sign, as most people were still unable to read. Pickpockets and cutpurses looked for victims among the throng.

The Renaissance in Britain

Since about 1500, Britain had felt the effects of the Renaissance. This "rebirth" had seen an outburst of fresh thinking and creativity throughout Europe. Starting in Italy in the 14th century, it had grown and spread. Painters, writers, sculptors and scholars began to look at the world in new ways, and use new techniques and theories.

In Britain, the painter Nicholas Hilliard produced exquisite miniature portraits of courtiers and monarchy, including Elizabeth herself. Thomas Tallis and William Byrd composed beautiful choral music and Robert Smythson designed stunning palaces. Writers, such as Christopher Marlowe and Ben Jonson, drew huge audiences to new city playhouses. William Shakespeare, the most famous playwright of all, created a new type of verse drama, which gave a

WILLIAM CAXTON

Caxton was a cloth merchant who learned the new craft of printing. He used single pieces of type for each letter. These were put together to form a page of print, then broken up and used again. Caxton published over 100 titles, covering history, religion and adventure. Among them were the life of St Jerome (*above*), Chaucer's *Canterbury Tales* and Malory's stories of King Arthur.

◁ *Ornate glassware and pottery, decorated with engraving or with designs in silver and gilt, were produced by craftsmen. A lot of precious metal and gemstones came from the Americas.*

▽ *The plays of William Shakespeare are still performed all over the world and in many languages. But the setting of the modern theatre, with its clever lighting and sloping stage, is very different from that of the Elizabethan Globe.*

▷ *The Globe playhouse was where Shakespeare's company performed plays. Spectators could pay one penny to stand as "groundlings" below the stage, or two pennies to sit in the sheltered galleries. A replica of the Globe has been built near the original site beside the river Thames in London.*

vivid picture of the Elizabethan world. In comedies such as *Twelfth Night* and tragedies such as *King Lear*, he explored the range of human feelings. Until late Tudor times, actors worked as travelling bands. But by 1600 several playhouses had been built in London, notably the Globe, where most of Shakespeare's greatest plays were first seen. These theatres boasted music and special effects.

The spread of Renaissance ideas was made easier by the development of printing. Until the 1470s there had been few books in Britain. Each one had to be copied out by hand. In 1476 William Caxton produced the first printed book in Britain, using techniques invented in Germany. Soon, new printing presses were set up, turning out quantities of cheap books and pamphlets. For the first time, information and ideas were available to anyone who could read. The printed word became an important way of forming public opinion.

△ **Shakespeare was born** in this house in Stratford-upon-Avon, Warwickshire in 1564. He left the town as a young man to work in London, but returned as a rich and successful playwright when he retired. His birthplace can be visited today.

1491 Death of William Caxton, printing pioneer.
1564 William Shakespeare born in Stratford-upon-Avon, Warwickshire.
1567 Opening of London's first proper theatre, the Red Lion.
1575 Tallis and Byrd publish a collection of their musical settings.
1580–1600 Nicholas Hilliard paints series of miniatures.
1589–91 Shakespeare's first plays written and performed.
1590 Edmund Spenser begins writing his poem *The Faerie Queene*, which glorifies Queen Elizabeth.
1591 William Smythson designs Hardwick Hall, Derbyshire.
1599 The Globe playhouse opens in London.
1616 Death of Shakespeare.

113

Explorers and Pirates

1497 John Cabot reaches coast of Newfoundland.

1553 Willoughby and Chancellor fail in their search for a northeast passage to China.

1555 The Muscovy Company founded to trade with Russia.

1562 John Hawkins begins carrying slaves from West Africa to the Caribbean.

1576–83 Attempts by Frobisher and Gilbert to find a northwest passage.

1577–80 Drake first leader to circumnavigate the world.

1585 First, unsuccessful New World colony founded on Roanoke Island.

1585–7 Davis explores Greenland and the Arctic.

1594 Lancaster sets up trading posts in the East Indies.

1595 Raleigh's vain trip to South America in search of El Dorado.

△ *The first kind of potato seen in Britain* was probably the sweet potato, which John Hawkins brought back from South America in 1564. Sir Walter Raleigh began planting the common potato on his estates in Ireland in about 1586. Potatoes were not widely grown in Britain until the 18th century.

1600 East India Company founded to trade with southern Asia.

1607 Colony of Virginia founded.

When the Tudor Age began, Europeans were on the brink of amazing discoveries about their world. Merchants were eager to expand their business, and find new trading routes. The cheapest and quickest way to do this was by sea.

There was one place above all they wanted to reach – the Far East. In Cathay (China) they could buy wonderful silks, gold and porcelain. In the Spice Islands (the Moluccas) they could buy precious cloves and nutmegs. The trouble was, nobody knew the way.

Then, in 1487, Portuguese ships rounded the southern tip of Africa. This opened up an easterly route to India and the Far East. In 1492, Spanish ships under Christopher Columbus set out for China in the opposite direction: westwards. To Columbus's surprise, he found the vast continents of the Americas instead.

Britain joined in the adventure. In 1497, John Cabot sailed westwards from Bristol in search of silks and spices. He landed on the coast of Newfoundland. There were no exotic goods to buy, but something that was just as valuable – fish. Soon, huge supplies of cod, as well as furs and timber, were being shipped back to Britain.

North America and the Caribbean became a crucial part of Britain's trading empire. In 1585, Sir Walter Raleigh founded the first colony on Roanoke Island, North Carolina. This failed, but a later colony gave England a firm foothold in North America. Sugar plantations were established in the West Indies, worked by slaves bought in from West Africa. This cruel trade brought great wealth to

▽ *Ships* sailed vast distances for explorers to find new sea routes for trade. The explorers aimed to reach the Far East, which they could do by sailing eastwards across the Indian Ocean or westwards across the Atlantic. But they found the American continents in the way!

△ *Plundered treasure.* Drake's *piratical expeditions made him very rich. On his round-the-world voyage, he captured treasure worth £25 million from one galleon!*

men such as the English naval commander and slave trader, Sir John Hawkins.

Meanwhile, other explorers were trying to find other ways to the Far East. In 1553 Sir Hugh Willoughby and Richard Chancellor searched for a northeast passage, to the north of Norway. They were blocked by ice, though Chancellor eventually reached Russia, and set up new trade links. In 1577, Francis Drake got past the Americas, sailing past the southern tip. He headed up the west coast of South America, before crossing the Pacific and Indian Oceans. He reached England again in 1580, becoming the first man to lead an expedition round the world.

FINDING YOUR WAY
Navigating a Tudor sailing ship was very difficult. The captain could find out his latitude (how far north or south he was) by using an astrolabe or a backstaff. By looking at the Sun through these, he could measure its angle above the horizon. But working out longitude (how far east or west) was much more difficult.

▷ *Spanish ships* carried gold, *silver and other treasures across the Atlantic to Spain from Mexico and Peru, which the Spanish had conquered by the 1540s. These ships, in turn, were prey to pirates and privateers such as Drake and Hawkins, who lurked in the Caribbean ready to attack.*

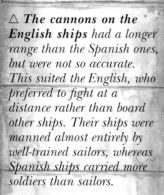

△ The cannons on the English ships had a longer range than the Spanish ones, but were not so accurate. This suited the English, who preferred to fight at a distance rather than board other ships. Their ships were manned almost entirely by well-trained sailors, whereas Spanish ships carried more soldiers than sailors.

The Spanish Armada

In 1558, King Philip II of Spain offered to marry Elizabeth I of England. In 1588, he sent a fleet to invade her realm. What caused the change? The answer, of course, was religion. Philip had hoped that by marrying Elizabeth he could ensure that England became a Catholic country again. But after the queen's Protestant Settlement of 1559 this hope disappeared. England was definitely Protestant.

In 1570 the Pope excommunicated Elizabeth, saying that she had "seized the kingdom" and was not the rightful ruler. This opened the way for Philip and his Catholic agents to try and get rid of her. In 1586, Philip assembled a huge fleet, or Armada, of ships to invade England and capture Elizabeth. But Philip's plans suffered a setback. In 1587, Francis Drake led an English attack on the Spanish port of Cadiz, sinking ships and burning vital supplies.

It took a whole year for the Armada to recover from this blow. At last, 130 Spanish ships set out from Lisbon. In July 1588 they reached the English Channel. The English fleet harassed the invasion force all the way up the narrow Channel. The Armada anchored off the French coast for safety.

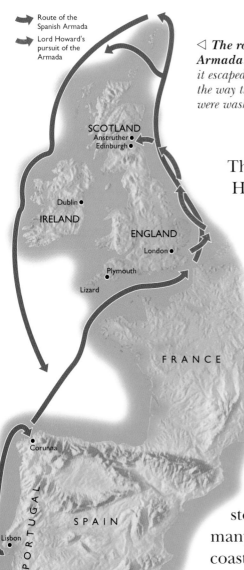

→ Route of the
Spanish Armada

⇒ Lord Howard's
pursuit of the
Armada

◁ *The route taken by the Spanish Armada.* *After the Battle of Gravelines, it escaped northwards because that was the way the wind blew. Many Spaniards were washed up on the Irish coast.*

Then the English leader Lord Howard sent in eight blazing "fireships". The terrified Spaniards were forced away from the shore and the two fleets clashed in a day-long battle off Gravelines. The Spaniards suffered terrible loss of life and decided to give up the invasion. They headed for Spain, round the north of Scotland and into the Atlantic. This was a disaster. Fierce storms scattered the fleet and many were wrecked on the coasts of Scotland and Ireland. Only 60 ships made it home.

FIRESHIPS
The eight ships were stuffed with anything which would burn – including tubs of butter! The guns were loaded with double shot, and went off when the fire reached them.
The ships were released at night, under full sail, to be blown towards the tightly packed Spanish fleet.

▽ *The Armada* was first sighted off the Isles of Scilly, to the west of Cornwall. A chain of beacon fires relayed the news along the south coast. The English fleet gathered to attack. It was bigger in number than the Armada, with 197 ships, but had fewer men.

Ireland and the Tudors

1494 "Poyning's Law" – English Parliament rules that all new laws in Ireland must be approved by them.

1534 Revolt by Thomas of Kildare against English rule crushed by Henry VIII.

1541 Irish Parliament accepts Henry as king, rather than simply lord, of Ireland.

1556 Mary begins "plantation" of Laois and Offaly.

1557 Irish Parliament repeals all laws imposing Protestantism.

1565 Court established to enforce Protestant religion.

1566–67 Revolt by Shane O'Neill to gain control of Ulster.

1569–71 English regional councils imposed in Connacht and Munster cause further uprisings.

1571 English president bans wearing of traditional Gaelic clothes in Munster.

1579–80 Revolt by James Fitzgerald in Munster is savagely crushed by English.

1584 Plantation of English settlers begins in Ulster.

1594 Hugh O'Neill, Earl of Tyrone, raises rebel army in Ulster; Nine Years' War begins.

△ *The ruins of a Franciscan monastery. Although forced to recognize Henry VIII as Supreme Head of the Irish Church in 1537, most Irish people remained loyal to Rome. Catholicism became an important symbol of Ireland's resistance to English domination, especially when the rebels were supported by Catholic leaders such as Philip of Spain.*

1598 O'Neill defeats the English at Yellow Ford, Ulster.

1599 Earl of Essex routed in County Wicklow and deserts his troops.

1603 O'Neill surrenders to Lord Deputy of Ireland.

Ireland was the only part of the British Isles which did not turn Protestant. Irish leaders rejected the Reformation, and in 1534 Thomas of Kildare rebelled against Henry VIII's rule. He offered the lordship of Ireland to the Pope or to the Holy Roman Emperor. Henry sent troops to defeat Kildare, and later forced the Irish to accept him as king.

All the same, English control over Ireland was weak, and most Irish people remained Catholic. During Elizabeth's reign, there were many attempts to "plant" English settlers on the island. Property was seized from Gaelic landowners and given to the Protestant newcomers. The crops grown on these plantations were used to feed the garrisons of English soldiers. In the 1570s, Elizabeth tried to extend her rule into the south and west, including Munster, Sligo and Monaghan.

It is not surprising that the Irish grew angry with English bullying, and frequently rose in rebellion. There were major revolts in 1569, 1571, 1576 and 1579.

IRISH HORSEMEN

Hugh O'Neill assembled an army of nearly 10,000 cavalry and infantry at the outset of the Nine Years' War. They were well-trained and equipped, and many had already fought in the Spanish army in Europe. Beside the old-fashioned knights in chain mail stood footsoldiers skilled in using pikes and firearms, such as muskets and a gun called an arquebus.

◁ *A war shield. Irish rebels in the early part of Elizabeth's reign used traditional weapons that had been common in tribal wars since the Middle Ages. They were mainly footsoldiers, wielding battle axes, bows and arrows, swords and spears. Their war shields were decorated with Celtic patterns.*

The most dangerous rising of all was the Nine Years' War, which started in 1594, when the Earl of Tyrone gathered a large army. He twice defeated the English in Ulster. In 1599, Elizabeth's favourite courtier, the Earl of Essex, failed to put down the rebels and fled back to England in disgrace. The war only ended in 1603 after the Irish were starved into surrender. For the first time, England ruled the whole of Ireland.

▽ *Irish footsoldiers, or kerns, were ferocious opponents of the English. Inspired by the sound of the bagpipes, they attacked settlements, burned buildings and stole or destroyed food stores. They were difficult to force into pitched battle because they preferred carefully prepared ambushes or lightning strikes.*

The Stuarts

1603 James VI of Scotland (1566–1625) becomes James I, first Stuart king of England and Ireland.

1604 End of war with Spain. Hampton Court Conference discusses church reform.

1605 Gunpowder Plot to blow up Parliament fails and conspirators are executed.

1609 "Plantation of Ulster" Protestant settlers move on to land taken from Irish Catholics.

1610 Negotiations for the "Great Contract" fail to solve financial problems.

△ **The manor house at Ashby St Ledgers** *in Northamptonshire. This house and estate belonged to the Catesby family until 1612, when it was sold. Robert Catesby was the leader of the Gunpowder plotters.*

1611 Publication of the Authorized Version of the Bible, known as the King James Bible.

1612 Death of Henry, eldest son of King James.

1621 Protestation of House of Commons stating their right to free speech.

1623 Prince Charles and George Villiers (later Duke of Buckingham) travel to Spain and try unsuccessfully to secure marriage between Charles and the daughter of King Philip IV.

1625 Death of James I.

In April 1603, the new king of England, James I, made a triumphal progress from Edinburgh, the capital of his native homeland of Scotland, to London. As he travelled slowly through his new kingdom, he was delighted by the rapturous reception from the crowds who greeted him with cheers and gifts. Remembering this happy time he described his new subjects, "their eyes flaming with nothing but sparkles of affection, their mouths and tongues uttering nothing but sounds of joy".

The Stuarts had ruled Scotland since 1371, but James VI of Scotland was the first Stuart king of England. James was the son of Mary, Queen of Scots, the bitter rival of Elizabeth I. Yet, without an heir to succeed her, on her deathbed Elizabeth named James as the next rightful king.

When he arrived in London, James was already a skilled and experienced ruler. He brought with him many Scottish courtiers, but he was also careful to appoint English ministers to advise him. Nevertheless, many people at the English court remained deeply suspicious of this new Scottish king.

James held very strong views about the powers of monarchs. He believed that his authority to rule came directly from God. His beliefs brought him into conflict with the House of Commons several times during his reign. He also wanted to unite the kingdoms of England and

◁ *James I surrounded by his courtiers. Many English contemporaries were very rude about the King's appearance and behaviour. They said that he was ugly and coarse, that he drank too much, that he had a tongue too big for his mouth, was difficult to understand, and that he dribbled!*

Scotland, but any such union was firmly rejected by his English ministers and by parliament.

The early years of James I's reign were successful in many ways. He ended the war with Spain, and he managed to achieve a balance between the different religious groups – Catholics, Anglicans and Puritans. But he spent money extravagantly, and his court gained a reputation for scandal and intrigue. Later in his reign, James fell under the spell of one of his courtiers, George Villiers, lavishing money on him and making him Duke of Buckingham. The Duke quickly became extremely powerful in the English court. He also became a friend of James's son, Prince Charles, and in the last year of the old king's life Charles and Buckingham took control of all political decisions.

△ *In 1605, a group of English Catholics* plotted to blow up the Houses of Parliament and with it King James I, his wife and his eldest son. The plotters were led by Robert Catesby (second from right), but the most famous of them all is Guy Fawkes (third from right). The plotters hoped that in the confusion after the explosion and murder of the King, English Catholics would be able to take over the country.

▷ *This is the lantern that* belonged to Guy Fawkes. It was Fawkes who put at least 20 barrels of gunpowder in a cellar beneath the Houses of Parliament. But the plot was discovered and he was captured and tortured to reveal the names of the other conspirators.

FEATHERY FASHIONS

Men's fashions in the 17th century were extravagant and colourful. During the 17th century, men gradually started to replace the stiff, frilled collars, known as ruffs, with large, floppy lace-edged collars. Their hats, made from felt or velvet, were decorated with ostrich feathers. However, this was the costume of the aristocrat. Puritans protested against such extravagance, and wore plain, simple clothes.

Pilgrims in the New World

1606 William Brewster leaves England with a group of Separatists and goes to Leiden, in the Netherlands.

1619 Brewster and William Bradford return to England.

1620 The Pilgrims set sail from Plymouth, England on 16 September. They sign the Mayflower Compact on 11 November. They land at Plymouth Colony, New England on 21 December.

1621 William Bradford succeeds John Carver as governor of the new colony. He serves as governor almost continuously until 1656. He negotiates a treaty with the local Wampanoag people.

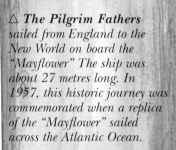

△ *The Pilgrim Fathers sailed from England to the New World on board the "Mayflower" The ship was about 27 metres long. In 1957, this historic journey was commemorated when a replica of the "Mayflower" sailed across the Atlantic Ocean.*

1625 Miles Standish returns to England and establishes the right of the colony to own its own land.

1629 Massachusetts Bay Company obtains charter from Charles I.

1630 About 1,000 Puritans settle in Massachusetts under Governor John Winthrop.

1691 Plymouth Colony is annexed to Massachusetts Bay.

In November 1620, a three-masted sailing ship called the *Mayflower* dropped anchor off the coast, near present-day Provincetown, Massachusetts. The ship carried 102 passengers from England, and it was far off its course. The intended destination of the *Mayflower* was Virginia, many hundreds of kilometres further south. This was where the English passengers had permission to set up a colony in the "New World". But storms and mistakes in navigation landed the colonists on the rocky Cape Cod coast.

Many of the colonists on board the *Mayflower* were dissenters. They belonged to a group of English Protestants called Puritans who disagreed with many of the practices of the Church of England. Their leader was William Brewster (1567–1644), who, in 1606, had broken away from the Church of England to form a separate congregation. At this time it was illegal to set up an independent congregation in England, and Brewster and his followers, known as Separatists, were persecuted. To escape arrest, Brewster and members of his breakaway congregation fled to the Netherlands, where they settled in Leiden.

▽ *In autumn 1621, the first autumn in their new colony, Governor William Bradford invited local Native Americans to join the settlers in three days of feasting to celebrate the harvest. This feast became known as Thanksgiving and is still celebrated throughout North America.*

◁ *The land on which the Pilgrim Fathers settled was already occupied by Native Americans of the Wampanoag people. The newcomers and the Native Americans negotiated trade agreements. The Native Americans also showed the settlers ways of growing food, hunting and fishing that were an essential part of their survival in this new colony.*

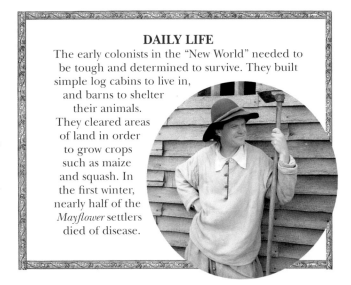

DAILY LIFE

The early colonists in the "New World" needed to be tough and determined to survive. They built simple log cabins to live in, and barns to shelter their animals. They cleared areas of land in order to grow crops such as maize and squash. In the first winter, nearly half of the *Mayflower* settlers died of disease.

In 1619, Brewster and another Separatist called William Bradford (1590–1657) returned to England. The Separatists were dissatisfied with life in the Netherlands. As foreigners they were not permitted to buy land, or to work in skilled trades. Their thoughts turned to the promise of the "New World" far across the Atlantic Ocean. Brewster and Bradford negotiated with the Virginia Company for some land, and found merchants willing to back their venture.

On 16 September 1620, 41 Separatists and 61 other would-be colonists boarded the *Mayflower* at Plymouth and set sail for the "New World". They reached Cape Cod in November, and spent a month exploring the coast before finally deciding on a site for their settlement, which they named Plymouth Colony. Before landing, 41 of the male passengers signed a document which became known as the Mayflower Compact. This document was an agreement for cooperation that became the foundation of the government of the new colony. The first settlers of Plymouth Colony became known as Founders, Forefathers, or – after a term used by William Bradford himself – Pilgrims.

One of the Pilgrim leaders, John Carver (1576–1621) became the first governor of the new colony, succeeded after his death by William Bradford.

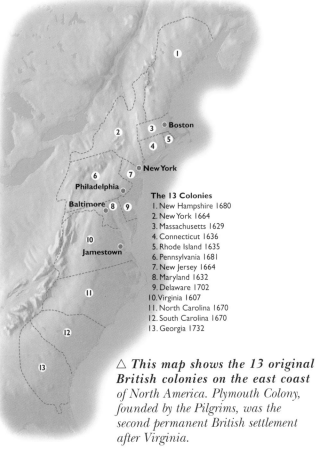

The 13 Colonies
1. New Hampshire 1680
2. New York 1664
3. Massachusetts 1629
4. Connecticut 1636
5. Rhode Island 1635
6. Pennsylvania 1681
7. New Jersey 1664
8. Maryland 1632
9. Delaware 1702
10. Virginia 1607
11. North Carolina 1670
12. South Carolina 1670
13. Georgia 1732

△ *This map shows the 13 original British colonies on the east coast of North America. Plymouth Colony, founded by the Pilgrims, was the second permanent British settlement after Virginia.*

123

Charles I

Like his father, Charles I believed that he was chosen by God to rule his kingdom. He was also very religious, devoted to the Church of England. These deeply held beliefs soon brought him into conflict with his subjects.

In the early years of his reign, Charles summoned parliament three times. He needed to raise money for wars with Spain and France. But both wars were unsuccessful, and parliament refused to cooperate with the King until he agreed to a 'Petition of Right' in 1628. Amongst other things, this Petition stated that the King could not impose taxes on his subjects without the consent of parliament. However, the King continued to try to raise taxes. In 1629, the third parliament of Charles's reign ended in confusion. Charles sent orders to dissolve parliament, but members of the House of Commons held the speaker down in his chair until three resolutions were passed condemning the behaviour of the King. This was revolutionary behaviour, and Charles did not call another parliament for 11 years.

△ *Portraits of King Charles I made him look more impressive and dignified than he was in real life. He was a small, shy man, with a slight stammer. But he was a good horseman, and he loved art – he brought the finest painters of the time to England including Anthony van Dyck and Peter Paul Rubens.*

△ *Although the present-day Houses of Parliament (above) were built almost two centuries after the time of Charles I, the Palace of Westminster has long stood on the same riverside site in the middle of London.*

1600 Birth of Charles, second son of James VI of Scotland and Anne of Denmark.
1624–30 War with Spain.
1625 Charles succeeds his father as Charles I. He marries Henrietta Maria.
1626–9 War with France.
1628 Assassination of the King's favourite, the Duke of Buckingham.
1629 Charles dissolves parliament. He does not call another for 11 years.
1637 Riot in Edinburgh after Charles tries to force Scots to use a new Anglican prayer book.
1639–40 Bishops' Wars fought between Charles and the Scots.
1640 Short Parliament lasts from April to May. Long Parliament is summoned in November.

HENRIETTA MARIA

In 1625, Charles I married Henrietta Maria, daughter of Henry IV of France and Marie de Medici. The first years of the marriage were difficult as Charles was still deeply under the influence of the Duke of Buckingham. But after the Duke's death, Charles came to love and rely on his wife.

War with Scotland

Although Charles I was king of Scotland as well as England he neglected his northern kingdom, visiting it only once in the first eight years of his reign. Then, in 1637, Charles tried to force the Scots to accept a new prayer book for use in their Presbyterian kirk (church) based on the practices of the Church of England.

The Scots were furious at the King's behaviour. People from all over Scotland signed a declaration called the National Covenant promising to defend their kirk. But the King would not back down, and he decided to go to war against the rebellious Scots. An English army went north in 1639 but lacking confidence in his troops – and enough money to pay for them – Charles was forced to make peace. The first Bishops' War ended before a shot was fired.

The King desperately needed money to raise a bigger army. For the first time in 11 years he called parliament, but MPs were unwilling to grant the King the funds he needed. The parliament lasted only three weeks and became known as the Short Parliament. Meanwhile, Scots armies marched into the north of England and seized Northumberland and Durham. And so the second Bishops' War ended with victory for the Scots. They knew that Charles had little choice but to agree to their demands. In 1640 he called parliament once again.

△ *A Scottish nobleman kneels before King Charles I with a petition.* The Scots wanted the King to give up his attempt to force a new prayer book upon them. Charles was advised and backed by William Laud, his Archbishop of Canterbury. Laud disapproved of traditional Scottish practices in the Presbyterian kirk where there was no set form of service or prayer book for use in all churches.

◁ *The official introduction of the new prayer book in Scotland was on 23 July 1637.* The Bishop of Edinburgh was to preside at a service in St Giles's Cathedral in Edinburgh. The congregation planned to stage a walk-out, but as the minister began to speak the first words of the hated service a more violent reaction erupted. A woman stood up and hurled her three-legged stool across the cathedral. The rest of the congregation joined in and soon the riot had spilled out on to the streets of Edinburgh.

Towards Civil War

1640 Start of Long Parliament (November).
1641 Triennial Act is passed in House of Commons stating that parliament must be summoned every three years (February).
King's authority to dismiss Long Parliament is removed (May).
Earl of Strafford is beheaded (12 May).
Charles travels to Scotland and negotiates peace with the Scots (August).
Uprising by Catholics in Ulster, Ireland (22 October).
"Grand Remonstrance" – a list of grievances against the King is passed by the House of Commons (23 November).

▽ *Re-enacting battles from the English Civil Wars is a favourite pastime for many people more than 300 years later. The first battle between Royalists and Roundheads was fought at Edgehill in October 1642.*

1642 Charles attempts unsuccessfully to arrest five MPs in the House of Commons and one peer in the House of Lords (4 January).
Charles leaves London for the north of England (10 January).
"Nineteeen Propositions" – set of proposals for peace rejected by King Charles.
Royalists and Roundheads rally support in preparation for First Civil War.

Parliament met in November 1640. This was the beginning of the Long Parliament, so called because it was not officially dismissed for 20 years. Once again, MPs condemned the king for his actions. They also removed William Laud and another of the King's most powerful advisers, the Earl of Strafford, from office. Charles was powerless to prevent the execution of Strafford in 1641. Laud was executed in 1645.

The King was forced to agree to other parliamentary reforms, too. These included a requirement that parliament should meet every three years, and that it should be dismissed only by its own, and not the King's, consent. In October 1641 there came news of an uprising in Ireland. Protestant settlers had been attacked by Irish Catholics in Ulster. The tales of murder and torture were horrifying and fuelled an increasing hysteria in England about Catholic conspiracies.

Once again, Charles needed money to raise an army and crush a rebellion. But MPs feared that any

▷ *This Roundhead soldier wears a "lobster-tail" helmet, so called because of the protective neck guard at the back. It has a triple-bar face guard and flaps at the sides to protect the ears. The peak was hinged to allow the helmet to be taken on and off.*

◁ *Supporters of the King were known as Cavaliers. This officer wears a buff coat – a thick leather jacket made from buffalo hide – and a metal breastplate. For battle he would have worn a metal helmet too.*

army loyal to the King might be used to fight against them. They tried to force Charles to hand over command of the army. Charles refused and, on 4 January 1642, he went with 400 men to the House of Commons to arrest five MPs for treason. But the MPs were warned and they escaped. The whole of London was in turmoil. Things were so dangerous in the capital for Charles that he abandoned the city and travelled north. Both sides began to prepare for war. The King and his followers, known as Royalists or Cavaliers, were initially based in York. Parliament supporters, known as Roundheads, controlled London and the southeast. The King formally declared war by raising his standard at Nottingham on 22 August 1642.

ROUNDHEADS

In contrast to the flowing hairstyles of fashionable noblemen at the court of Charles I, the supporters of parliament tended to wear their hair closely cropped to their heads. This earned them the name "Roundheads". Queen Henrietta Maria may have been the first person to use this term.

▽ *Charles I left London on 10 January 1642. He headed for Hull where there were large stores of military supplies, but he was unsuccessful in his attempt to take the city. At the same time, Queen Henrietta Maria went to the Netherlands to raise money for the Royalist cause by pawning the crown jewels.*

Winning the War

1640 Oliver Cromwell is elected Member of parliament.
1642 First battle, at Edgehill near Warwick (23 October).
1642 Cromwell organizes Roundhead armies in his Cambridgeshire constituency.
1643 Leads his army to victory over Royalists in Battle of Gainsborough.
1643 Charles moves his headquarters to Oxford. Charles negotiates peace in Ireland in order to free troops to fight in England.

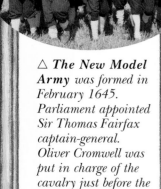

△ *The New Model Army was formed in February 1645. Parliament appointed Sir Thomas Fairfax captain-general. Oliver Cromwell was put in charge of the cavalry just before the great Battle of Naseby in June 1645.*

1644 Scottish armies join with the Parliamentarians against the King. Parliamentary victory at Marston Moor (2 July).
1645 New Model Army is formed. Defeat of Royalists at Naseby, near Leicester (14 June).
1646 Royalists surrender Oxford. Charles escapes and takes refuge with the Scots.

The first objective for King Charles was to regain control of the capital, London. The Royalist and Roundhead armies met at Edgehill in Warwickshire in October 1642, but the fighting ended inconclusively. Then the Royalists marched towards London, but they got only as far as Turnham Green before being forced by enemy troops to turn back.

This was the closest the Royalist army came to capturing London. Charles set up his new headquarters in Oxford and spent the winter of 1642–3 preparing for new campaigns. In 1643, a peace proposal was presented to the King by a group of Parliamentarians. However, the two sides could not agree and so the fighting continued.

In the summer of 1644 the Scots invaded England once again. Roundhead leaders had negotiated with the Scots, promising to set up a Presbyterian kirk in England in return for their help against the Royalists. At the Battle of Marston Moor on July 2, the combined Roundhead and Scots forces defeated the King's army. However, the advantages gained by the Roundheads were all but lost as they quarrelled amongst themselves about how and whether to continue the campaign against the King. In parliament, MPs listened to the arguments of Oliver

◁ *Oliver Cromwell at the head of his cavalry regiment. Cromwell trained his troops carefully and demanded the highest standards of all those under his command.*

△ *Oliver Cromwell was born on 25 April 1599 in Huntingdon. He was first elected as an MP in 1628. He was a Puritan, but he preached "liberty of conscience", believing that most people should be allowed to follow their own faiths and beliefs.*

◁ *This map shows the main battles of the English Civil Wars. The pink shading shows the areas held by the Royalists after the Battle of Marston Moor (1644).*

Cromwell, the Puritan MP for Cambridge. He said that the only way to end the war was to improve the military training and resources of the Roundhead armies. And so the Roundheads set up the "New Model Army".

The year 1645 proved to be a decisive one in the Civil War. The highly trained and well-disciplined New Model Army defeated the Royalist forces at Naseby on June 14. This was the first of a succession of Roundhead victories that led to the surrender of the Royalist headquarters in Oxford in 1646. Charles escaped, but was quickly handed over to Parliament. However, the victorious Roundheads were still deeply divided. parliament was suspicious and fearful of the New Model Army – particularly after the army kidnapped the King and held him under guard at Hampton Court.

THE NEW MODEL ARMY
The "lobster-tailed pot", the rounded helmet worn by the Roundheads, made up part of their uniform of war. Metal breastplates, riding boots, spurs and other body armour completed it.

129

Executing a King

On 11 November, King Charles I escaped his captors at Hampton Court and attempted to flee to France. He got as far as the Isle of Wight. There he stayed in Carisbrooke Castle, under the watchful eye of the governor of the island, who was a parliament supporter.

Charles was prepared to strike deals to regain power, and he was skilful at playing one party off against another. He negotiated with the Scots, promising if they restored him to power that he would accept the Presbyterian kirk in Scotland, and establish Presbyterianism in England for three years. At the same time he discussed peace terms with parliament. During 1648, there were Royalist uprisings across the country, but they were not co-ordinated and were easily put down by the army. The King's final hope of a military solution was dashed when the Scots were defeated by the New Model Army at the Battle of Preston in August.

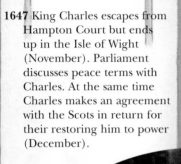

1647 King Charles escapes from Hampton Court but ends up in the Isle of Wight (November). Parliament discusses peace terms with Charles. At the same time Charles makes an agreement with the Scots in return for their restoring him to power (December).

1648 Second Civil War: Royalist rebellions across country put down by army. Scottish invasion defeated at Battle of Preston by New Model Army (17 August). Colonel Thomas Pride prevents MPs entering the Palace of Westminster (6 December). Start of the Rump Parliament.

1649 Trial of King Charles in Westminster Hall (20 January). Charles is sentenced to death. Execution of King (30 January). Government of the Commonwealth declared (May).

△ *Oliver Cromwell views the dead body of King Charles I.* Cromwell was on campaign with his army in the north when the army removed many MPs from parliament in December 1648. He was ordered back to London by Sir Thomas Fairfax and was one of the 135 judges who took part in the trial of the King in Westminster Hall.

▷ *Charles I was tried by a High Court of Justice* hurriedly established by the Rump Parliament. The King did not give the speech he had written in his defence, but its text was published only a few days later for all to read. There was great popular support for the King.

▷ *Charles I was dignified and calm* in the face of death. On the scaffold he said: "All the world knows I never did begin a war with the two Houses of Parliament...They began these unhappy troubles, not I..." As he placed his head on the block he spread out his arms, the signal of his readiness for the executioner to bring down the axe on his neck.

Six years of civil war had left the country in tatters and ordinary people desperate for peace. Many MPs still believed that the answer was to reinstate the King. But the army leaders believed that their victories in the war made them the rightful representatives of the people. In December 1648, Colonel Thomas Pride prevented any MPs who opposed the army from entering the House of Commons. In the end, only about one third of the parliament remained. It became known as the Rump Parliament.

The King was brought to trial in January 1649. He stood accused of making war on his own people. The trial lasted for five days, and when the King refused to answer the charges his silence was taken as an indication that he pleaded guilty. He was sentenced to death as a tyrant, traitor, murderer and public enemy. On his death warrant there were 59 signatures, including that of Oliver Cromwell.

On 30 January 1649, Charles Stuart went to the scaffold. It was a bitterly cold day. Charles wore two shirts so that he should not shiver and seem afraid. As the axe came down upon his neck there was a groan from the crowd. The executioner held up the King's head and said the traditional words: "Behold the head of a traitor."

JOHN BRADSHAW'S HAT

Many people were unwilling to have anything to do with the King's trial. The Lord Chief Justice refused to preside, so a little-known judge called John Bradshaw was appointed president. He was so afraid of assassination attempts that he wore a hat lined with iron for the duration of the trial.

Ireland and Scotland

1649 Cromwell lands in Ireland (August) and prepares to attack combined Royalist and Catholic opposition. Massacres at Drogheda and Wexford.

1650 Charles II makes an agreement with Scots to accept Presbyterianism in return for their support to restore him to English crown. Cromwell leads an army to Scotland (July). Cromwell defeats Scottish army at Dunbar (September).

1651 Scottish armies defeated at Stirling. Charles II enters England but is defeated at Worcester (3 September).

Despite the defeat of Royalist forces in England, supporters of the monarchy were still active in both Ireland and Scotland. It was vital for the new Commonwealth in England that these rebels should be subdued. In August 1649, Oliver Cromwell and the New Model Army landed in Ireland.

The Royalists in Ireland were supported by the Irish Catholics. Cromwell fought a very harsh campaign in Ireland – he held the rebels responsible for the horrors of the massacres in 1641. The English army took its revenge by attacking and killing the inhabitants of Drogheda, a garrison town north of Dublin. Cromwell reported to parliament that such actions were justified because they would "...tend to prevent the effusion [shedding] of blood for the future..." A similar massacre took place at Wexford in the south of Ireland.

Next, Cromwell turned his attention to Scotland. After the execution of Charles I, his son was proclaimed Charles II of Scotland. In 1650 Charles II landed in Scotland and gathered together an army of loyal followers. Cromwell marched northwards with the New Model Army and inflicted a crushing defeat on the Scots at Dunbar in September. Nevertheless, the fighting dragged on for

△ *A Pikeman. Pikes were up to 4.5 metres long. Pikemen were carefully trained to handle their weapons when marching and attacking.*

▽ *Oliver Cromwell leads the New Model Army outside Edinburgh. In 1650 Cromwell was appointed captain-general of the army in place of Sir Thomas Fairfax who refused to invade Scotland. Even Cromwell was unwilling to fight the Scots, who were fellow Puritans. But when forced to fight he defeated the Scots at Dunbar, east of Edinburgh.*

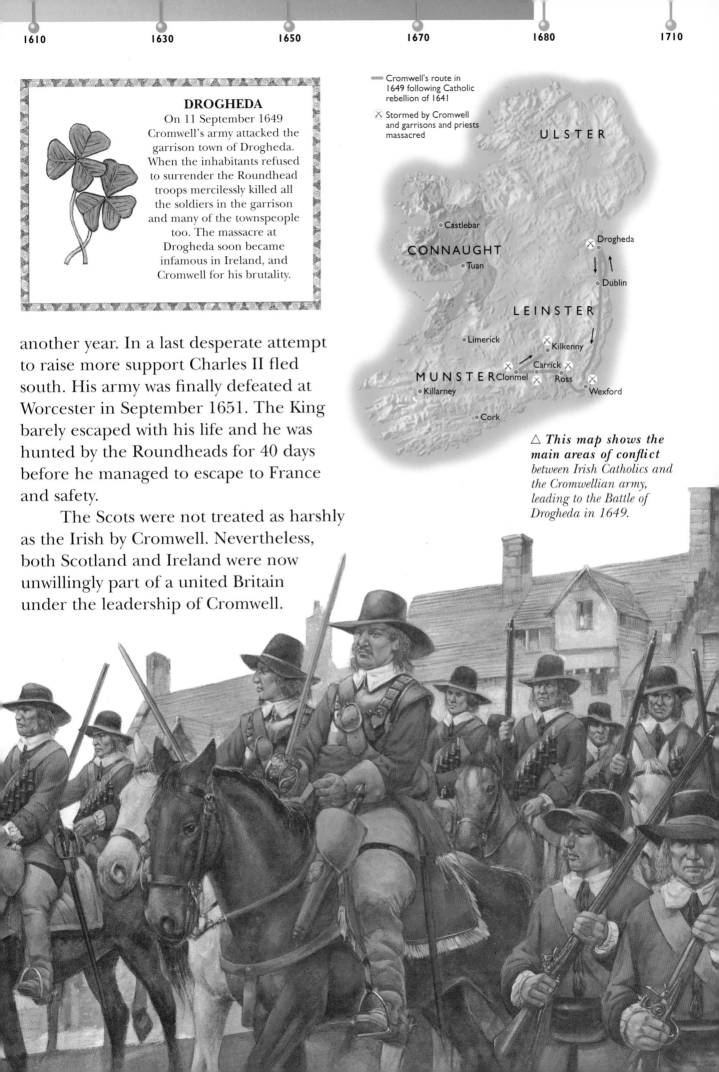

DROGHEDA

On 11 September 1649 Cromwell's army attacked the garrison town of Drogheda. When the inhabitants refused to surrender the Roundhead troops mercilessly killed all the soldiers in the garrison and many of the townspeople too. The massacre at Drogheda soon became infamous in Ireland, and Cromwell for his brutality.

another year. In a last desperate attempt to raise more support Charles II fled south. His army was finally defeated at Worcester in September 1651. The King barely escaped with his life and he was hunted by the Roundheads for 40 days before he managed to escape to France and safety.

The Scots were not treated as harshly as the Irish by Cromwell. Nevertheless, both Scotland and Ireland were now unwillingly part of a united Britain under the leadership of Cromwell.

Cromwell's route in 1649 following Catholic rebellion of 1641

⊠ Stormed by Cromwell and garrisons and priests massacred

△ *This map shows the main areas of conflict between Irish Catholics and the Cromwellian army, leading to the Battle of Drogheda in 1649.*

The Commonwealth

1652 Act of Settlement – six Irish counties are cleared of Catholic landholders and settled by English Protestants.

1653 Cromwell forcibly dismisses the Rump Parliament (20 April). "Nominated Parliament" hands back power to Cromwell (12 December). Cromwell becomes Lord Protector.

1654 End of war with the Netherlands. First Parliament of the Protectorate (3 September).

On 20 April 1653, Cromwell called his musketeers into the chamber of the House of Commons. He declared to the astonished MPs that they were "corrupt and unjust men" before removing the Speaker. The Rump Parliament was dismissed.

Cromwell's anger with the MPs of the Rump Parliament was caused by their unwillingness to act on the many reforms he and the army considered necessary. Cromwell ordered a new parliament to be chosen from a list drawn up by church representatives but this "Nominated Parliament" did little better than its predecessor. In December, its members handed back power to Cromwell. So a new plan was drawn up, in which Cromwell became "Lord Protector" of England, Scotland and Ireland.

Many people remained suspicious of Cromwell and fearful of the power of the army. After an unsuccessful Royalist uprising in the West Country, Cromwell divided

◁ *A Puritan family in typical sombre dress.*
The Puritan movement began in the late 1500s and gathered strength through the 1600s. Puritans wished to purify the Church of England from Catholic ways. They were noted for their earnestness.

▽ *Cromwell dismisses the Rump Parliament. "You are no parliament; I will put an end to your sitting..." he told the MPs. The Rump was unwilling to pass reforms required by Cromwell and the army.*

1655 Royalist uprising in the West Country led by Colonel John Penruddock is put down by New Model Army. Military leaders, major-generals, are appointed to each region to keep the peace.

1656 Second Parliament of the Protectorate.

1658 Death of Oliver Cromwell (3 September).

LORD PROTECTOR

The first parliament of the Protectorate was held in 1654. Cromwell had several aims. He wanted to set up a Puritan Chuch, but wished to allow freedom of worship. He was very interested in education and wanted to reform the legal system. He believed that capital punishment (execution) should be used only for major crimes such as murder, treason and rebellion.

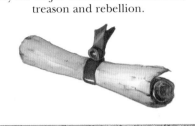

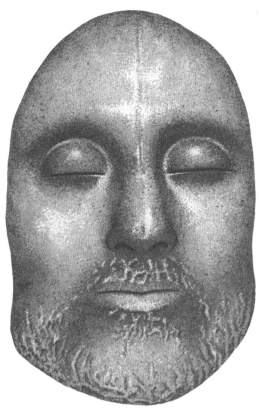

▷ *The death mask of Oliver Cromwell who died on 3 September 1658. He was buried in Westminster Abbey. In 1661, after King Charles II was restored to the throne, Cromwell's remains were dug up and hung at Tyburn where criminals were executed. His head was stuck on a pole on top of Westminster Hall.*

the country into 11 districts and appointed military leaders to run them. Some were strict Puritans who were unpopular because they closed down alehouses and stopped popular pastimes and sports. Nevertheless, this was a time of relative religious tolerance and prosperity after the strife of the Civil Wars. In 1658, on his deathbed, Cromwell named his son Richard as his rightful successor.

▽*After the horrors of the Civil Wars, the Commonwealth was a time of peace for most ordinary people in England. Trade flourished in busy coastal towns such as this. However, Puritan rule was strict – theatres were closed, and Christmas became a fast-day.*

Charles II

On 25 May 1660, King Charles II landed at Dover. After 15 years in exile the King was returning to his kingdom.

It had soon become apparent that Richard Cromwell was not capable of running the country. "Tumbledown Dick" was quickly removed from office, and parliament invited Charles to return and take up his crown. People across the country rejoiced that the strict Puritan regime of the Commonwealth was at an end.

The terms of the Restoration were worked out between 1660 and 1662. The New Model Army was disbanded and sent home. The Church of England became more powerful. Charles himself wished for religious tolerance, particularly towards Roman Catholics – he himself was a Protestant but the rest of his family were Catholics, and his new Portuguese wife was also Catholic. But there was still deep suspicion of Roman Catholic "popery" in parliament and across the country.

△ *Nell Gwynne was one of the King's many mistresses. She was an actress who first came to the King's attention in 1668. Their relationship lasted until the end of the King's life. Charles had many illegitimate children by his mistresses. The eldest and best-loved of these was James, Duke of Monmouth, son of Lucy Walter.*

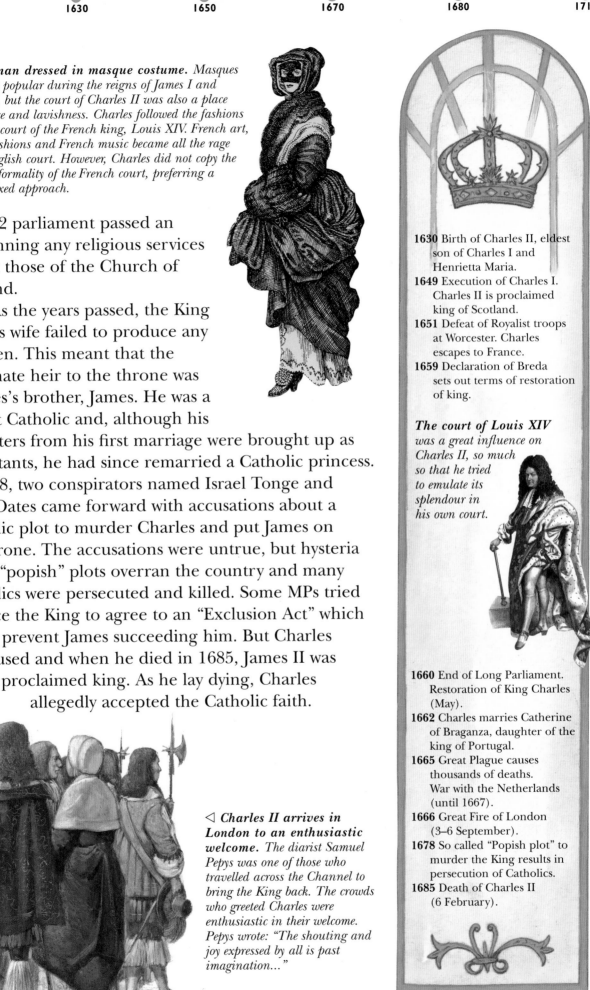

▷ *A woman dressed in masque costume. Masques were most popular during the reigns of James I and Charles I, but the court of Charles II was also a place of elegance and lavishness. Charles followed the fashions set by the court of the French king, Louis XIV. French art, French fashions and French music became all the rage at the English court. However, Charles did not copy the excessive formality of the French court, preferring a more relaxed approach.*

In 1662 parliament passed an act banning any religious services except those of the Church of England.

As the years passed, the King and his wife failed to produce any children. This meant that the legitimate heir to the throne was Charles's brother, James. He was a devout Catholic and, although his daughters from his first marriage were brought up as Protestants, he had since remarried a Catholic princess. In 1678, two conspirators named Israel Tonge and Titus Oates came forward with accusations about a Catholic plot to murder Charles and put James on the throne. The accusations were untrue, but hysteria about "popish" plots overran the country and many Catholics were persecuted and killed. Some MPs tried to force the King to agree to an "Exclusion Act" which would prevent James succeeding him. But Charles refused and when he died in 1685, James II was proclaimed king. As he lay dying, Charles allegedly accepted the Catholic faith.

1630 Birth of Charles II, eldest son of Charles I and Henrietta Maria.
1649 Execution of Charles I. Charles II is proclaimed king of Scotland.
1651 Defeat of Royalist troops at Worcester. Charles escapes to France.
1659 Declaration of Breda sets out terms of restoration of king.

The court of Louis XIV was a great influence on Charles II, so much so that he tried to emulate its splendour in his own court.

1660 End of Long Parliament. Restoration of King Charles (May).
1662 Charles marries Catherine of Braganza, daughter of the king of Portugal.
1665 Great Plague causes thousands of deaths. War with the Netherlands (until 1667).
1666 Great Fire of London (3–6 September).
1678 So called "Popish plot" to murder the King results in persecution of Catholics.
1685 Death of Charles II (6 February).

◁ *Charles II arrives in London to an enthusiastic welcome. The diarist Samuel Pepys was one of those who travelled across the Channel to bring the King back. The crowds who greeted Charles were enthusiastic in their welcome. Pepys wrote: "The shouting and joy expressed by all is past imagination…"*

137

Life in 17th-Century Britain

△ *This horn book was used to teach children the letters of the alphabet. Sons of the nobility and the gentry were usually sent to public or grammar schools. Girls were mostly educated at home.*

The 17th century was a time of dramatic events in Britain: a king beheaded and civil war across the country. The war had a devastating effect on ordinary people in some areas, but many people remained largely untouched by the political turmoil.

Most ordinary people, such as farm labourers, cottagers and servants, lived on pitifully low incomes. The less fortunate – paupers and vagabonds – relied on poor relief, paid for by the richer members of each parish. Even better-off households grew their own food, made their own clothes and brewed their own beer to drink. Travel between towns and villages was an adventure. The roads were appalling – most were little more than muddy tracks. People travelled by foot or on horseback. If they could afford it, they went by stage-coach which, by the 1660s, linked some of the main towns and cities in England.

In the parts of the country affected by the civil wars, the civilian population suffered badly. Local villagers or

△ *A 17th-century gentleman. Many of the gentry were landowners who had inherited estates and could easily live off the rents of their tenants.*

◁ *Between 1660 and 1669, Samuel Pepys kept a detailed diary of his life. Amongst other things, he recorded the effects of the Great Plague and the Great Fire in London. He wrote of the plague: "But Lord, what a sad time it is, to see no boats upon the River – and grass grow all up and down Whitehall-court – and nobody but poor wretches in the streets."*

COSTUME

During the time of the Commonwealth, frivolity and excess were frowned upon. This was reflected in the drab clothes worn during that time. With the Restoration of Charles II came a new glamour. Men wore curled wigs and replaced the wide boots of earlier years with stockings and buckled shoes.

△ *Coffee was introduced from Arabia into Europe* in the 16th and 17th centuries. *Together with tea and chocolate, coffee changed the drinking habits of many British people, replacing beer as the main beverage. Coffee drinking became a craze for the well-to-do, and after the 1650s coffee houses opened all over London and in many other cities and towns.*

townspeople were often obliged to provide lodging and food for the army passing though or occupying their area. Sometimes they were paid, but when there was no money they were given vouchers which were rarely honoured. Their horses often were confiscated by the army and their crops trampled to the ground by marching feet. Even worse, the soldiers brought with them disease, particularly typhus. It is little wonder that many ordinary people cared little about who won the war so long as it came to an end.

During the Commonwealth, which followed the end of the civil wars, the Puritans banned many festivals and pastimes that they considered frivolous. For example, in 1652 Christmas was abolished and in 1654 cock-fighting, a popular sport in town and country, was banned. In the towns, theatres were closed down and alehouses shut. After the Restoration of Charles II in 1660, people greeted the return of merriment with relief. Sports such as football and, in the south of England, cricket were very popular. In London there were many colourful pageants on the River Thames, such as the Lord Mayor's Show and celebrations held by craft. Once again, Christmas, May Day and harvest time became important festivals and were enjoyed by both rich and poor.

◁ *A coffee house pictured in 1668. Coffee houses became important meeting places for politicians and intellectuals. Opponents of Catholicism, and in particular of King Charles II's brother, James, met to discuss matters in coffee houses all over London. The writer John Dryden had his own chair at Will's Coffee House in Covent Garden.*

139

1633 Birth of James, second son of Charles I and Henrietta Maria.

1634 Created Duke of York.

1642–6 Lives in Oxford during Civil Wars.

1648 Escapes to Netherlands.

1660 Restoration of brother Charles I. Marries Anne, daughter of Earl of Clarendon. They have two daughters, Mary and Anne.

1668/9 James is admitted to Roman Catholic Church.

1673 Marries Catholic princess Mary of Modena.

1677 Eldest daughter, Mary, marries William of Orange.

1685 Succeeds his brother as James II (6 February).

1688 "Glorious Revolution". James II is allowed to escape.

1689 Parliament declares abdication of James II (12 February).

1690 James lands in Ireland. James defeated at Battle of Boyne.

1701 Death of James II.

△ *The young William III of Orange. William was born in The Hague on 14 November 1650, eight days after his father's death. Not surprisingly, he was trained to be a ruler from his earliest years.*

The Glorious Revolution

When James II came to the throne in 1685, memories of the horrors of civil war were still present in people's minds. No one wanted more conflict. But the new king was a Roman Catholic and many feared the outcome if he tried to impose his religion on his subjects. In the end, his reign was short, brought to an abrupt conclusion by the events of the "Glorious Revolution".

Shortly after he became king, James was faced with a rebellion by the Duke of Monmouth, the eldest of the illegitimate children of Charles II. The rebellion was short-lived and the Duke and his followers were punished with great ferocity.

The main hope for Protestant leaders lay in the fact that James's heir was his eldest daughter, Mary, borne by his first wife. She was a Protestant and was married to William III of Orange, ruler of the Dutch Protestants. However, even this hope faded when it was announced that James's second wife was pregnant. In June 1688 she gave birth to a son – the new heir to the throne who would undoubtedly be brought up in the Catholic faith.

William began to make preparations for an attack by sea. James could not believe that his own daughter and son-in-law would attack him, and he thought that the Dutch preparations were for war against the French king,

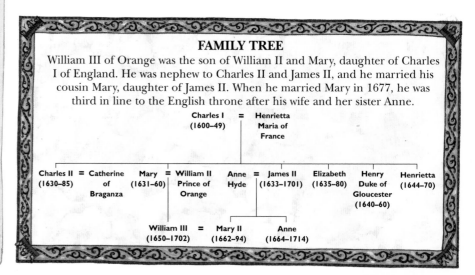

FAMILY TREE

William III of Orange was the son of William II and Mary, daughter of Charles I of England. He was nephew to Charles II and James II, and he married his cousin Mary, daughter of James II. When he married Mary in 1677, he was third in line to the English throne after his wife and her sister Anne.

Charles I (1600–49) = Henrietta Maria of France

Charles II (1630–85) = Catherine of Braganza   Mary (1631–60) = William II Prince of Orange   Anne Hyde = James II (1633–1701)   Elizabeth (1635–80)   Henry Duke of Gloucester (1640–60)   Henrietta (1644–70)

William III (1650–1702) = Mary II (1662–94)   Anne (1664–1714)

BROADSHEETS

Before the first newspapers were set up, the main method of spreading printed information was by leaflets called broadsheets. These contained rhymes, called ballads, relating the latest events, as well as black and white illustrations.

△ *The title of this picture* is *"Popery's downfall and the Protestant's uprising".* It celebrates the victory of the Protestant King William over James II.

◁ *When James II ordered freedom* of worship for Catholics and other Dissenters, the Archbishop of Canterbury and six other bishops sent a petition to the King asking him to withdraw the order. James's reaction was to send them to the Tower of London. The bishops were tried and found not guilty.

▽ *The first time James II tried* to flee from England, he was captured by some fishermen on the coast of Kent. He returned to London, but the victorious William of Orange ordered James to leave the capital. James was escorted to Rochester in Kent by a guard of Dutch troops, and this time James "escaped" successfully, landing safely in France where he was reunited with his wife and son.

Louis XIV. So he was unprepared when William's fleet landed in Torbay, Devon, on 5 November 1688.

At the news of the Dutch invasion, James panicked. He refused to send his army to confront the invaders because he thought they were too unreliable. Indeed, many Protestant officers deserted and went to join the Dutch force. When he heard that his second daughter, Anne, had also deserted him for the Protestant cause, James made plans to flee. After one unsuccessful attempt, he escaped to France to join his wife and baby.

William and his army marched to London without a shot being fired. This was the "Glorious Revolution" – a military campaign without bloodshed.

Towns and Trade

1600 Creation of the East India Company.
1602 Dutch East India Company set up to protect Dutch trade in Indian Ocean.
1615 Trading post granted at Surat in India.
1650s First coffee houses open.
1651 Navigation Act prevents foreign ships from taking part in trade with English colonies or carrying imports into Britain.
1661 Bombay becomes British trading post, ceded by Portugal.
1663 Royal African Company set up to trade in slaves, ivory and gold.
1664 French East India Company is set up. British seize New Amsterdam from Dutch and rename it New York.

△ *Together with chocolate, coffee (left) and tea (right) became very popular drinks in the 17th century. Tea was advertised as a "China Drink" and chocolate as an "excellent West India drink". All three drinks were sweetened with sugar imported from plantations in the English West Indies.*

1666 Great Fire of London.
1673 Rebuilding of St Paul's Cathedral, London, begins.
1686 East India Company base established at Calcutta, India.
1694 Bank of England set up.
1695 Bank of Scotland set up.
1696 Royal Board of Trade set up.

"Some of our maids sitting up late last night to get things ready for our feast today, Jane called us, about 3 in the morning, to tell us of a great fire they saw in the City..."

With these words Samuel Pepys describes the beginning of the Great Fire of London. It started on 2 September 1666 in a baker's shop, but because there were so many timber buildings, it quickly raged out of control. On 4 September, St Paul's Cathedral was burned down. A large part of the city was destroyed and about 100,000 people were left homeless.

King Charles II was determined that fire should not so easily sweep through the city again. He ordered that all new buildings must be made from brick and stone. An architect called Christopher Wren produced a grand plan for rebuilding the city, but it was not accepted. However, Wren was kept very busy designing St Paul's Cathedral and many other fine churches.

No other town in 17th-century Britain could equal London in size and importance. Not only was it the seat of government but it was also a major port and commercial centre. The second town in terms of population was Norwich

WOMEN IN SOCIETY

Women in the 17th century wore their skirts caught back to reveal the petticoats beneath. Dresses were often cut low, and were finished with delicate lace collars and cuffs to match. In the winter, a thick, hooded cloak kept the wearer warm. Long gloves were very fashionable, and women often also carried fur muffs. In the earlier part of the century, court ladies wore masks whenever they went outside. Hair was drawn off the face and curled into ringlets. Older women often wore elaborate curled wigs. Women were responsible for running their households and caring for their children. In poorer families, many women also brought in much-needed extra income by spinning, or seasonal work in the fields.

(20,000 in the 1660s). Norwich was a centre for the textile trade. In the West Country, Bristol was the most important town – a busy and expanding port.

During the second half of the 17th century, Britain became an increasingly powerful trading nation. Trade routes reached far beyond Europe to overseas colonies in North America and the Caribbean, as well as the trading posts established in Asia. Goods such as tobacco, sugar, spices and textiles flooded into Britain.

The boom in trade made ship owners and merchants very rich. But there was a human cost. English ships sailed to West Africa where they exchanged iron goods, textiles and guns for African captives. These captives were transported across the Atlantic Ocean in appalling conditions. They were sold as slaves to work on the plantations in the colonies. The ships then sailed back to England with cargoes of sugar and tobacco. This terrible trade became known as the "Triangular Trade".

△ *Merchants of the Dutch East India Company trade with locals on the Cape of Good Hope.* The Dutch East India Company was set up in 1602 to protect Dutch trade in the Indian Ocean. The English East India Company was incorporated by Royal Charter in 1600. Both companies imported spices and textiles such as silks, and calico, chintz and muslin all made from cotton.

▽ *A busy scene in a coffee house.* Much business was done in the coffee houses that opened in the second half of the 17th century. Samuel Pepys wrote in his diary in 1660: "To the coffee-house where was a great confluence of gentlemen; ...admirable discourse until 9 at night..." There were over 2,000 coffee houses in London by 1700.

New Ideas and Discoveries

The 17th century saw great advances in all branches of science in England. Men such as William Harvey, Robert Hooke and Isaac Newton laid the foundations for the modern sciences as they are studied today.

These advances were part of an intellectual movement across Europe which saw new ideas and discoveries being exchanged across frontiers. For example, William Harvey studied at the University of Padua in Italy, which had a brilliant reputation for its medical school. With a thorough grounding in anatomy, Harvey dissected every kind of living thing, including human corpses. From his observations he demonstrated how the blood circulates around the body, pumped by the heart. His findings made him famous throughout Europe – although many disagreed with him.

▽ The first Eddystone lighthouse was designed by Henry Winstanley. It was one of the first lighthouses to be exposed to the open sea. Constructed from timber, it was anchored by 12 iron cables and stood 136 metres tall. The lighthouse stood from 1699 to 1703 when it was swept away by a ferocious storm. Its designer, Winstanley, was in the lighthouse at the time and was drowned in the storm.

ARCHITECTURE

In the 1660s, Christopher Wren visited Paris to see for himself the glories of the Louvre Palace and the Palace of Versailles. He also met the famous Italian architect Bernini. On his return he began to design a dome for St Paul's Cathedral. But his plans were cut short by the Great Fire of London which destroyed the old cathedral. Wren's plans for a new, grand cathedral were accepted in 1675 and the building was completed in 1711.

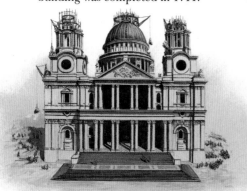

◁ **Isaac Newton was born in 1642,** the same year that Galileo Galilei died. At Trinity College, Cambridge, Newton learned about Galileo's theories of motion and went on to develop them into laws of motion and gravity which provide the basis of modern-day physics.

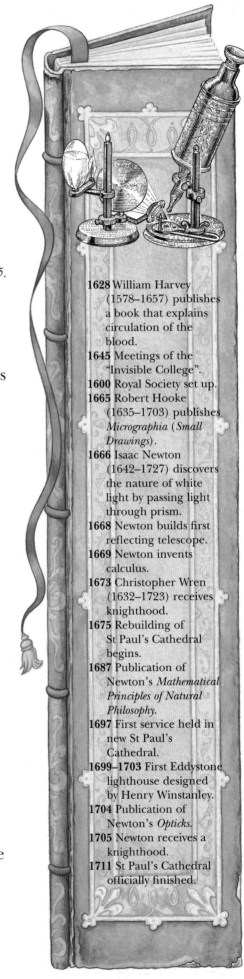

▷ **Robert Hooke used a microscope** to study the structures of natural objects such as snowflakes. He described his findings in "Micrographia" (Small Drawings) published in 1665. The first powerful lens microscope was built by the Dutch scientist Antonie van Leeuwenhoek in 1674.

1628 William Harvey (1578–1657) publishes a book that explains circulation of the blood.
1645 Meetings of the "Invisible College".
1600 Royal Society set up.
1665 Robert Hooke (1635–1703) publishes *Micrographia (Small Drawings)*.
1666 Isaac Newton (1642–1727) discovers the nature of white light by passing light through prism.
1668 Newton builds first reflecting telescope.
1669 Newton invents calculus.
1673 Christopher Wren (1632–1723) receives knighthood.
1675 Rebuilding of St Paul's Cathedral begins.
1687 Publication of Newton's *Mathematical Principles of Natural Philosophy*.
1697 First service held in new St Paul's Cathedral.
1699–1703 First Eddystone lighthouse designed by Henry Winstanley.
1704 Publication of Newton's *Opticks*.
1705 Newton receives a knighthood.
1711 St Paul's Cathedral officially finished.

Isaac Newton was also influenced by European thinkers such as the French philosopher René Descartes and Italian mathematician and scientist Galileo Galilei. Newton also drew on the work of other English scientists, such as the chemist Robert Boyle (1627–91) who built the first air pump. Newton applied his brilliant mind to many different problems. His discoveries about light, his laws of force, motion and gravity, and his formulation of calculus in mathematics provide the basis for our modern-day understanding of the world around us. Newton's new ideas were frequently challenged – one of his main rivals being Robert Hooke (1635–1703). Hooke was also interested in optics and gravity, and his ideas brought him into frequent conflict with Newton. However, Newton's genius was recognized in his own lifetime, and he was the first scientist to be knighted for his work.

In 1703, Newton was made president of the Royal Society. This society was set up in 1660 by a group of English scientists including Robert Boyle and Christopher Wren. It grew out of earlier meetings held either in Oxford or in Gresham College in London, when scientists would discuss astronomy, mathematics and other scientific subjects. They called themselves the "Invisible College". In 1662, Charles II granted a royal charter to the society, giving it its full name of the "Royal Society of London for the Promotion of Natural Knowledge".

William and Mary

Although Mary had the first claim to the English throne, William refused to accept an inferior role to his wife – he said that he would not be tied to the "apron strings". So parliament decided to make William and Mary joint king and queen. They received the Scottish crown in May 1689.

At the coronation of William and Mary a Declaration of Rights was presented. This stated that the monarch could not be a Catholic, or be married to a Catholic. It also limited the powers of the monarchy. In future, no king or queen could suspend a law without the consent of parliament. The Bill of Rights passed through parliament in October, 1689.

William had taken the English throne without a fight, but holding on to it was more of a problem. With the backing of the French king, Louis XIV, James invaded Ireland and defeated Protestant forces there. William himself led an army to Ireland and crushed James's forces at the Battle of the Boyne (1690).

In Scotland, William also faced dissent and rebellion. Fighting in the early 1690s brought no definite conclusion.

1688 Glorious Revolution.
1689 William and Mary accept Declaration of Rights and become joint monarchs (February). James II lands in Ireland with French troops. William and Mary accept Scottish crown (May).
1690 William defeats French troops at Battle of the Boyne (1 July). James flees to France.
1691 Battle of Aughrim (July). Treaty of Limerick sets out toleration for Irish Catholics but is soon proved worthless.
1692 1 January: date by which Highland chiefs to swear allegiance to William and Mary. Massacre in Glencoe, Scotland (13 February).
1694 Death of Queen Mary.

△ *Mary (above) had no children*, so her sister Anne succeeded to the throne on William's death in 1702.

1697 Treaty of Ryswick: William is recognized by French king as rightful ruler of Britain.
1701 Act of Settlement.
1702 Death of William. He is succeeded by Queen Anne.

◁ **Irish Catholics flee from their homeland.** *After Protestant victories at the Battle of the Boyne and Aughrim (1690), the English Parliament confiscated the estates of many Catholic landowners. This was despite the Treaty of Limerick which aimed to protect Irish Catholics, but which proved worthless.*

William was persuaded to offer peace terms to the Highland clans if they would swear allegiance to him. When the leader of the MacDonalds of Glencoe missed the deadline for the oath of allegiance, William decided to make an example of him. He ordered the massacre of the MacDonald clan in Glencoe – an act of violence which lives on to this day in Scottish memory.

▽ **The Battle of the Boyne** *was fought on 1 July 1690. The two sides were drawn up on either side of the river Boyne. William's cavalry managed to cross the river and began to surround James's troops. James fled and his troops withdrew. The battle is still celebrated today in Northern Ireland as a landmark Protestant victory.*

TAX ON WINDOWS
During the reign of William and Mary a new tax was introduced on windows. Houses were allowed only six untaxed windows. Many people bricked up windows in their houses in order to avoid paying this tax.

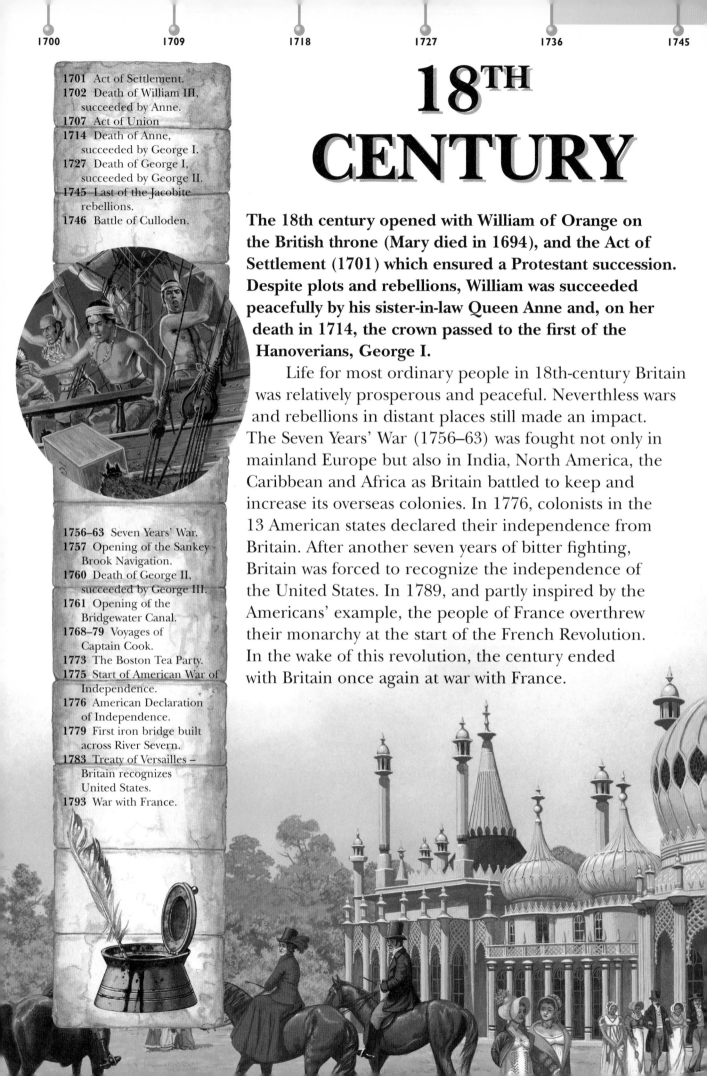

18TH CENTURY

1701 Act of Settlement.
1702 Death of William III, succeeded by Anne.
1707 Act of Union
1714 Death of Anne, succeeded by George I.
1727 Death of George I, succeeded by George II.
1745 Last of the Jacobite rebellions.
1746 Battle of Culloden.

1756–63 Seven Years' War.
1757 Opening of the Sankey Brook Navigation.
1760 Death of George II, succeeded by George III.
1761 Opening of the Bridgewater Canal.
1768–79 Voyages of Captain Cook.
1773 The Boston Tea Party.
1775 Start of American War of Independence.
1776 American Declaration of Independence.
1779 First iron bridge built across River Severn.
1783 Treaty of Versailles – Britain recognizes United States.
1793 War with France.

The 18th century opened with William of Orange on the British throne (Mary died in 1694), and the Act of Settlement (1701) which ensured a Protestant succession. Despite plots and rebellions, William was succeeded peacefully by his sister-in-law Queen Anne and, on her death in 1714, the crown passed to the first of the Hanoverians, George I.

Life for most ordinary people in 18th-century Britain was relatively prosperous and peaceful. Neverthless wars and rebellions in distant places still made an impact. The Seven Years' War (1756–63) was fought not only in mainland Europe but also in India, North America, the Caribbean and Africa as Britain battled to keep and increase its overseas colonies. In 1776, colonists in the 13 American states declared their independence from Britain. After another seven years of bitter fighting, Britain was forced to recognize the independence of the United States. In 1789, and partly inspired by the Americans' example, the people of France overthrew their monarchy at the start of the French Revolution. In the wake of this revolution, the century ended with Britain once again at war with France.

Meanwhile, two different sorts of revolution were happening in Britain. Both were, in fact, gradual changes that gathered pace throughout the century. The first, often known as the Agricultural Revolution, involved different ways of organizing and owning land, and the application of scientific principles to growing crops and breeding animals. The second, known as the Industrial Revolution, started in around the 1760s although pioneers such as Abraham Darby, Thomas Newcomen and John Kay were at work earlier in the century. Industrialization involved new methods of powering machinery and of manufacturing goods.

The Hanoverians

1660 Birth of George Ludwig, son of Elector of Hanover and Sophia (granddaughter of James I of England).

1682 George Ludwig marries Sophia Dorothea of Celle. Birth of son George Augustus (1683).

1698 George succeeds father as Elector of Hanover.

1701 English Parliament passes Act of Settlement ensuring Protestant succession to throne.

1714 Death of Queen Anne (1 August). The Elector of Hanover is proclaimed George I.

△ *Men in 18th-century Britain* wore powdered, curled and perfumed wigs.

1727 Death of George I. He is succeeded by Prince of Wales as George II.

1760 Death of George II. George III becomes king.

1776 American Declaration of Independence.

1788 Illness of king provokes "Regency Crisis".

1810 King ill once again, Prince of Wales is made Prince Regent.

1820 Death of George III. He is succeeded by Prince Regent as George IV.

In 1714, two British ministers sent word to the exiled son of James II, James Edward (the "Old Pretender"). If he would renounce his Roman Catholic faith and become an Anglican, they would support his claim as heir to the British throne. But James Edward refused. And so, when Queen Anne died in her sleep on 1 August 1714, the crown passed peacefully to a German prince, George, Elector of Hanover.

George I excluded from office the ministers who had tried to place James Edward on the throne instead of him. These ministers belonged to the political party known as the Tories. In their place he promoted ministers of the opposing party – the Whigs. One of these ministers, Robert Walpole, became an extremely powerful figure in government.

▷ *George I was the first of the Hanoverians to rule in Great Britain. He could not speak English, so he talked with his ministers in French. He was backed by the Whig political party. Many members of the other main political party, the Tories, would have preferred James Edward, son of James II as their king.*

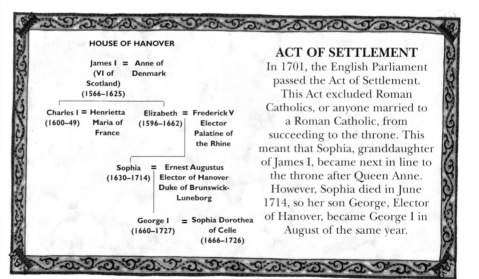

HOUSE OF HANOVER

James I = Anne of
(VI of   Denmark
Scotland)
(1566–1625)

Charles I = Henrietta   Elizabeth = Frederick V
(1600–49)   Maria of   (1596–1662)   Elector
       France   Palatine of
                       the Rhine

Sophia = Ernest Augustus
(1630–1714)   Elector of Hanover
           Duke of Brunswick-
           Luneborg

George I = Sophia Dorothea
(1660–1727)   of Celle
           (1666–1726)

ACT OF SETTLEMENT

In 1701, the English Parliament passed the Act of Settlement. This Act excluded Roman Catholics, or anyone married to a Roman Catholic, from succeeding to the throne. This meant that Sophia, granddaughter of James I, became next in line to the throne after Queen Anne. However, Sophia died in June 1714, so her son George, Elector of Hanover, became George I in August of the same year.

He was the first prime minister of the British Parliament.

George I was succeeded by his son. George II took a close interest in matters at home and abroad. He was the last British monarch to appear in person on the battlefield – at the Battle of Dettingen in 1743, where he showed great personal courage.

George II's son, Frederick Louis, died, so his heir was his grandson, also called George. The reign of George III was a turbulent one. War in the American colonies ended with the American Declaration of Independence in 1776. Revolution was in the air in Europe too, boiling over in France in 1789. George III battled with illness and insanity throughout his life. In 1811 his son became Prince Regent, standing in for his father until George III's death in 1820.

△ *Georgian townhouses from the 18th century. The kitchens and tradesmen's entrance were situated in the basement, below street level. Servants for this well-off household slept in rooms in the attics. The grand main entrance was slightly raised from street level. Inside, the ground floor was given over to reception rooms, the first floor contained drawing room and salon, and the second floor family bedrooms.*

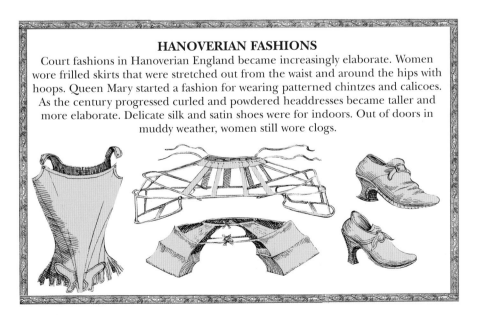

HANOVERIAN FASHIONS

Court fashions in Hanoverian England became increasingly elaborate. Women wore frilled skirts that were stretched out from the waist and around the hips with hoops. Queen Mary started a fashion for wearing patterned chintzes and calicoes. As the century progressed curled and powdered headdresses became taller and more elaborate. Delicate silk and satin shoes were for indoors. Out of doors in muddy weather, women still wore clogs.

The Enlightenment

Just as the scientific advances of the 17th century were part of a Europe-wide movement, so the Enlightenment grew out of ideas that were discussed across the Continent. The ideas of the Enlightenment led people to question the traditional teachings of the Church and to celebrate the power of human reason.

Enlightenment thinkers believed that knowledge about the universe and the world around them could be gained only by experience. This idea grew partly out of the work of the 17th-century scientists, particularly Sir Isaac Newton. Newton used experiment and the rigorous application of logic to arrive at ideas that helped people understand the universe, such as his law of gravity.

A major figure of the Enlightenment, John Locke, wrote many books setting out the power of reason. In his *Essay Concerning Human Understanding* Locke said that at birth the human mind was empty (a "clean slate") and that it was experience that created every individual character. As a result, Locke insisted on the importance of a good and broad education for every child. He also wrote about government in the influential *Two Treatises of Government*. He insisted that the rulers of any country were entrusted with the "public good", and if they failed to fulfil that trust then the people could

△ *In the 18th century ballet was performed in public for the first time. The clothes that dancers wore became less restrictive and much easier to dance in.*

▽ *An evening of music, readings and conversation in a 17th-century middle-class house. The "middle sort" ranged from farmers to professionals such as clergymen and lawyers. They were better educated and had more money to spend than ever before leading to a growth in publications such as magazines and novels.*

◁ **The "Encyclopédie" was** *published in parts between 1751 and 1772 in France. It was inspired by the success of an English publication called "Cyclopaedia" published in 1728. The "Encyclopédie" was edited by the philosopher Denis Diderot, and it embraced the tolerance and open-mindedness of Enlightenment ideas.*

verthrow them. Together with the work of other writers such s Jeremy Bentham and the French author Voltaire these ideas ventually led to revolution in America and France, and eform in Britain.

　Britain in the 18th century was regarded with great dmiration by many European thinkers and writers. They rote about the civilized character of English society and the ay in which there was tolerance and moderation in all things. oltaire wrote: "The English nation is the only one on earth hich has succeeded in controlling the power of kings... and in hich the people share in the government without confusion."

　　Although this was rather an optimistic view, Britain did come closer to the ideals of the Enlightenment than other European countries of the day.

1632 Birth of John Locke.
1668 Locke becomes a member of the Royal Society.
1675–9 Locke lives in France.
1689 Publication of *Essay Concerning Human Understanding* by Locke.

▽ **Many of the great writers** *of the Enlightenment were French, including Denis Diderot, Jean-Jacques Rousseau and Voltaire. In England, leading Enlightenment writers included John Locke and Thomas Hobbes.*

1690 Publication of *Two Treatises of Government* by Locke.
1693 Publication of *Some Thoughts Concerning Education* by Locke.
1694 Birth of Voltaire.
1704 Death of John Locke.
1726–8 Voltaire exiled in England.
1728 Publication of Ephraim Chambers' *Cyclopaedia*.
1734 Publication of Voltaire's *Lettres Philosophiques*.
1737 Birth of Thomas Paine.
1751–72 Publication of the French *Encyclopédie* edited by Denis Diderot.
1776 Declaration of American Independence.
1789 Publication of *An Introduction to the Principles of Morals and Legislation* by Jeremy Bentham. Revolution in France.
1791 Publication of the *Rights of Man* by Thomas Paine defending the French Revolution.

The Agricultural Revolution

The Agricultural Revolution was not a sudden, revolutionary change as its name might suggest. It was a slow change that took place throughout the 18th century and continued into the 19th.

1674 Birth of Lord "Turnip" Townshend (d.1738) who pioneered crop rotations. Birth of Jethro Tull (d.1741).

1700–60 About 200 Acts of Enclosure passed through parliament.

1701 Introduction of Jethro Tull's horse-drawn seed drill.

1725 Birth of Robert Bakewell of Dishley, Leicestershire (d.1795).

1731 Publication of *The New Horse Houghing Husbandry* by Jethro Tull.

△ *This type of windmill was known as a tower mill. The vane (on the right) turned the top part of the mill, called the head, so that the sails were always facing into the wind. The sails turned to provide power for grinding wheat and other grains.*

1741 Birth of Arthur Young (d.1820) writer and supporter of agricultural improvements.

1753 Birth of George Culley of Northumberland (d.1813) who worked on selective breeding of sheep.

1754 Birth of Thomas Coke of Holkham Hall, Norfolk (d. 1842).

1760–80 Over 1,000 Acts of Enclosure passed through Parliament.

In the 18th century, agriculture had to provide enough food to feed the entire population of Britain. Grains such as wheat, barley, oats and rye provided the staple diet together with foods such as potatoes, peas, beans and cheese. Most ordinary families ate very little meat. The only foods that were usually transported into the country at this time were exotic and expensive imports such as spices, chocolate, sugar, coffee and tea. The amount of food produced in Britain rose steadily throughout the 18th century. This happened because of two main changes: an increase in land enclosures and improvements in agricultural techniques.

From medieval times, much of the land across Britain was open land or common land. Often, the open land was divided into strips each cultivated by one farmer and animals were kept on the common land. But in some areas land was enclosed by hedges or ditches to make fields. The process of enclosing land had been going on for centuries, but it speeded up in the 18th and early 19th centuries. In some cases, wealthy landowners bought up land cultivated by poorer farmers. In others, the land was enclosed by an Act of Parliament. The result was more large farms on which the land was leased (rented) to tenant farmers. And it was mainly on these larger farms

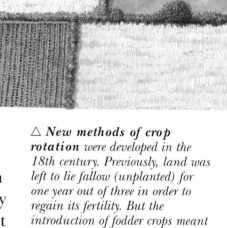

△ *New methods of crop rotation were developed in the 18th century. Previously, land was left to lie fallow (unplanted) for one year out of three in order to regain its fertility. But the introduction of fodder crops meant that the land could be planted continuously. The "Norfolk rotation" was usually wheat, turnips, barley and clover. The turnips provided food for livestock; the clover fertilized the soil.*

▽ *Jethro Tull invented the horse-drawn seed drill* and introduced it in 1701. Traditionally, seed was scattered by hand which meant that quite a lot of seed went to waste. But the seed drill planted seeds in neat rows, called furrows.

▷ *A farmer takes wheat* to the mill to be ground into flour. Wheat was the most important of the grain crops because it was used to make bread – the staple food for most families in 18th-century Britain.

Mill to grind Flower

that experiments with new methods of agriculture were carried out.

Jethro Tull was one of the first of the pioneers who applied their minds to the improvement of agricultural techniques. He invented a horse-drawn seed drill which sowed the seeds in rows. Another improvement introduced from the Netherlands was the cultivation of "fodder" crops such as clover or turnips. Fodder crops improved the fertility of the soil and provided food for livestock. The manure from livestock was also used to fertilize the soil.

It was not only arable farming (growing crops) that was subject to improvement. Men such as Robert Bakewell (1725–95) experimented with breeding animals to give the best meat, milk and wool (called selective breeding). In Norfolk, another pioneering landowner Thomas Coke (1754–1842) lived at Holkham Hall. Coke bred sheep, pigs and cattle and held huge sheep shearing meetings at Holkham which were the forerunners of the modern-day agricultural show.

▽ *Farmers employed labourers such as cowhands, ploughmen, milkmaids and shepherds* to work on their farms. They often lived in the farm house with the farmer and his family. Many labourers worked on one farm for 12 months at a time.

155

A Trading Nation

1717 Birth of John Metcalfe (d.1810) who improved road building and constructed over 300 kilometres of road, mainly in Pennines.

1736 Smugglers Act imposed harsh penalties on smugglers.

1751–60 Over 180 Turnpike Acts passed through Parliament.

1756 Birth of John McAdam (d.1836) who invented mixture of tar and small stones known as "tarmac" used to surface roads.

1757 Birth of Thomas Telford (d.1834) engineer who oversaw building of London to Holyhead road and Menai Bridge.

1761–72 Over 200 turnpike Acts passed through parliament.

1773 Stock Exchange founded.

1807 Slave trade abolished by Britain.

1833 Slavery abolished in British Empire.

△ *The wealth that the triangular trade brought to ports such as Liverpool and Bristol had a terrible human cost. As part of the trade, African captives were taken from their homeland to work on plantations in the West Indies. Their treatment at the hands of the European traders was often both cruel and inhumane.*

Daniel Defoe, writing in the 1720s, described Britain as the "most flourishing and opulent country in the world". And so it must have seemed as communications within Britain improved, and trade into and out of Britain continued to expand throughout the 18th century.

Trade within Britain at the opening of the 18th century still depended largely on markets and fairs. In London, there were large specialized markets at Billingsgate (fish), Smithfield (meat) and Covent Garden (vegetables). Supplies for these markets came from all over the country. There were smaller markets in regional centres where people came to buy and sell goods. Transporting goods from one place to another was both difficult and expensive. Each parish was responsible for looking after roads in its area. In the early 18th century, local businessmen began to set up turnpike trusts to improve stretches of road and links to the main cities and travelling around the country became easier. However, most heavy goods were not sent by road but by river and on the new canals that were constructed in the late 18th and early 19th centuries.

By the beginning of the 18th century the "triangular trade" between Britain, West Africa and the Caribbean was thriving. As demand for imports such as tobacco and sugar rose, ports along the west coast of Britain flourished. Bristol, Liverpool and Glasgow all expanded rapidly. In 1700 Liverpool had a population of about 5,000 people. One hundred years later, it was a major transatlantic port with a population of over 80,000.

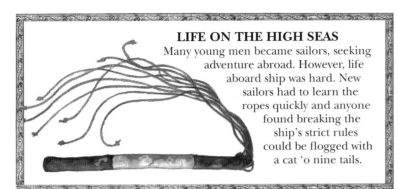

LIFE ON THE HIGH SEAS
Many young men became sailors, seeking adventure abroad. However, life aboard ship was hard. New sailors had to learn the ropes quickly and anyone found breaking the ship's strict rules could be flogged with a cat 'o nine tails.

△▷ *These fancy vases come from China. Trade with Asia brought many exotic goods to Britain including Chinese porcelain and tea, spices such as pepper and cinnamon, and – most important – cheap cotton from India.*

Many goods that were imported, such as tobacco, tea, coffee and sugar, were re-exported to other destinations in Europe. In addition, exports of manufactured goods to Britain's colonies, for example in North America, became an increasingly valuable market. However, throughout the 18th century the most important export from Britain was textiles. The manufacture of woollen textiles was centred in the West Country, East Anglia and Yorkshire. But, after the 1780s, cotton manufacture began to replace wool in importance. Cotton was to play a major role in the Industrial Revolution in Britain.

▽*Ships were frequently wrecked along the rocky shores of southwest Britain and often provided welcome supplies of luxury goods such as brandy or tea for local communities. Smuggling was also common in coastal areas. Goods such as tea, tobacco, brandy and lace were all subject to customs duties (taxes), so smuggling these items into the country was a widespread and lucrative business.*

Jacobite Rebellion

1707 Act of Union unites England and Scotland to form Great Britain.
1708 "Old Pretender" James Edward (son of James II) attempts unsuccessfully to invade Scotland.
1715 John Erskine, Earl of Mar, raises support for Jacobite cause. James arrives in Scotland (December).
1716 Jacobite rebellion dies out. James and Earl of Mar flee to France.
1720 Birth of Charles Edward (the "Young Pretender")
1745 Young Pretender lands in Scotland (July). British army defeated at Battle of Prestonpans (September). Jacobite army marches south as far as Derby.
1746 British army defeats Jacobites at Battle of Culloden (16 April). Escape of Young Pretender to France.

△ *James Stuart became known as the "Old Pretender" to distinguish him from his son, the "Young Pretender". The word "Pretender" comes from the French word "prétendant", meaning claimant. Both father and son were claimants to the British throne.*

1766 Death of Old Pretender.
1788 Death of Young Pretender.

Although the Glorious Revolution took place without bloodshed, many people in Britain still looked on James II as the rightful king. Supporters of James were known as "Jacobites" from the Latin equivalent for James, "Jacobus".

James II died in France in 1701, but the fight for the Jacobite cause continued for many years. After the massacre of Glencoe, Jacobite support strengthened in Scotland. The Act of Union (1707) which joined Scotland and England was also bitterly opposed by many in Scotland. The scene was set for Jacobite supporters to try to put James II's son, James Edward (known as the "Old Pretender"), on the throne.

The Old Pretender had the backing of the French king, Louis XIV, but attempts to invade Britain in 1708, 1715 and 1719 all failed. The task of reclaiming the British throne was left to his son, Charles Edward, also known as "Bonnie Prince Charlie" and the "Young Pretender". Charles Edward was born and brought up in Rome yet when he landed for the first time on Scottish soil in 1745 he declared: "I am come home."

The Young Pretender raised an army of Highlanders and after defeating the British army at the Battle of Prestonpans, he marched southwards as far as Derby. But with little support, the Jacobites were forced to retreat to Scotland once more. At Culloden the Highlanders were overcome by the British army, led by George II's son, the Duke of Cumberland. Charles Edward escaped, and after many adventures, he sailed for France. He was never again to set foot on British soil. This was the end of any real Jacobite threat in Britain.

INTO BATTLE
The clansmen of the Highlands carried some fearsome weapons including short daggers called dirks and long, two-handed swords known as claymores. They protected themselves with small metal shields called targes. However, at the Battle of Culloden they proved no match for the Duke of Cumberland's troops. The Highlanders were exhausted and hungry after their long marches and they could not withstand the British artillery and cavalry charges.

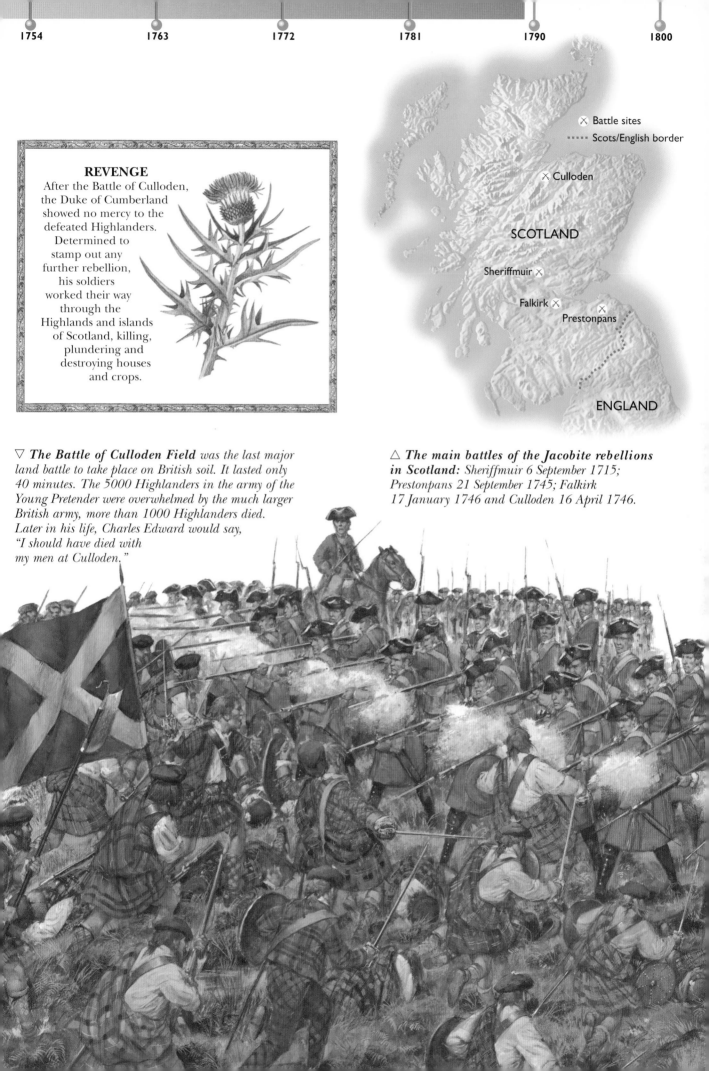

X Battle sites
····· Scots/English border

X Culloden

SCOTLAND

Sheriffmuir X

Falkirk X
Prestonpans X

ENGLAND

REVENGE

After the Battle of Culloden, the Duke of Cumberland showed no mercy to the defeated Highlanders. Determined to stamp out any further rebellion, his soldiers worked their way through the Highlands and islands of Scotland, killing, plundering and destroying houses and crops.

▽ *The Battle of Culloden Field* was the last major land battle to take place on British soil. It lasted only 40 minutes. The 5000 Highlanders in the army of the Young Pretender were overwhelmed by the much larger British army, more than 1000 Highlanders died. Later in his life, Charles Edward would say, "I should have died with my men at Culloden."

△ *The main battles of the Jacobite rebellions in Scotland: Sheriffmuir 6 September 1715; Prestonpans 21 September 1745; Falkirk 17 January 1746 and Culloden 16 April 1746.*

The Loss of America

One of the outcomes of the Seven Years' War was that British colonists in America no longer feared a French invasion from the north. Many colonists thought that there was little need for the British army and navy to remain in North America – especially as the colonists had to pay towards their upkeep. But the British government had different ideas.

Ministers in the British Parliament were determined to protect the valuable trade to and from North America. In order to meet some of the expense of keeping a military force in North America the government decided to impose new taxes on the colonists. As they had no representatives at Westminster, there was no one to argue the colonists' cause. During the 1760s and 1770s, the government in Britain imposed a whole series of taxes on the American colonists. Finally, in 1775, the colonists' resentment boiled over into armed resistance.

In April 1775, British troops were sent from Boston to destroy military supplies held by the colonists at Concord,

◁ *The army of the American colonists* was made up not of professional soldiers, like the British troops, but of untrained, working men such as farmers. However, the Americans used guerrilla tactics such as ambushing and sniping to surprise and outwit the British troops.

△ *British soldiers were often called "Redcoats"* because of the bright red coats of their uniforms. About 42,000 British soldiers fought in the American War of Independence.

TAXES ON GOODS
The British government attempted to force the American colonists to pay taxes on many different commodities including lead, glass, paint, tea and paper. The new taxes were met with fierce opposition from the Americans. The eventual outcome was war and the declaration of American independence.

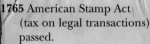

▽ **On 16 December 1773, American colonists**
*disguised as Native Americans boarded ships belonging
to the British East India Company in Boston Harbour.
In protest at the tax imposed on tea by the British
government they threw more than 300 chests
of tea overboard. This event became known
as the Boston Tea Party.*

Massachusetts.
However, the
colonist rebels were
warned and the first battles
of the American War of Independence were fought at
Concord and nearby Lexington. The American colonists
declared themselves independent from Britain on 4 July
1776, but the fighting continued until 1783.

    Under their general, George Washington, the
Americans used their local knowledge to harass the
British troops. In 1778, help came for the Americans when
France declared war on Britain. The French sent armies
and fleets to America, but they also attacked British
colonies in India and the West Indies. Similarly, Spain
and the Netherlands joined the fighting in 1779 and 1780.
Britain had to withdraw troops from North America to
defend its other colonies. Finally, Lord Cornwallis, who
commanded the British army in America, was forced to
surrender. In 1783, Britain formally recognized the
independence of the United States of America.

1765 American Stamp Act
(tax on legal transactions)
passed.
1767 Townshend's Act passed
imposing taxes on various
goods imported into
America.
1770 Act passed to remove
taxes on paper, glass and
paint, but not on tea.
1773 Boston Tea Party (16
December).
1775 First battles of American
War of Independence at
Concord and Lexington
(19 April). George
Washington appointed
commander of rebel
armies (15 June).

▽ **President Thomas
Jefferson (1743–1826)**
*was the main author of the
Declaration of Independence
which set out the reasons for
the break of the 13 American
colonies with Britain.*

1776 American Declaration
of Independence (4 July).
1777 Surrender of British at
Saratoga (17 October).
1778 Treaty signed between
France and American
rebels. France declares
war on Britain (17 June).
1779 Spain declares war
on Britain (21 June).
1780 Britain declares war on
Netherlands (20 December).
1781 Cornwallis surrenders at
Yorktown (19 October).
1783 Treaty of Versailles signed
by Britain, France, Spain and
the United States. Britain
recognizes United States
(3 September).
1784 Treaty signed with the
Netherlands.

161

The Industrial Revolution

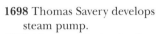

1698 Thomas Savery develops steam pump.
1709 Abraham Darby develops coke-fired blast furnace.
1712 Thomas Newcomen develops steam-powered pumping engine for use in mines.
1733 John Kay develops flying shuttle.
1764 James Hargreaves develops "Spinning Jenny".
1769 Richard Arkwright patents water-frame (water-powered spinning machine). James Watt patents improved steam engine.
1776 Adam Smith writes *Wealth of Nations*.
1779 First iron bridge built across River Severn.

△ *Machinery in a factory.*
Many people were suspicious of the new machines and the changes they brought. In 1811–12 there were riots in which a group called the Luddites broke into factories and destroyed machinery.

1782 Watt develops rotary steam engine.
1784 Henry Cort develops puddling iron.
1785 Edmund Cartwright invents power loom.
1815 Invention of Davy safety lamp for use in mines by Sir Humphry Davy.
1825 Stockton to Darlington railway opens.

Like the Agricultural Revolution, the phrase Industrial Revolution is used to describe a gradual rather than a sudden change. The Industrial Revolution is usually said to have started around the 1760s. By 1830, Britain was the most industrially advanced country in the world.

Britain was the first country to experience an Industrial Revolution, although industrial advances soon followed in Europe, America and elsewhere. There were many reasons for Britain's industrialization. Improved roads and the construction of canals and railways meant that transporting goods was relatively cheap and easy. There were rich natural resources such as coal and iron. Britain also had overseas colonies to provide cheap raw materials, such as cotton from India. These same colonies provided a ready market for manufactured goods.

The improvements of the Agricultural Revolution meant that there were ample supplies of food for the rapidly

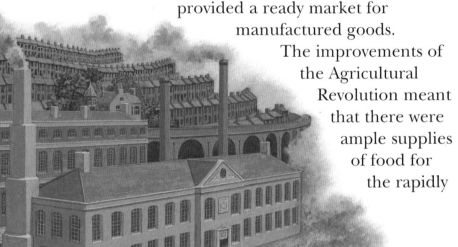

◁ *Children at work in a mine.*
Children and women were usually
cheaper to employ than men.
However, in 1842 a parliamentary
report on conditions in the mines
shocked people so much that an
Act was passed forbidding the
employment of women and girls
underground, and setting a
minimum age of 10 for boys.

STEAM POWER

Steam power was in use as early as 1698
when Thomas Savery developed a steam-
driven engine to pump water out of mines.
The engine was improved by Thomas
Newcomen and later by James Watt. Steam
gradually took over as the main power
source to drive machinery in mines,
factories and mills. By 1800 there were
over 50 steam-driven cotton mills
in Manchester.

▽ *The Industrial Revolution completely*
changed the landscape in parts of Britain.
Factories, smoking chimneys and powerful
machinery appeared in places where there
were once only green fields. Many people
were awestruck by the industrial
landscapes of northwest
England or South Wales,
but not everyone
approved.

growing population of Britain. This
increasing population provided the
workforce for industrial development.

As new mines, mills and factories
opened, many people left the rural areas
and moved into towns and cities. London,
the industrial towns of northwest England and
South Wales all grew rapidly – Bradford, for
example, had a population of 13,000 in 1800
which increased to over 100,000 by 1850.

The power that drove the Industrial
Revolution was steam. In 1769 the Scottish
engineer James Watt patented a much
improved steam engine. Other inventors
who had a major impact in the development
of the Industrial Revolution included
Abraham Darby (coke-smelting),
John Kay (flying shuttle),
James Hargreaves
(Spinning Jenny) and
Richard Arkwright
(water-powered
spinning
machine).

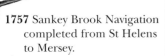

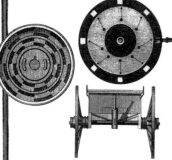

△ *The first half of the 19th century was the age of great engineers and engineering. This period is famous for names such as Isambard Kingdom Brunel, George Stephenson, Thomas Telford and James Brindley.*

Canals and Railways

In 1761, an 11 kilometre canal was opened between Worsley and Manchester. It was planned and paid for by the wealthy Duke of Bridgewater.

The Duke owned coalmines in Worsley, but taking the coal 11 kilometres to Manchester by road was very expensive. After the opening of the Bridgewater Canal, he was able to transport his coal for a much lower price. The success of this canal aroused a lot of interest. Soon, landowners and business people were forming companies to raise money to build canals.

The canals brought many different benefits. They provided cheap transportation for goods such as coal, and linked up parts of the country that had previously been without access to navigable waterways, such as the Potteries area around Stoke on Trent. The building of canals also called upon considerable engineering skills to construct tunnels, locks and aqueducts. Engineers such as James Brindley and Thomas Telford worked on many famous canal-building projects.

▷ *This map shows the main centres of industrial activity after 1760 for cotton, wool and iron. It also shows the route of the Grand Union Canal which linked the northwest, the Midlands and the southeast.*

△ Cotton
○ Wool
◇ Iron

Another engineer, George Stephenson designed the first railway. It went from Stockton to Darlington and was opened in 1825. Like the canals, its purpose was to carry coal. The first passenger-carrying railway opened in 1830. It ran from Liverpool to Manchester. This was the beginning of the age of railway construction. Between 1830 and 1850 about 10,000 kilometres of track was built.

The engines that ran along the railway tracks were powered by steam. The first engineer to design a successful steam engine that would run along an iron track was Richard Trevithick in 1804.

Another use of steam was to power ships. The 1830s, 40s and 50s saw the launch of three great steam-powered ships all designed by Isambard Kingdom Brunel. The *Great Eastern*, launched in 1858 was iron hulled and twice a large as any other ship of the time.

▽ *Travel by railway in the middle of the 19th century. Railways provided a cheap, efficient and fast way to move both people and goods around the country, and Britain was soon exporting its railway technology to countries around the world.*

IRON BRIDGE

The first bridge to be made out of iron was erected in 1779 across the river Severn at Coalbrookdale. The bridge was constructed at the ironworks of the Darby family. It was Abraham Darby (1687–1717) who, in 1709, had discovered how to smelt iron ore using coke (made from coal) rather than charcoal (made from wood) as a fuel – an important breakthrough.

Highland Clearances

△ *Many highland families suffered injustice at the hands of heartless landlords who dispossessed them of their property. Entire families were removed from their land and sent to a life of hardship overseas.*

The Jacobite rebellion in 1745 ended in decisive victory for the Duke of Cumberland's army. But it had given ministers in London a severe fright and made them determined to stamp out any possibility of further rebellion. The result was wholesale killing and looting throughout the Scottish Highlands by British troops.

In the wake of the rebellion, laws were passed to prevent Highlanders carrying weapons and wearing their traditional tartan kilts. Even the bagpipes were banned. These laws were repealed in 1782, but it was to be another 40 years before a British monarch visited his northern kingdom. In 1822 George IV appeared in Edinburgh dressed in full tartan outfit. However, it was his niece, Queen Victoria, who loved Scotland and the Highlands so much that she spent every summer holiday in the north. By the time of Queen Victoria's reign, the Highlands were a quite different place from the well-populated region of the early 18th century. Many landowners no longer felt a sense of responsibility towards the people who scraped a living on their land. They became much more interested in making the most profit from their vast

GLENCALVIE

In 1845, 18 families were thrown out of their houses in Glencalvie, Ross-shire. Their own place of refuge was the churchyard at Croick where they attempted to shelter under a makeshift tent. Before they finally left to move to a town, or to emigrate, some scratched their names and messages on to the windows of the church. The scratches are still there today.

THE BEST AND CHEAPEST ROUTES
TO MOST PLACES IN
AMERICA
ARE THOSE OF THE
"ALLAN" LINE,

△ *An advertisement* for the "Allan" line, one of the many companies that promised to transport desperate Highlanders across the seas and to a new life in "all parts of Canada and the United States".

▽ *Many of the people evicted from* the Highlands emigrated to North America. Some found work on farms and plantations in Canada and the United States, but life was very hard, and many of the new immigrants suffered extreme hardship.

Highland estates. And the easiest way to do this was to use the land for sheep or cattle farming.

After about 1760 and well into Queen Victoria's reign, landowners systematically turned people off the land they had farmed for hundreds of years and replaced them with sheep, cattle and, later, deer forests. This process became known as the "Highland Clearances".

Some farmers continued to make a living of sorts on small crofts, or by fishing. Some joined up with the Scottish regiments that fought in the Napoleonic Wars. Thousands more decided to leave Scotland altogether. Many Highlanders emigrated to North America and to one of Britain's newest colonies – Australia.

1728 James Cook born in Marton-in-Cleveland, Yorkshire (27 October).

1746 Cook apprenticed to shipowner in Whitby.

1755 Cook joins the Navy.

1756–63 Seven Years' War. Cook sees action in Bay of Biscay, at Louisburg and Quebec.

1762 Cook marries Elizabeth Batts.

1763–8 Cook surveys coast of Canada.

1768–71 First voyage on *Endeavour*. Scientific voyage to Pacific Ocean.

1769 Observes transit of Venus on Tahiti (3 June). Charts New Zealand.

1770 Sails along east coast of Australia.

△ *James Cook made contact with the people of New Zealand, Australia and many of the smaller Pacific islands. He took care to treat the local people with respect. He wrote of the Aborigine people in Australia "They live in Tranquillity which is not disturbed by the Inequality of Conditions..."*

1772–5 Second voyage on ships *Resolution* and *Adventure* to circumnavigate and investigate the Antarctic.

1773 Ships cross the Antarctic Circle (17 January).

1776 Third voyage on ships *Resolution* and *Discovery* to look for northwest passage around Canada and Alaska.

1779 Cook is killed in Hawaii (14 February). His body is buried at sea (21 February).

1780 *Resolution* and *Discovery* return to Britain.

Captain Cook

In 1768, the Royal Society decided to send a scientific expedition to the Pacific Ocean. The scientists were to include astronomers, botanists and artists. The little-known James Cook was appointed commander of the voyage.

Cook had been at sea since the age of 18, and having worked on merchant ships he then joined the navy and saw action in the Seven Years' War. He spent the years after the war making charts of the coast of Canada for the navy. His talents as a navigator, surveyor and astronomer, and his powers of command, made him an ideal choice to lead the Royal Society's scientific expedition.

One of Cook's orders was to look for a great Southern Continent. At the time, Europeans had little idea about the geography of the southern hemisphere. People thought that there was a large landmass to balance the huge landmass of Europe and Asia in the northern hemisphere. On his first round-the-world voyage (1768–71), Cook sailed around New Zealand and up the east coast of Australia. On his second voyage (1772–5), he explored the southern Pacific Ocean, crossing the Antarctic Circle and sailing further south than anyone had ever ventured before. His voyages proved that there was no Southern Continent. Cook wrote in his journal that there was at last a "final end put to the searching after a Southern Continent".

△ *Captain Cook's voyages are commemorated on these stamps. Cook was an excellent commander who took good care of his sailors. He insisted that the crew's quarters should be clean and well ventilated. He also avoided scurvy by including cress, sauerkraut and a kind of orange marmalade in the sailors' diet.*

PLANTS

One of the scientists on Cook's first voyage was the young botanist, Joseph Banks. He was the first European to see the plants and wildlife of New Zealand and Australia. After his return to Britain, Banks became famous for his reports of the plants and animals of the southern hemisphere.

Janzoon (1605)
Tasman (1642–1644)

Cook's first voyage (1768–1771)
Cook's second voyage (1772–1775)
Cook's third voyage (1776–1779)

◁ *The routes of Captain Cook's* **three** *voyages are shown here. Black is the "Endeavour" 1768–71; red is "Resolution and Adventure" 1772–5; blue is "Resolution and Discovery" 1776–80.*

▽ *The "Endeavour" was a sturdy ship about 30 metres in length. It was designed to carry coal along the east coast of Britain, but Cook had the cargo hold converted to carry stores and water for the expedition. The "Endeavour" carried 94 people on the long voyage to the Pacific Ocean.*

The aim of Cook's third and final voyage (1776–9) was to find a northwest passage around Canada and Alaska. But disaster struck in Hawaii. After a bad-tempered exchange with the local people of the islands, Cook was killed. His body was buried at sea on 21 February 1779.

▽ *Captain Cook meets the Maori people of New Zealand in 1769. To help him understand the language of the Maoris, Cook had with him an interpreter from the island of Tahiti. Cook then spent five months sailing around the coast of New Zealand and making an accurate chart of the two islands.*

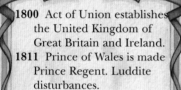

1800 Act of Union establishes the United Kingdom of Great Britain and Ireland.

1811 Prince of Wales is made Prince Regent. Luddite disturbances.

1815 Battle of Waterloo.

1819 "Peterloo Massacre" in Manchester.

1820 George III dies. Prince Regent becomes George IV.

1830 Death of George IV. Succeeded by his brother as William IV.

1832 Reform Act gives vote to men living in property worth £10 per year.

1837 Death of William IV. Succeeded by Queen Victoria.

1839 First Chartist petition presented to parliament.

1840 Marriage of Queen Victoria to Prince Albert of Saxe-Coburg-Gotha. Penny Post introduced.

1842 Second Chartist petition rejected by parliament.

1845–9 Potato famine in Ireland.

1846 Repeal of Corn Laws.

1848 Revolutions in Europe.

1851 Great Exhibition in Crystal Palace.

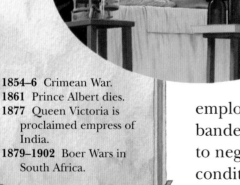

1854–6 Crimean War.

1861 Prince Albert dies.

1877 Queen Victoria is proclaimed empress of India.

1879–1902 Boer Wars in South Africa.

19TH CENTURY

By the beginning of the 19th century, the process of industrialization was already well under way in Britain. By 1858, as Britain's factories turned out textiles, pottery, ironware and many other goods, Benjamin Disraeli was able to describe Britain as the "workshop of the world". About one-quarter of all world trade passed through British ports, and over 90 percent of exports from Britain were goods manufactured in British factories.

This increase in trade and industrial production brought huge wealth to people such as factory owners and landowners. For the thousands of people who flocked to the new industrial centres, it brought dramatic changes in ways of living and working. Many people, particularly women and children, suffered from working long hours under harsh, often dangerous, conditions. Throughout the 19th century, governments passed a series of Factory Acts to control the way that employers treated their workers. Workers also banded together to form "combinations" (trade unions) to negotiate improvements in pay and working conditions. These unions became increasingly powerful throughout the 19th century.

Unrest and reform were ever-present issues in the 19th century, from the Luddite riots and Peterloo

Massacre in the early years, to the fight for Home Rule that gathered pace in Ireland towards the end of the century. Despite the Reform Act of 1832, which gave the right to vote to many more men than ever before, demands for electoral reform continued in the 1840s, as campaigners called the Chartists presented huge petitions to parliament. They were all rejected.

The 19th century was an age of railway-building in Britain. By 1880 there were about 25,000 kilometres of track open in Britain. Long-distance travel was safe and affordable for the first time for many ordinary people. Millions of people began to enjoy day trips, or weekend excursions to seaside resorts. And in 1851 there was a new attraction – the Great Exhibition, held in London.

War with France

In July 1789, a mob in Paris stormed the Bastille prison. This event marked the beginning of the French Revolution. Inspired by the example of the Americans, the revolutionaries declared that France was no longer to be ruled by a monarch but by the National Assembly.

In Britain many people welcomed the revolution and its slogan "liberté, égalité, fraternité". Others feared that violence would break out in Britain's towns and cities. The British prime minister, William Pitt, waited to see which side would emerge victorious in the Revolution. However, Pitt was forced to take action when France declared war on Britain in 1793.

The British government agreed to help its European allies to fight France on the Continent by contributing towards the cost. Meanwhile, the British army and navy concentrated on fighting the French at sea, and defending the British colonies. Pitt was forced to raise new taxes to pay for the war, and in 1795 there were widespread riots in protest. To make matters worse, a brilliant new military commander had emerged in France and was winning victories over Britain's allies. His name was Napoleon Bonaparte.

△ *Lord Nelson was born in Norfolk in 1758. He died at the Battle of Trafalgar, hit by a bullet from a French sniper. Although Trafalgar was an important victory for the British, the whole nation went into mourning for their great hero.*

▽ *The Battle of Waterloo marked the turning point in Britain's war against France. Napoleon met his final defeat near Waterloo, in Belgium, on 18 June 1815. He abdicated soon after and was eventually exiled to St Helen, an island in the Atlantic, where he died in 1821.*

▷ *This map shows the French Empire* under Napoleon I and the dependent states that were virtually part of it. The main battles of the Napoleonic Wars are also shown.

- ■ The empire
- ■ Dependent states
- X Battles

Borodino X

X Friedland   X Smolensk

X Leipzig
X Lutzen
X Jena

X Waterloo

Hohenlinden X

X Austerlitz
X Wagram

Vittoria X

Marengo X

X Torres Vedras

X Trafalgar

In 1798, Napoleon invaded Egypt in an attempt to cut off Britain from its colonies in India. He was driven back when the British fleet, under the command of Lord Nelson, defeated the French at the Battle of the Nile. Nelson scored another momentous victory in 1805 when he defeated a combined French and Spanish fleet at Trafalgar. This battle put an end to the threat of a French invasion – but not to the wars.

Napoleon continued to inflict defeats in Europe until 1812, when he attempted to invade Russia. His troops were caught by the savage Russian winter, and thousands died. Napoleon went into exile, but escaped in 1815. His final defeat was at Waterloo in Belgium.

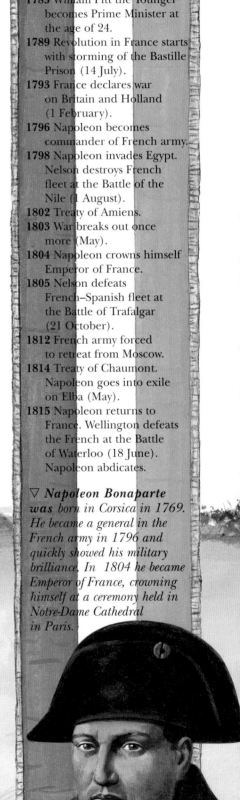

1783 William Pitt the Younger becomes Prime Minister at the age of 24.
1789 Revolution in France starts with storming of the Bastille Prison (14 July).
1793 France declares war on Britain and Holland (1 February).
1796 Napoleon becomes commander of French army.
1798 Napoleon invades Egypt. Nelson destroys French fleet at the Battle of the Nile (1 August).
1802 Treaty of Amiens.
1803 War breaks out once more (May).
1804 Napoleon crowns himself Emperor of France.
1805 Nelson defeats French–Spanish fleet at the Battle of Trafalgar (21 October).
1812 French army forced to retreat from Moscow.
1814 Treaty of Chaumont. Napoleon goes into exile on Elba (May).
1815 Napoleon returns to France. Wellington defeats the French at the Battle of Waterloo (18 June). Napoleon abdicates.

▽ *Napoleon Bonaparte was* born in Corsica in 1769. He became a general in the French army in 1796 and quickly showed his military brilliance. In 1804 he became Emperor of France, crowning himself at a ceremony held in Notre-Dame Cathedral in Paris.

Regency Britain

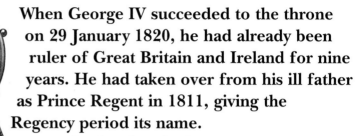

When George IV succeeded to the throne on 29 January 1820, he had already been ruler of Great Britain and Ireland for nine years. He had taken over from his ill father as Prince Regent in 1811, giving the Regency period its name.

1785 Prince of Wales has relationship with Maria Fitzherbert.
1795 Prince of Wales marries Caroline of Brunswick.
1810 George III becomes ill.
1811 Prince of Wales is made Prince Regent. Beginning of Luddite disturbances.
1814 Abdication of Napoleon.
1815 Defeat of Napoleon at Waterloo.
1819 "Peterloo Massacre" in Manchester.
1820 George III dies. Prince Regent becomes George IV.
1821 Riots in London at funeral of Queen Caroline.
1830 Death of George IV. Succeeded by his brother as William IV.

By the time he became Regent, the Prince already had a reputation as a man rather "too fond of women and wine". In 1785 he had become informally and secretly married to Maria Fitzherbert, who was a Roman Catholic. This marriage was never acknowledged and, in 1795, he officially married Caroline of Brunswick. Only a year later the two separated. Caroline's behaviour was outrageous, but her harsh treatment at the hands of the Prince Regent earned her public sympathy. He refused to allow her to attend his coronation in 1821, and after her death a few weeks later there were riots at her funeral.

Unrest and riot characterized much of the Regency period. After 20 years of Napoleonic War, people across Britain were sick of the hardships it brought. Many workers received pitifully low wages and others were losing their jobs. High food prices and poor harvests created widespread fear of starvation. In 1811 there were attacks on machinery and mills by people who claimed allegiance to a man called Ned Ludd. He probably did not exist, but the protestors became known as Luddites.

△ *Three well-dressed Regency ladies. These simple, high-waisted gowns became fashionable in Britain in the late 18th century. They were a reaction to the fussy frilled and hooped gowns worn during the earlier years of the century.*

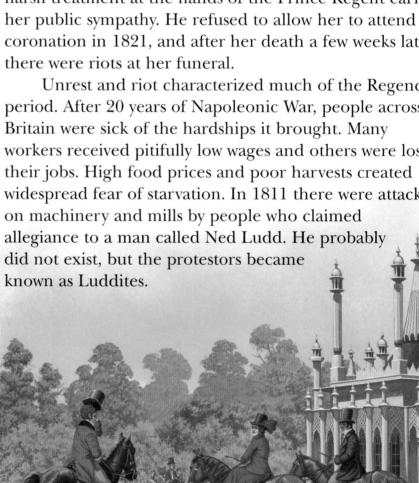

The attacks ended in 1812, only after the arrest and execution of 17 Luddites. Further evidence of the bitterness felt towards the government came when Prime Minister Spencer Perceval was shot in the House of Commons. His assassin was a businessman who had gone bankrupt as a result of the war. By many, he was hailed as a hero.

▽ *The artist and caricaturist Thomas Rowlandson (1756–1827)* illustrated everyday life in 18th-century and Regency England. Here he shows a tradesman trying to sell his ducks in a fashionable Regency town square.

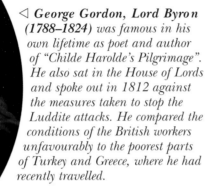

◁ *George Gordon, Lord Byron (1788–1824)* was famous in his own lifetime as poet and author of "Childe Harolde's Pilgrimage". He also sat in the House of Lords and spoke out in 1812 against the measures taken to stop the Luddite attacks. He compared the conditions of the British workers unfavourably to the poorest parts of Turkey and Greece, where he had recently travelled.

▽ *The Royal Pavilion in Brighton* was one of the projects of the Prince Regent. He first went to Brighton in 1783 and it was there that he met Maria Fitzherbert in 1784. As a result of the Prince's patronage, Brighton quickly became a fashionable resort. The Prince used his favourite architect, John Nash, to create the Royal Pavilion in Indian style with Chinese decorations.

Victorian Britain

1837 Death of William IV. Succeeded by Queen Victoria.

1840 Marriage of Queen Victoria to Prince Albert of Saxe-Coburg-Gotha.

1851 Great Exhibition in Crystal Palace.

1854–6 Crimean War.

1861 Prince Albert dies (December 14th).

1877 Queen Victoria is proclaimed empress of India.

1879–1902 Boer Wars in South Africa.

1901 Death of Queen Victoria (January 22nd).

In the early hours of June 20, 1837, a carriage raced as fast as possible from Windsor Castle to Kensington Palace in London. Inside were two men bearing important news – King William IV was dead. At Kensington they greeted their new queen, the 18-year-old Victoria. The Victorian age had begun.

At first, the young queen was a lonely figure relying heavily on the advice of her prime minister, the leader of the Whig party, Lord Melbourne. Victoria's friendship with Lord Melbourne and her enthusiasm for the Whigs caused several scandals in the early years of her reign. However, after her marriage to Prince Albert in 1840, she was more careful to avoid favouring one party over another, working closely with her ministers whatever their political beliefs. In fact, Victoria's nine pregnancies obliged her to hand over many of the responsibilities of monarchy to her husband, and he became an increasingly powerful figure.

When Albert died in 1861, Queen Victoria was distraught. She went into mourning and withdrew almost entirely from public life. As the years passed, public sympathy gave

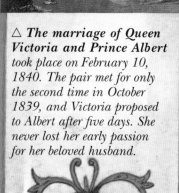

△ *The marriage of Queen Victoria and Prince Albert took place on February 10, 1840. The pair met for only the second time in October 1839, and Victoria proposed to Albert after five days. She never lost her early passion for her beloved husband.*

▷ *Queen Victoria was the first British monarch to be photographed. She also travelled widely around her kingdom thanks to the new railway network. She and Albert especially loved Scotland, where they stayed at Balmoral Castle, and the Isle of Wight, where they stayed at Osborne House.*

△ **The Salvation Army was formed by Catherine and William Booth in 1878.** *It was made up of members from their Whitechapel Christian Mission. The Salvation Army offered help to the poor, homeless and sick during the Victorian period. Today it is a worldwide organization that helps those in poverty.*

way to discontent with the absent monarch. Only the persuasiveness of the Tory prime minister, Benjamin Disraeli, eventually brought Victoria back to her public duties. Her Golden and Diamond jubilees in 1887 and 1897 (celebrating 50 and 60 years on the throne) were huge successes.

When she died in 1901, she was buried alongside the love of her life, Albert, in a mausoleum near Windsor. Of Victoria and Albert's nine children, the first in line to the throne was Edward, Prince of Wales, who became Edward VII on the death of his mother in 1901. Many of Victoria's children married members of other European royal families. At her death, Victoria had 37 great-grandchildren.

▽ **A Victorian lady of fashion.** *Women's fashion during the Victorian era was dominated by the bustle gown, with its exaggerated, full skirts and tiny waist.*

▷ **Dancing at the Royal Cremorne Gardens in Chelsea, London.** *There were all sorts of amusements in these pleasure gardens including fireworks, dancing, puppet shows and hot-air balloons.*

1840 Introduction of Penny Post by Rowland Hill improved the postal service.

1842–4 Prime Minister Sir Robert Peel introduces reduction or abolition of duty on many goods.

1844 Bank Charter Act.

1846 Repeal of Corn Laws. Free trade in corn established.

1848 Revolutions across Europe.

1850 Over 10,000 kilometres of railway track open.

1851 Great Exhibition held in Crystal Palace, Hyde Park, London.

1860 Final abolition of duties on many goods.

1880 Over 25,000 kilometres of railway track open.

Trade and Industry

In 1858, Benjamin Disraeli called Britain the "workshop of the world". Both trade and industry were booming. About one-quarter of all world trade passed through British ports, and most of this was carried in British ships. By the middle of the 19th century, over 90 percent of the exports from Britain were goods manufactured in British factories.

The most important of the exports were textiles. In 1830, textiles made up 75 percent of all Britain's exports, and half of this amount was cotton goods. Raw cotton was imported from North America and turned into cloth in the factories and mills in northern Britain. It was then exported either as cloth, or manufactured into cheap goods. Many of these cotton goods were sold in India.

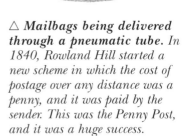

△ *Mailbags being delivered through a pneumatic tube. In 1840, Rowland Hill started a new scheme in which the cost of postage over any distance was a penny, and it was paid by the sender. This was the Penny Post, and it was a huge success.*

△ *The Great Exhibition in 1851 was held in a massive glass building, known as the Crystal Palace, built in Hyde Park. It lasted for five months and attracted over six million visitors.*

▷ *Rioting breaks out in Germany in 1848. While Europe was in a state of turmoil, British industry went from strength to strength. Britain soon became a leading industrial nation.*

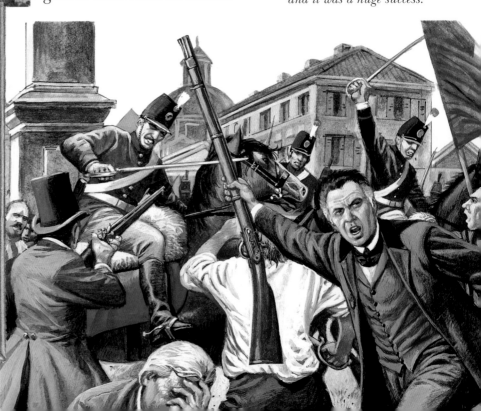

The amount of railway track in Britain increased rapidly in the 19th century. The railways revolutionized travel, providing cheap and efficient transport. Soon, British engineering and technology was being used in many overseas countries for railway building projects. From the 1840s, iron became a major British export – much of it destined for the construction of railways.

The introduction of free trade in the middle of the 19th century also helped to boost trade. For many years, British products had been protected by charging duties (taxes) on goods imported from overseas. These duties were gradually removed, making the importing of raw materials, such as cotton, cheaper.

The event that best showed off the power of British trade and industry was the Great Exhibition of 1851. It displayed the finest British technology and engineering, proving Britain's leadership in industry at the time.

△ *Bank notes being printed. The British banking system started in the late 17th century. At first, each bank issued its own notes. However, the Bank Charter Act of 1844 aimed to control the number of banknotes issued, and gradually limited the issue of notes to the Bank of England.*

HORSEDRAWN CARRIAGES

The arrival of the railways in the 19th century brought an end to long-distance journeys by carriage. The railways were far more efficient, and more reliable than the old stagecoaches. However, carriages continued to be used for shorter journeys, and town streets were choked with horse-drawn traffic.

▽ *Labourers at work on a new railway track. Thousands of miles of track were laid in Britain in the 19th century. Gangs of construction workers often came from Scotland or Ireland and were known as 'navvies' (short for 'navigation', another word for canal). The building of the railways provided unskilled work for many thousands of labourers.*

Life in Victorian Britain

1799 Combination Act prevents "combinations" of workers.

1824 Repeal of Combination Act.

1825 New Combination Act confines combinations to peaceful negotiation over wages and hours.

1834 Trade unions join together to form Grand National Consolidated Trades' Union (GNCTU). "Tolpuddle Martyrs" sentenced to transportation for swearing illegal oaths in connection with Friendly Society of Agricultural Labourers. Public outcry and demonstrations lead to pardon of the six men.

1868 First Trades Union Congress in Manchester.

1893 Keir Hardie sets up Independent Labour Party.

△ *This early bicycle was known as the "boneshaker". Its frame was made from iron and steel and its tyres from rubber. It made its appearance on the roads in the 1860s.*

▷ *A bustling scene on London Bridge. The streets of Victorian London were usually filthy and choked with traffic. For short journeys in town, people travelled by foot, on horseback, or by carriage – for example in a two-wheeled hansom cab (front left).*

One of the effects of the Industrial Revolution was that large numbers of people moved to work in the factories and mills of the industrial areas. These workers had to become accustomed to new ways of working – including long hours, and the discipline of factory life.

Life in the country was not easy either. A 12-hour day was normal, and it could be longer during busy times of year, such as harvest. However, during the winter, shorter daylight hours meant that the working day was also shorter. In the factories, the 12-hour working day operated throughout the year and workers had to be far more disciplined. For example, if they turned up late for work the factory gates were shut, and they lost pay.

In some places, workers combined into groups to demand better conditions. These groups were known as "combinations" (and later as "unions"). Although they faced many legal challenges, the unions grew in importance throughout the 19th century.

For many working-class women, jobs in factories or mills offered an opportunity to earn their own money for the first time, although they were usually paid less than men for the same work. The largest group of women workers was domestic servants.

△ *Ladies' summer fashions of 1844.* These full skirts would have been supported by several starched petticoats. In the 1850s crinolines appeared. They were frameworks of steel and whalebone that were lighter and more comfortable than thick, heavy petticoats.

◁ *Two wealthy ladies visit the home of a poor family.* Many well-off people in Victorian times were deeply concerned with the plight of the poor. Many charities were set up, as well as voluntary hospitals and the "Ragged Schools" – free schools for poor children.

CHILDHOOD

Most children in middle-class homes in the 19th century were brought up largely by nurses and governesses. Parents were often remote figures, to be treated with respect. Great emphasis was laid on good manners, and children would often address their father as "Sir". Boys were usually sent away to school but, until the later years of the century, most girls were educated at home by a governess.

Unrest and Reform

Since Elizabethan times, there had been a system in England of helping those who were sick or who could not find work, as well as poor widows and orphans. Known as the "Poor Law", the money for this system came from the householders in each parish.

In 1832, a government commission was set up to look into the workings of the Poor Law. Many people were unhappy with the cost of the system and the way it was run. The New Poor Law, passed in 1834, targeted people who were able-bodied yet unemployed. Out-of-work labourers were no longer to get relief (money). Instead they were to go to the workhouse, where they would be separated from their families and fed the poorest food. The New Poor Law saved money, but it caused misery to thousands of people.

For those in work, life was sometimes little better. Conditions in many mines, mills and factories were atrocious, with women and

▽ *Women at work* in the workroom of a Victorian workhouse. The inhabitants of a workhouse were made to wear uniforms and were not allowed to receive visitors or to leave the building. The workhouse was loathed and dreaded by the poor.

△ *Mounted police move in to quell a riot* in Trafalgar Square on November 13, 1887. The disturbance started after a meeting of unemployed people. Such clashes were common throughout the 19th century, as workers demanded reforms and rights.

▷ *A scene from one of Charles Dickens's novels, "Oliver Twist".* Oliver is famous as the workhouse boy who dared to ask for more food because he was hungry. In "Oliver Twist", Dickens highlighted the conditions and the treatment of poor children in workhouses.

children working long hours with dangerous equipment. Various Factory Acts limited working hours and the age of children being put to work, but the Acts were largely ineffective until inspectors were employed to check that the new laws were being obeyed.

In the late 1830s, unrest over working conditions and the New Poor Law broke out in the north of England. Out of this unrest grew the movement called Chartism. Chartists believed that the only way towards fairer laws was if more working men had the vote. Until 1832, only wealthy landowners were allowed to vote. In 1839 a group of Chartists presented the People's Charter to parliament. It called for the vote for men of 21 years and over, but it – and further petitions – were rejected. After 1848, Chartism died out, but parliamentary reform continued.

1819 Factory Act limits working day for children in cotton mills to 12 hours.
1832 Reform Act gives vote to men living in property worth £10 per year.
1833 Factory Act limits work for children in textile factories.
1834 New Poor Law Act.
1839 First Chartist petition presented to parliament.
1842 Second Chartist petition rejected by parliament.
1847 Factory Act limits women and children to 58-hour working week.

△ *The author Charles Dickens* used his novels to reveal the plight of the poor. He painted a vivid picture of the appalling conditions in workhouses, in factories, and in the slums of London.

1848 Feargus O'Connor presents third Chartist petition. It is rejected by parliament.
1850 Factory Act establishes standard working day.
1867 Second Reform Act gives vote to about one in three working men.
1885 Third Reform Act.

SERVANT EMPLOYMENT

In the 19th century, domestic service was a large source of employment for both men and women. Even modestly well-off households employed a maid or two, and in larger households there were teams of maids and men servants. The servants' living quarters were usually in the basement and at the top of a large house (*right*). Their employers lived and slept in greater luxury in the main rooms (*left*).

1838 Poor Law introduced in Ireland.

1841 Population of Ireland is 8,175,000.

1845 Potato blight first reported in southern England (August). Blight appears in Ireland (September). Beginning of famine in Ireland. Peel orders shipment of corn from United States to feed starving people in Ireland.

1846 Repeal of the Corn Laws. Sir Robert Peel resigns and Lord John Russell becomes prime minister (June). Potato crop fails again and famine worsens. More than 100,000 people emigrate from Ireland.

1847 Potato crop succeeds but it is very small and insufficient to feed the population. About 215,000 people emigrate from Ireland.

1848 Blight reappears and potato crop fails.

1849 Only partial failure of potato crop brings an end to famine.

1851 Population of Ireland has fallen to 6,552,000. Over 250,000 people emigrate this year.

△ *The potato plant was first brought to Europe from North America in the 16th century. The fungus that killed the Irish potato crop also came from America, arriving in 1845. The fungus destroyed both the leaves and the roots of the potato plant, leaving a rotting mess behind.*

Great Hunger

Between 1845 and 1849 a famine struck Ireland, killing an estimated one million people from starvation or disease. Many thousands more emigrated across the Atlantic to the United States to escape the great hunger.

In 1841, just over eight million people lived in Ireland. About half depended on potatoes as their main food source. In 1845 a fungus affected the potato crop in southern England. It soon moved to Ireland, and in an unusually cold, wet year the fungus quickly swept across the country. Many people found that their potatoes had rotted in the ground. Others picked seemingly sound potatoes only to find that they rotted later on.

The situation was made worse by the Corn Law, which protected British landowners by taxing imported corn. This kept the price of British corn too high for the Irish to afford to buy. Prime Minister Sir Robert Peel ordered £100,000 worth of corn to be imported from the USA. It was sold cheaply in Ireland, helping to prevent starvation. In 1846 Peel persuaded MPs to vote for the repeal (cancellation) of the Corn Laws. Many Conservative MPs were landowners and they saw the repeal of the Corn Laws as a threat to their profits. The vote split the Tory party and led to Peel's resignation. He was replaced by a Whig, Lord John Russell. When the harvest failed in 1846, the famine worsened.

△ *A starving woman and her children search for edible potatoes in Ireland. Starvation was not the only cause of death during the great famine. Diseases such as typhus and dysentery spread, killing thousands of people.*

▷ *Irish emigrants wait at the dockside* to board ships to the United States of America. Between 1846 and 1849 thousands of people emigrated, desperate to escape from the famine in Ireland. Conditions on board ship were often appalling. One in nine emigrants from the Cork region died before they reached their destination.

The new government did little to help the people of Ireland. Russell expected Irish landowners to take responsibility for their starving tenants. The government limited its help to building extra workhouses and opening soup kitchens. The crop failures and famine continued, and it was not until 1849 that conditions slowly began to improve.

▽ *Famine-struck Ireland in 1845.* One writer said of the scenes he saw: "In many places the wretched people were seated on the fences of their decaying gardens, wringing their hands, and bewailing bitterly the destruction that had left them foodless."

The Crimean War

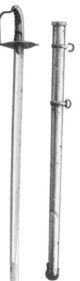

1853 Ottoman Empire (Turkey) declares war on Russia. Turkish fleet destroyed by Russians at Sinope. French–British fleet goes to Black Sea to protect Turkish coast.

1854 France and Britain declare war on Russia. Siege of Sevastopol begins. Major battles at Alma River, Balaklava and Inkerman. Florence Nightingale and a team of nurses arrive in Scutari.

1855 French capture Malakhov and Russians evacuate Sebastopol.

1856 Russians accept peace. Treaty of Paris (March).

1857 Royal Commission on the Health of the Army set up. Foundation of Army Medical School.

△ *The Victoria Cross is a medal presented to members of the British armed forces for acts of extreme bravery. It was set up by Queen Victoria during the Crimean War, and the first crosses were awarded to soldiers who fought in this war.*

The Crimean War takes its name from the region where the war was fought – the Crimean Peninsula, on the Black Sea in present-day Ukraine. The war was fought between Russia and the allied armies of Britain, France and the Ottoman Empire (Turkey), with the army of Sardinia–Piedmont joining this alliance in 1855.

The war started because of religious conflicts between Russia and the Ottoman Empire. Britain also had concerns about Russia's wish to expand its territories and any threat this might present to British colonies and trade. In 1853 Russia invaded Turkish-held provinces on the river Danube and declared war on the Ottoman Empire. Most British ministers wanted a peaceful settlement to the conflict, but public opinion forced Britain and France to declare war on Russia.

The Russian armies withdrew from the Danube provinces in the summer of 1854, but the British and French decided to send a force to attack their stronghold at Sebastopol on the Crimea. The aim was to launch a swift attack to frighten the Russians and increase security for the Ottoman Empire. What actually happened was a year-long siege in which many thousands of soldiers died.

The end came when French troops captured the Russian position at Malakhov. The Russians blew up their forts and ships at Sebastopol and withdrew. A peace treaty was signed in March 1856.

△ *The Battle of Alma started on September 20, 1854 when British and French troops forced the Russians to retreat towards Sevastopol. The Crimean War was the first to be closely recorded in the press, with reporters sending daily accounts of the realities of war.*

Many of the British troops who died in the Crimea were killed not by Russian attacks but by disease. The sick were taken to makeshift hospitals at Scutari in Turkey, where they were left to die of typhus or of their wounds. Their suffering was described in *The Times* by its correspondent Sir William Russell. His reports caused a public outcry, and prompted the minister for war to ask Florence Nightingale to go to Scutari with a team of nurses. She had soon earned her well-known nickname: "the lady with the lamp".

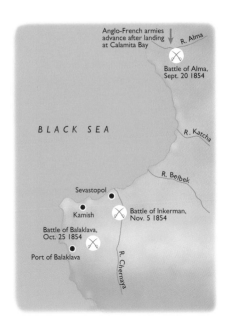

◁ **Florence Nightingale** *was called the "lady with the lamp" because of her late-night ward rounds on which she comforted the sick troops. When she arrived in Scutari, Florence Nightingale found filthy hospitals full of dying men lying on bare boards. She ordered 200 scrubbing brushes, and then she cleaned the wards. Next, she organized the delivery of mattresses and sheets, and opened a kitchen to prepare food for her patients.*

△ **This map shows the main battles of the Crimean War,** *including the famous Battle of Balaklava in which the charge of the Light Brigade took place.*

▽ **The charge of the Light Brigade** *happened at the Battle of Balaklava on October 25, 1854. A set of confused orders sent the Light Brigade towards a well-armed Russian outpost and as a result about 250 out of the 673 men died. The event was made famous in a poem by the English poet, Alfred, Lord Tennyson.*

1800 Act of Union establishes the United Kingdom of Great Britain and Ireland.

1828 Daniel O'Connell elected as an MP, although as a Catholic he could not take up the post.

1829 Catholic Emancipation Act gives Catholics political equality.

1843 Meeting at Clontarf to promote repeal of the Union put down by troops.

1845–9 Great famine.

1848 Leaders of Young Ireland movement arrested and transported after unsuccessful uprising.

1858 Founding of Fenian Brotherhood to fight for Irish independence.

1870 Home Rule League founded in Dublin by Isaac Butt.

1880 Charles Stewart Parnell becomes leader of Home Rule League.

△ *Eamon de Valera (1882–1975) continued the Irish struggle for independence after the turn of the century. De Valera went on to become president of Ireland in 1959.*

1884 Franchise Act gives vote to many supporters of Home Rule.

1886 First Home Rule Bill defeated in House of Commons.

1893 Defeat of Second Home Rule Bill.

Ireland and Home Rule

In 1800, the Act of Union joined Great Britain and Ireland to form the United Kingdom. Ireland was now represented by 100 MPs at Westminster in London. However, Irish Catholics, who made up 90 percent of the Irish population, could not vote or become MPs.

The fight for political equality for Catholics was led by Daniel O'Connell. Although he could not legally become an MP, he stood for election in County Clare in 1828 and won a huge number of votes. In 1829, Catholics gained the right to become MPs. O'Connell wanted the Act of Union to be repealed (cancelled), and Ireland to be independent and to have its own parliament again. O'Connell died in 1847, but the agitation for repeal continued with the Young Ireland movement and the Fenian Brotherhood.

In 1870, Isaac Butt founded an organization that used the slogan "Home Rule". Under the leadership of Charles Stewart Parnell, the Home Rule League played a major part in the fight for independence.

▽ *An Irish tenant farmer and family are evicted by their landlord. Tenants were thrown out if they could not pay their rent. Some landlords tried to "clear" their estates by offering tenants incentives of money to emigrate.*

△ *Trying petty cases in an Irish courtroom in 1853.* *Justice was weighted heavily in favour of the English landlord in 19th-century Ireland. The fate of Irishmen brought to court was often already decided before the trial began.*

In 1884, the Franchise Act gave the vote to many more Catholics, and in 1885 over 80 Irish "Home Rulers" were elected. Prime Minister William Gladstone was convinced of the need for Home Rule. However, between 1886 and 1893 two Home Rule bills were defeated in parliament.

▽ *In March 1867, there was a Fenian uprising. It was unsuccessful, lasting only one night. Many of the Fenian leaders had already been rounded up and imprisoned by the government.*

Health and Education

The first half of the 19th century saw a massive movement of people from the countryside to industrial centres such as Manchester and Leeds. Huge numbers of houses were built to accommodate these workers, but towns quickly became overcrowded and unhealthy places.

The most basic problem was one of sanitation. The new houses were built back to back, or around a courtyard. They were overcrowded, and there was often just one privy (toilet) and one clean-water pipe for the occupants of several houses. There were no sewerage systems, so sewage often drained directly into rivers or was dumped in heaps. It is not surprising that water for drinking was often dirty, spreading fatal diseases such as cholera.

In the 1840s, people began to accept the links between the filthy conditions in towns and the spread of disease. Plans were drawn up for water and sewerage systems, and conditions in towns slowly began to improve.

1828   Thomas Arnold becomes headmaster of Rugby School and begins the reform of public schools.

1833   Factory Act includes education for children working in textile factories, and provides government fund for education.

1844   "Ragged Schools" set up for poorest children.

1848   Public Health Act to set up boards of health.

1870   Education Act sets up School Boards and aims to "cover the country with good schools".

1875   Public Health Act sets up authorities to oversee housing, sanitation and so on.

1880   Education Act makes school compulsory for children aged 5–10.

1891   Assisted Education Act funds each child, allowing schools to stop having to charge fees.

△ *This ornamental washstand is typical of the style of the late 19th century. Fitted bathrooms were found in the houses of the well-to-do at this time.*

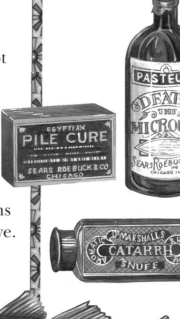

MEDICINE
Health and cleanliness became an important issue during the Victorian era. Various medicines and sanitary products were introduced and a number of medical discoveries made. One of the most important medical breakthroughs of the age was the use of Joseph Lister's carbolic antiseptic spray during operations.

▷ *A Victorian schoolroom. In many schools pupil-teachers helped with the teaching. The pupil-teachers were boys and girls of 13 and over. After five years of apprenticeship they could themselves become teachers.*

KING CHOLERA
Cholera is a disease spread through dirty water, although the way it spread was not understood in the 19th century. There were outbreaks of cholera in 1831, 1848, 1853 and 1866, each time killing thousands of people.

However, in the 1860s a writer could still complain that the town of Kidderminster in the West Midlands "stank from end to end"! For most children of working-class families in the early 19th century, there were few opportunities for education. Church organizations ran some Sunday schools, and there were "Dame" schools (so called because they were run by women) for young children. In 1844, "Ragged Schools" were set up to provide basic education for orphans and very poor children. As more men were given the right to vote, people began to realize the importance of educating future voters.

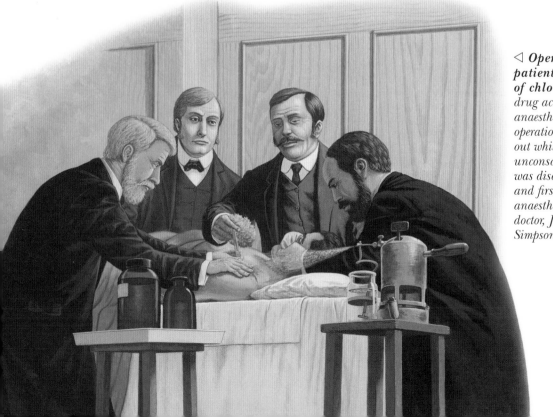

◁ *Operating on a patient with the use of chloroform. This drug acted as an anaesthetic, allowing operations to be carried out while the patient was unconscious. Chloroform was discovered in 1831 and first used as an anaesthetic by a Scottish doctor, James Young Simpson, in 1847.*

Inventions and Discoveries

The 19th century saw major developments that made travel, communications and trade easier for many people. The railways allowed people to travel cheaply and rapidly, opening up new possibilities for both rich and poor. The postal service expanded after the introduction of the "Penny Post".

The first practical electric telegraph was demonstrated by two British inventors, William Fothergill Cooke and Charles Wheatstone in 1837. It used electric signals running along a wire to make a needle point to specific letters and numbers at the receiving end. It provided, for the first time, a method of fast, long-distance communication. Soon telegraph wires were being laid alongside railway tracks, and strung between poles to link towns and cities. In 1876, there was another breakthrough in communications when the Scottish-born inventor Alexander Bell sent a voice message along a telegraph line. This was the first telephone message.

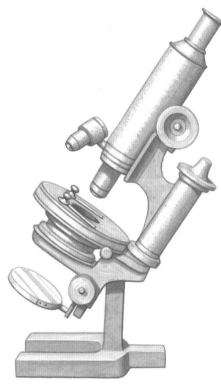

△ *A microscope was one of the essential pieces of equipment for scientists in the 19th century. Charles Darwin's microscope still sits on his desk in his study at his house in Kent. Darwin's controversial theories were backed up by the discovery of dinosaur fossils and other evidence of early life on Earth, and were soon accepted by many people.*

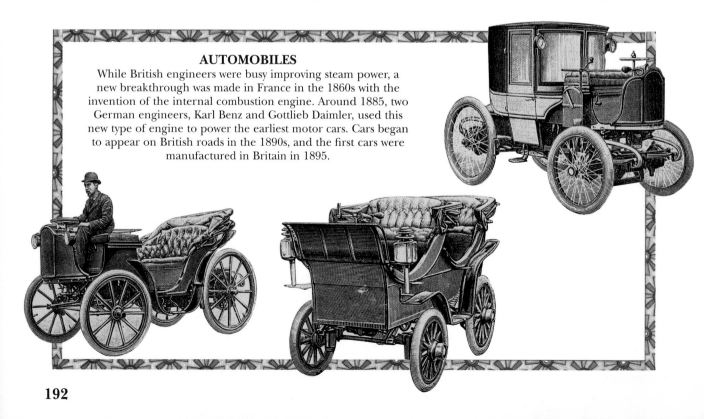

AUTOMOBILES

While British engineers were busy improving steam power, a new breakthrough was made in France in the 1860s with the invention of the internal combustion engine. Around 1885, two German engineers, Karl Benz and Gottlieb Daimler, used this new type of engine to power the earliest motor cars. Cars began to appear on British roads in the 1890s, and the first cars were manufactured in Britain in 1895.

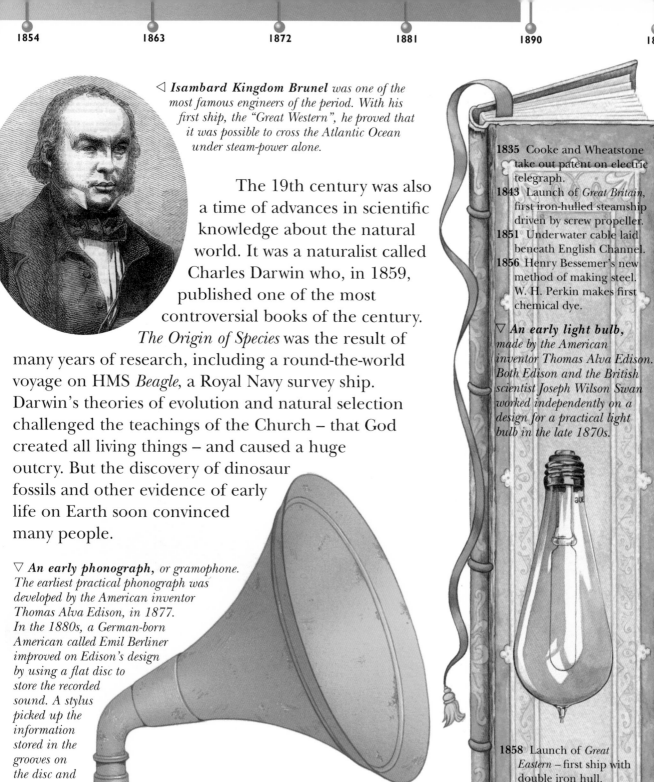

◁ *Isambard Kingdom Brunel was one of the most famous engineers of the period. With his first ship, the "Great Western", he proved that it was possible to cross the Atlantic Ocean under steam-power alone.*

The 19th century was also a time of advances in scientific knowledge about the natural world. It was a naturalist called Charles Darwin who, in 1859, published one of the most controversial books of the century. *The Origin of Species* was the result of many years of research, including a round-the-world voyage on HMS *Beagle*, a Royal Navy survey ship. Darwin's theories of evolution and natural selection challenged the teachings of the Church – that God created all living things – and caused a huge outcry. But the discovery of dinosaur fossils and other evidence of early life on Earth soon convinced many people.

▽ *An early phonograph, or gramophone. The earliest practical phonograph was developed by the American inventor Thomas Alva Edison, in 1877. In the 1880s, a German-born American called Emil Berliner improved on Edison's design by using a flat disc to store the recorded sound. A stylus picked up the information stored in the grooves on the disc and converted it back into sound.*

1835 Cooke and Wheatstone take out patent on electric telegraph.
1843 Launch of *Great Britain*, first iron-hulled steamship driven by screw propeller.
1851 Underwater cable laid beneath English Channel.
1856 Henry Bessemer's new method of making steel. W. H. Perkin makes first chemical dye.

▽ *An early light bulb, made by the American inventor Thomas Alva Edison. Both Edison and the British scientist Joseph Wilson Swan worked independently on a design for a practical light bulb in the late 1870s.*

1858 Launch of *Great Eastern* – first ship with double iron hull.
1866 *Great Eastern* used to lay underwater cable beneath Atlantic Ocean.
1876 Alexander Bell sends first voice message along a telegraph line.
1878 Joseph Swan makes successful light bulb.
1879 Thomas Edison also develops light bulb.
1885 Karl Benz and Gottlieb Daimler develop first motor cars.

The British Raj

On May 10, 1857, sepoys (soldiers) in the service of the East India Company in Meerut shot their British officers. This was the start of the uprising known to Indians as the First War of Independence, and to the British as the Indian Mutiny.

By the middle of the 19th century, British rule was well established in India. The East India Company, set up in the 17th century to trade with countries in the East, was responsible for administration across British-ruled India.

The immediate cause of the mutiny that broke out amongst the sepoys in 1857 was the introduction of a new kind of rifle. The cartridges for this rifle had to have the ends bitten off before the bullet inside could be used. A rumour began that the grease used in these cartridges was made of a mixture of cow's and pig's fat. This was unacceptable to both the Hindu and Muslim sepoys,

△ *Rudyard Kipling*
was born in India in 1865. He was sent to school in England from the age of six, but returned to India in 1882 to work as a journalist. He became famous for his poems and short stories about life in India. He also wrote many children's stories including "The Jungle Book" and the "Just So Stories".

1833 East India Company becomes administrative agent in India on behalf of the British government.
1845–56 Lord Dalhousie pursues policy of introducing Western ideas about religion and education into India.
1857 Indian Mutiny begins at Meerut 10 May.

△ *A British soldier in tropical uniform. The British army in India was made up of a mixture of British and Indian troops.*

1858 Peace proclaimed. British government assumes control of India.
1876 Queen Victoria is created empress of India.
1885 Indian National Congress founded.
1892 First Indian members sit on legislative council.

CARRIAGE AND BEARERS
The British officials of the British East India Company were often very wealthy and could afford to be carried around in an enclosed litter, called a *palanquin*. After the Indian Mutiny, most British officials in India lived in well-guarded military towns, or camps, built outside local towns.

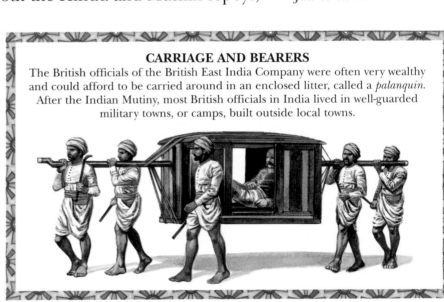

◁ **Indian cavalry of the British army** *fight a battle in Burma. There were three wars between Britain and Burma in 1824–6, 1852 and 1885. Britain invaded Burma in order to protect the safety of India, but also because of greed for Burma's valuable natural resources of teak, oil and rubies.*

as Hindus consider the cow to be a sacred animal, and Muslims consider pigs to be unclean. When the sepoys in Meerut refused to use the new cartridges, they were thrown into prison. Their comrades then mutinied against the British officers.

The main battles of the mutiny were fought in Delhi, Cawnpore and Lucknow. The massacre of 200 women and children at Cawnpore outraged the British. However, they took equally violent revenge on the sepoys, killing hundreds of Indian soldiers. Peace was finally declared on July 8, 1858. The Indian Mutiny shocked the British, and changes were made to prevent future similar uprisings. The administration was taken away from the East India Company and a new government department was set up to run India. Before the mutiny, British policy was to introduce Western ideas about religion and education, which threatened both Hindu and Muslim ways of life. After 1858, a new British policy aimed to prevent interference with religious matters in India.

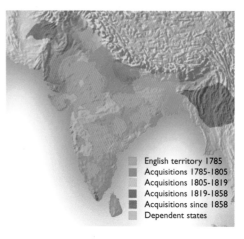

English territory 1785
Acquisitions 1785-1805
Acquisitions 1805-1819
Acquisitions 1819-1858
Acquisitions since 1858
Dependent states

△ **This map shows how the British expanded their rule over India.** *The British took over some states by force, others were occupied when their rulers died and there was no obvious heir. The dependent states were ruled by Indian princes under British protection. Until 1947, India also included the countries of Pakistan and Bangladesh (which was East Pakistan until 1971).*

◁ **Chintz** *was made in India for export to Europe. It is printed and glazed calico (a type of Indian cotton), and became popular for clothes in India and in Britain, where it was also used for furniture coverings. Different patterns were used on the cloth that was for the home market and that for export, following the fashions of the time. The word "chintz" comes from a Hindu word meaning "spotted".*

195

Opium Wars

1839 Chinese officials seize opium from British merchants. Start of First Opium War (until 1842).

1841 Guangzhou captured by British forces (24 May).

1842 Shanghai captured (19 June). Treaty of Nanjing (29 August). Hong Kong leased to Britain and five Chinese ports opened for foreign trade.

1856 Chinese seize British ship *Arrow* (October). Start of Second Opium War (until 1860).

1858 Treaty of Tientsin.

1859 Construction of Suez Canal begins (April 25th).

1860 British and French forces occupy Beijing. Treaty of Beijing (October 24th).

1869 Opening of Suez Canal (November 17th).

Although China exported large amounts of tea and silk to countries in Europe, the Chinese government restricted imports. Foreign traders were allowed to do business in only one Chinese port, Guangzhou.

British merchants tried to get round these restrictions by illegally importing opium from India into China. Although the dangers of opium were well known, the British government backed the merchants in their illegal trade. In 1839, Chinese officials seized all the opium stored in the British warehouses in Guangzhou. The First Opium War started in 1839 and ended with the British imposing a settlement on the Chinese in 1842. Under this treaty, Hong Kong became a British colony.

In 1856, the Second Opium War began. The British government wanted to extend its trading rights in China, and forced the Chinese to settle in the Treaty of Tientsin. When the Chinese tried to block this treaty, British and French troops occupied Beijing, the Chinese capital. In 1860, the Chinese signed the Treaty of Beijing in which they agreed to accept the terms of the Treaty of Tientsin.

△ *Two addicts smoking opium in China. Opium is a drug made from the juice of the opium poppy. It is the source of several pain-relieving medicines, but if it is misused it can be addictive.*

1875 British government buys shares in Suez Canal.

1882 British take control in Egypt.

1883 Sudanese defeat Egyptian army led by British commander.

1885 General Gordon is killed by Sudanese forces.

1888 International convention agrees that Suez Canal open to all nations.

▽ *The British steamship "Nemesis" attacked Chinese junks (sailing vessels) in 1841 during the First Opium War. Opium addiction became a problem in China in the 18th and 19th centuries. By 1890, it was estimated that about 80 percent of all Chinese men used the drug.*

Egypt and Sudan

The opening of the Suez Canal was important for trading nations in Europe. Instead of sailing around the southern tip of Africa, ships between Europe and Asia could now take a short cut from the Mediterranean Sea to the Red Sea.

The British government took no part in the canal's funding or construction. Nevertheless, the canal was vital for British trade. When political disturbances in Egypt threatened the canal, Britain quickly stepped in and took control of Egypt. In 1888, an international convention agreed that the canal should open for use by ships of all countries.

British rule in Egypt coincided with rebellion in neighbouring Sudan. Under their leader, the Mahdi, Sudanese rebels defeated an Egyptian army in 1883. Prime Minister Gladstone sent General Charles Gordon to oversee the withdrawal of Egyptian troops from Sudan. Gordon tried to overthrow the Mahdi. By March 1884 he was besieged in Khartoum, and in 1885 Gordon was killed. Sudan came under British and Egyptian control in 1898.

△ *Benjamin Disraeli was prime minister in 1868 and again from 1874 to 1880. In 1875 he bought a large number of shares in the Suez Canal Company from the Khedive (viceroy) of Egypt, Isma'il Pasha. This purchase gave the British government a financial interest in the management of the canal.*

▷ *Ships sail along the Suez Canal at its opening on November 17, 1869. The canal is 190 kilometres long and unites the Mediterranean Sea and the Red Sea. The opening of the canal reduced the sea journey from Britain to India by 9,700 kilometres. Funds for the construction of the canal were raised by the Suez Canal Company, and the project was organized by a French diplomat, Ferdinand de Lesseps. The canal took over 10 years to build.*

The Boer War

1836–44 "Great Trek" northwards of the Boers.
1854 Boers form Orange Free State.
1857 Boer Republic established in Transvaal.
1869 onwards Discovery of diamonds near Kimberley.
1877 Britain annexes Transvaal.
1880 Boers proclaim their independence.
1881 British defeated at Battle of Majuba (February 27th). Convention of Pretoria (April 5th) restores the independence of Transvaal.
1886 Gold discovered in Witwatersrand.
1897 Paul Kruger signs military alliance with Orange Free State.
1899 War is declared between Britain and the Boer alliance (October). The Boers besiege the towns of Ladysmith, Mafeking and Kimberley.

△ *Thousands of Boer farmers* trekked northwards from Cape Colony in southern Africa in the late 1830s and early 1840s, in what became known as the "Great Trek". The Boers left in rebellion against British rule.

1900 Reinforcements arrive from Britain and end sieges of Kimberley and Ladysmith (February). End of siege in Mafeking (May). Boer capital captured (June).
1902 Treaty of Vereeniging.

Cape Colony, the largest European settlement in Africa, came under British rule in 1806. Most of the colonists were descendants of Dutch farmers, known as Boers. Many Boers quickly came to dislike the new administration and in the 1830s, thousands of them started a long trek northwards, known as the "Great Trek". They founded two Boer states: Orange Free State and a Boer Republic in the Transvaal.

In the 1870s the British government tried to persuade the Boers to unite its states with the British colonies (Cape Colony and Natal). The British not only wanted to increase their power in southern Africa, they also wanted a share of the diamond deposits that were coming to light along the Vaal River, particularly around Kimberley. When British troops were sent to force the Boers to accept these proposals, the Boers fought back. The British were defeated at the Battle of Majuba in 1881.

In 1886 major gold deposits were discovered in the Transvaal. Britain feared the growing power and wealth of the Boer states and war broke out again in 1899. The Boer armies attacked the British settlements at Ladysmith, Mafeking and Kimberley. It was not until reinforcements arrived in early 1900 that these sieges ended. The British went on to capture Pretoria, the capital of Transvaal. By mid-1900 there were about 250,000 British troops in southern Africa compared to

▽ *This map shows* two Boer States: the orange free state and a state in the Transvaal

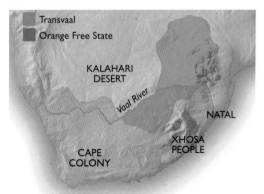

Transvaal
Orange Free State

KALAHARI DESERT

Vaal River

NATAL

XHOSA PEOPLE

CAPE COLONY

▷ *Zulu troops attack British soldiers.* *When the Boers trekked northwards in the 1830s, they moved into traditional Zulu homelands. The Boers attempted to set up a republic in Natal, but they were defeated by the Zulus.*

OGDEN'S "GUINEA GOLD" CIGARETTE

IS "A WELCOME COMRADE."

△ *An advertisement* for *Ogden's cigarettes, with a Boer War theme. The Boers used guerrilla tactics very successfully against the British. The British under Lord Kitchener responded by using a scorched-earth policy, burning Boer farms and crops and driving the people into concentration camps.*

only 30,000 Boer soldiers. Yet the Boers continued to fight a guerrilla war, attacking the British in raids. The British retaliated by burning Boer farms. The women and children were put in concentration camps. The conditions were appalling, and over 40,000 people died from disease. The Boers finally surrendered to the British and signed the Treaty of Vereeniging in 1902.

▽ *A diamond mine in southern Africa.*
The mines were owned by European companies, and many used slave labour.

The Scramble for Africa

1880 Leopold II, king of Belgium, claims large area of the Congo as his own personal territory.

1882 British take control in Egypt.

1884–5 Berlin Conference. European countries negotiate over control of West Africa.

1885 Leopold II proclaims his personal territory the "Congo Free State".

1888 The British conquer the Matabele people and take their land (later Rhodesia).

1889 British South Africa Company founded.

1890 Cecil Rhodes becomes prime minister of Cape Colony.

1891 British Protectorate in Nyasaland (present-day Malawi).

1894 Uganda becomes a British protectorate.

1895 Kenya becomes a British protectorate, called British East Africa.

1899 Start of Boer War.

▽ *The British attack the Zulus in southern Africa in 1879. The Zulu army, under its leader Cetswayo, defeated the British army at Iswandhlwana, killing 1,700 British soldiers. However, the Zulus were later defeated at Rorke's Drift.*

Between 1880 and 1900, European nations took over most of the African continent. The activities of these 20 years have become known as the "Scramble for Africa" as Europeans rushed to stake their claims and establish new colonies.

By the 1860s, France, Germany and the United States had all become successful industrial nations, threatening Britain's position as the leading power in both industry and trade. Across Europe, factories were producing cheap manufactured goods and European nations looked to Africa as a massive potential market in which to sell them. Europeans also believed that Africa was a source of valuable raw materials, such as rubber from the tropical forests. The discovery of diamonds and gold in southern Africa only added to these expectations.

In the late 1870s and early 1880s, several European nations laid claim to regions in Africa. The French laid claim to the north bank. The Germans proclaimed rights to areas in west and southwest Africa. In order to avoid conflict over Africa, the European nations held a conference in Berlin, Germany, from 1884–5.

The Europeans decided how to divide up Africa between them without regard for African peoples and their cultures. After the Conference, the "Scramble" began. The African people fought to defend their lands, but the invention of

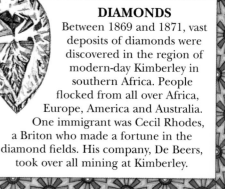

DIAMONDS
Between 1869 and 1871, vast deposits of diamonds were discovered in the region of modern-day Kimberley in southern Africa. People flocked from all over Africa, Europe, America and Australia. One immigrant was Cecil Rhodes, a Briton who made a fortune in the diamond fields. His company, De Beers, took over all mining at Kimberley.

◁ **Explorers Henry Stanley and David Livingstone** *meet at Ujiji on the shores of Lake Tanganyika. Stanley was a journalist who went to Africa to look for Livingstone. When he found him, the story made the headlines in newspapers all around the world.*

▽ **The map of Africa in 1914,** *after European nations had established colonies in almost every region. The only two remaining independent countries were Ethiopia and Liberia.*

British
French
German
Italian
Portuguese
Belgian
Spanish

the Maxim-gun (a type of machine-gun) gave European armies a major advantage over their African opponents. Many thousands of Africans died in the wars against European powers.

By the beginning of the 20th century, almost all Africa was ruled by seven European nations – Britain, France, Germany, Spain, Portugal, Belgium and Italy.

▽ **The exploration of Africa** *by Europeans in the 19th century marked a turning-point in African history as European nations scrambled to claim their "share" of the continent.*

MOROCCO
ALGERIA
LIBYA
EGYPT
RIO DE ORO
SAHARA
FRENCH WEST AFRICA
ANGLO EGYPTIAN SUDAN
ITALIAN SOMALILAND
GAMBIA
IVORY COAST
NIGERIA
SIERRA LEONE
ETHIOPIA
LIBERIA
BELGIAN CONGO
BRITISH EAST AFRICA
GOLD COAST
TOGOLAND
GERMAN EAST AFRICA
CAMEROUNS
ANGOLA
UNION OF SOUTH AFRICA
MADAGASCAR
GERMAN SOUTH WEST AFRICA
PORTUGUESE EAST AFRICA

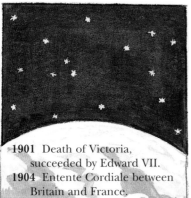

1901 Death of Victoria, succeeded by Edward VII.
1904 Entente Cordiale between Britain and France.
1909 Lloyd George's People's Budget.
1910 Death of Edward, succeeded by George V.
1914 Start of World War I defers question of Home Rule in Ireland.
1914–18 World War I.
1916 Easter Uprising in Dublin.
1921 Signing of Anglo-Irish Treaty. Miners' strike.
1924 First Labour government takes office.
1926 General Strike.
1928 Vote given to all women over age of 21.
1936 Death of George V and abdication of Edward VIII. George VI becomes king.
1939–45 World War II.
1951 Festival of Britain.
1952 Death of George VI, succeeded by Elizabeth II.
1968–9 Civil Rights marches in Northern Ireland.
1969 Provisional IRA begins terrorist campaign. British troops are sent to Northern Ireland.

1972 Britain joins EEC.
1979 Margaret Thatcher is first woman prime minister.
1982 Falklands War.
1993 Channel Tunnel opens.
1998 Good Friday Agreement in Ulster.

20TH CENTURY

As the 20th century dawned, Queen Victoria was in her 63rd year on the throne. Despite threats from other imperial powers, Britain remained at the centre of the largest empire the world has ever known – covering over one-fifth of the planet's land surface. Motor cars were still a startling and unusual sight on the streets of Britain. Most British men could vote for their member of parliament, but the right to vote was denied to women. As the century progressed, all these things were to change.

The first shock to the nation was the death of Victoria in January 1901. She was succeeded by her elderly son, Edward. The 'Edwardian era' is often regarded as an idyllic time – the 'calm before the storm' of World War I. In fact, the prewar years were a time of political uncertainty and social unrest, and they seem peaceful only in comparison with the terrible carnage that followed.

The 20th century will be remembered for its two terrible world wars. During the four years of World War I, from 1914 to 1918, over 900,000 soldiers of the British Empire died, wiping out almost a whole generation of young men. After the

Kill him – with War Savings

horrors of this slaughter, people hoped that World War I would be the "war to end all wars", but the rise of Fascism in Germany and other parts of Europe eventually sparked off World War II in 1939. For six years Britain and its allies fought against Germany and the Axis powers. This war spread around the globe, with action in Europe, Africa, Asia and the Pacific.

As the century progressed, Britain lost most of its empire as well as its dominance as an industrial nation. It joined the European Union, and became a multicultural society as people from the Caribbean, Asia and Africa made their homes in Britain.

Since the 1960s, the worst violence in Britain has been suffered by the people of Northern Ireland as rival parties have battled over its future. As Britain heads into the 21st century, there is hope of a solution to the problems in Ireland, and an end to violence there.

Edwardian Britain

Only three weeks after celebrating New Year in 1901, people were mourning Queen Victoria, who died on January 22nd. She was succeeded by her son, Edward.

The glamorous King Edward VII was hugely popular. His favourite activities were racing, sailing and shooting and he had a wide social circle both in Britain and on the continent. His willingness to speak French was put to good use when he visited Paris in 1903 and prepared the ground for the Entente Cordiale ("Friendly Relationship") which was signed between Britain and France in 1904.

Edward was king not only of the United Kingdom, but also of the world's biggest empire. But despite the wealth and power that the Empire continued to bring, there were some concerns about Britain's world position. Several countries that had industrialized later than Britain were now threatening British trade – the USA and Germany in particular. Worse, Germany was building a navy to rival Britain's. In response, the government ordered the construction of several new and up-to-date warships, the dreadnoughts.

For rich people, life in the first decade of the 20th century was good. The wealthy enjoyed their money openly, with fine food, large houses staffed with servants, and a social life based around their favourite outdoor pursuits. However, the gap between rich and

1901 Death of Queen Victoria. Succeeded by Edward VII (January 22nd). Start of Edwardian era.

1903 Edward VII visits Paris and opens more friendly relations with France.

1904 Entente Cordiale between Britain and France (April).

1906 Labour Party formed.

1909 Lloyd George's "People's Budget" rejected by House of Lords. Trade Boards fix wages in low-paid industries.

△ *King Edward VII and Queen Alexandra at the King's coronation in 1902. Alexandra was the eldest daughter of the king of Denmark. She and Edward had married in 1863.*

1910 Death of King Edward VII. Succeeded by George V. Strike by miners in South Wales lasts 10 months.

1911 Parliament Act passes through House of Lords, abolishing Lords' power of veto (August).

1912 Miners strike in support of national minimum wage.

1914 Start of World War I.

▷ *Edwardian schools were often run by clergymen,* sometimes helped by their wives who acted as matrons. Academic subjects such as reading, writing and mathematics were taught, along with a stern respect for the Church and British Empire.

poor was huge. A tiny minority of people enjoyed this affluent lifestyle – one estimate is that 13 percent of the population owned 92 percent of the wealth at that time. For the poor, the story was rather different.

In 1901, the manufacturer Seebohm Rowntree published a report called *Poverty: A Study of Town Life.* It was the result of his own investigations into poor households in York and it showed that even in a small cathedral city, many people lived in desperate conditions. Rowntree found that 28 percent of adults could not afford enough food to keep themselves healthy, and that 40 percent of children suffered illness and stunted growth from lack of food. A similar survey on a much larger scale was carried out by Charles Booth in London. He collected information over a period of 17 years, publishing his report in 1903.

△ *Alexandra Palace,* built in 1875, was named after the Princess of Wales. Its concert hall, containing one of the largest organs in the world, could seat 14,000 people. It burned down just days after opening and had to be completely rebuilt.

△ *A motor car,* in the Edwardian era, was a luxury only the rich could afford. Nevertheless, by 1910 there were over 100,000 cars registered in Britain.

Social and Political Change

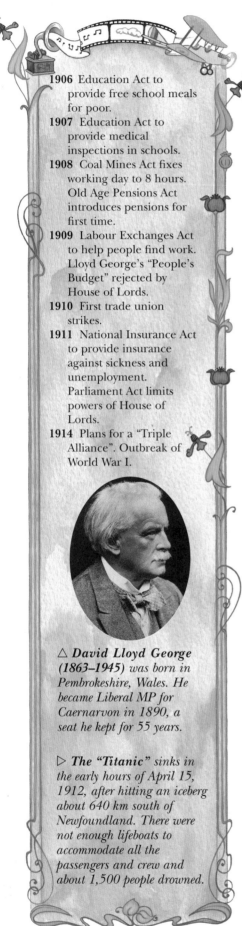

△ *David Lloyd George (1863–1945) was born in Pembrokeshire, Wales. He became Liberal MP for Caernarvon in 1890, a seat he kept for 55 years.*

▷ *The "Titanic" sinks in the early hours of April 15, 1912, after hitting an iceberg about 640 km south of Newfoundland. There were not enough lifeboats to accommodate all the passengers and crew and about 1,500 people drowned.*

The work of Seebohm Rowntree in York and Charles Booth in London focused public attention on poverty in Britain. As a result of these and other reports, the period from 1906 until the outbreak of war in 1914 saw the introduction of laws that formed the basis of the welfare state.

In 1906, the Liberal Party won 84 seats more than any other party in the general election and introduced a programme of welfare. The two ministers most active in these reforms were David Lloyd George and Winston Churchill. Their ideas were not new – Germany already had a system of old-age pensions and national insurance against unemployment and sickness.

They started in 1906 with an Act that gave free schoolmeals for poor children. This was followed by other measures including medical inspections in schools and pensions for the poorest people aged 70 and over. In 1909, Lloyd George read out the details of his "People's Budget" in the House of Commons. He wanted to tax the rich more heavily, to pay for the fight against "poverty and squalidness". Conservative MPs complained, but they did not have enough power in the House of Commons to

▷ *At work in a coal mine. In 1908 the Coal Mines Act limited the working day of a miner to eight hours. Nevertheless, miners in South Wales went on strike for 10 months in 1910. When the government sent in troops to help the police, there were riots. The miners went on strike again in 1912.*

defeat the budget. However, the Budget was thrown out by the House of Lords. The Liberals called and won a general election, forcing the Lords to back down. The Liberals were now determined to go further. With the support of the new king, George V, they forced the Lords to pass the Parliament Act which limited the powers of the Lords for good.

Throughout the 1900s membership of trade unions grew steadily. Workers' demands for better conditions and pay resulted in a series of strikes between 1910 and 1912. In 1914, three of the main unions agreed to work together to form a powerful "Triple Alliance". However, their plans were interrupted by the outbreak of war.

MOVIEMAKING

Cinema started when Auguste and Louis Lumière showed their films to an audience in Paris in 1895, while the first purpose-built cinema opened in Britain in 1907. Early films had no soundtrack. The Italian actor Rudolph Valentino was one of the biggest stars of these films, known as "silent movies".

World War I

June 28 1914 Assassination of Archduke Franz Ferdinand of Austria at Sarajevo.

July 1914 Austria–Hungary declares war on Serbia.

August 1914 Germany invades Belgium. Austria–Hungary invades Russia. Britain declares war on Germany and Austria–Hungary.

September 1914 First Battle of the Marne.

November 1914 Britain declares war on Ottoman Empire. First Battle of Ypres.

April 1915 Allied troops (mainly Australian, New Zealand and Indian) land at Gallipoli.

▷ *World War I was the first war in which aeroplanes were widely used. They were first used to spy on enemy trenches and later in air combat and bombing raids.*

May 1915 Second Battle of Ypres. Germans use poison gas for the first time. German submarine sinks British liner *Lusitania.* Over 1,000 people drown including 128 Americans: USA protests but does not enter war. Italy enters war on side of the Allies.

In June 1914, Archduke Franz Ferdinand and his wife Sophie visited the Austrian–Hungarian province of Bosnia. On June 28th, they were shot in the streets of the capital, Sarajevo. Their deaths sparked the outbreak of World War I.

The Archduke was assassinated by a Serbian terrorist who was protesting about Austrian–Hungarian rule in Bosnia. This caused Austria–Hungary to declare war on Serbia on July 28th. Germany supported Austria–Hungary's action, but Russia promised to defend Serbia, and France backed Russia. Germany declared war on Russia and France and the German army marched through Belgium and into France. The German invasion of the neutral country of Belgium brought Great Britain into the war on August 4th.

The pressures that led to war had been building up for years, with increasing rivalry between the countries of Europe. They competed for industrial power, control of trade, and for colonies. Germany built up a strong, well-trained army and navy. Other European nations felt threatened and expanded their own forces.

In an attempt to increase their security, several countries made agreements to support each other. Germany, Austria–Hungary and Italy formed the Triple Alliance, promising to go to war in the case of an attack. France, Russia and Great Britain had a similar

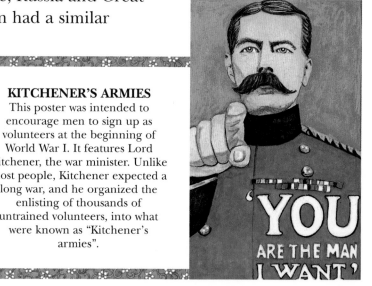

KITCHENER'S ARMIES
This poster was intended to encourage men to sign up as volunteers at the beginning of World War I. It features Lord Kitchener, the war minister. Unlike most people, Kitchener expected a long war, and he organized the enlisting of thousands of untrained volunteers, into what were known as "Kitchener's armies".

YOU ARE THE MAN I WANT'

▷ **This map shows neutral countries,** *and the groupings of Allies and Central Powers. It also shows the main battle fronts, including the Western Front.*

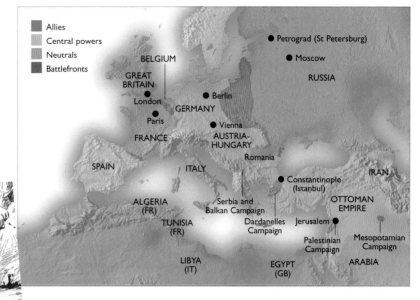

Allies
Central powers
Neutrals
Battlefronts

Petrograd (St Petersburg)
Moscow
RUSSIA
BELGIUM
GREAT BRITAIN
London
Berlin
GERMANY
Paris
Vienna
FRANCE
AUSTRIA-HUNGARY
Romania
SPAIN
ITALY
IRAN
Constantinople (Istanbul)
ALGERIA (FR)
Serbia and Balkan Campaign
OTTOMAN EMPIRE
TUNISIA (FR)
Dardanelles Campaign
Jerusalem
Palestinian Campaign
Mesopotamian Campaign
LIBYA (IT)
EGYPT (GB)
ARABIA

agreement, called the Triple Entente. After the outbreak of war, Germany and Austria–Hungary were known as the Central Powers. The nations who fought against the Central Powers were known as the Allies.

In 1914, the Germans were confident of victory on the Western Front in France. They wanted to reach the English Channel ports, but the Allies blocked their advance. By November 1914, neither side could gain any advantage. The deadlock lasted for over three years.

'The Rib of Life'
Michelin Tyre Co., Ltd., 81 Fulham Rd., Chelsea, London, S.W.

△ **An advert for Michelin tyres.** *The French Michelin company was founded by two brothers in 1888. They were the first to show that pneumatic tyres (tyres filled with air) could be used on motor vehicles. Here, the famous "Michelin man" supplies a spare tyre to replace a flat tyre on an Allied army ambulance during World War I.*

▽ **A British MK IV tank and HMS Dreadnought.** *The tank was a British invention during World War I. It was designed to batter its way across trenches and through barbed wire. HMS Dreadnought was a new type of battleship, built for the British navy in 1906. By 1914, the British navy had 22 dreadnoughts.*

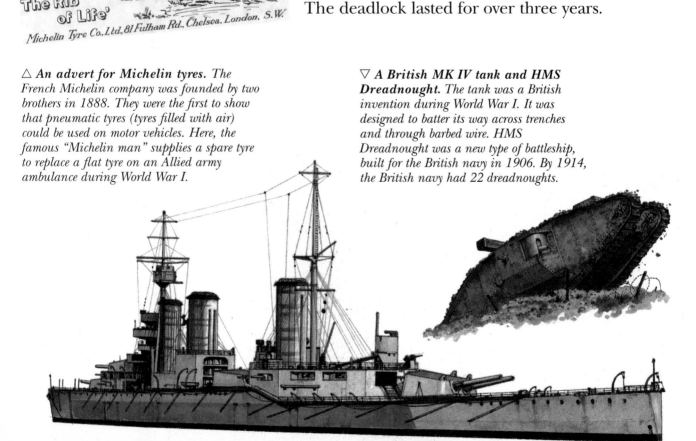

Life in the Trenches

January 1916 Evacuation from Gallipoli. Over 250,000 Allied troops wounded or killed.

May 1916 Conscription introduced in Britain.

June 5, 1916 Lord Kitchener, British secretary of state for war, is drowned when a German mine hits HMS *Hampshire*.

July–November 1916 Battle of the Somme. Over 400,000 British soldiers die.

December 1916 Lloyd George becomes prime minster.

April 1917 USA declares war on Germany. Revolution in Russia. Battle of Vimy Ridge.

December 1917 Over 300,000 British and Canadian soldiers die. Russia signs an armistice with Germany.

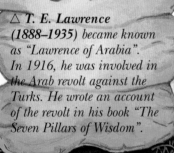

△ *T. E. Lawrence (1888–1935) became known as "Lawrence of Arabia". In 1916, he was involved in the Arab revolt against the Turks. He wrote an account of the revolt in his book "The Seven Pillars of Wisdom".*

By the end of 1914, the Western Front stretched over 700 kilometres from the English Channel to Switzerland. Thousands of Allied and German troops had dug themselves into parallel lines of trenches.

Trench warfare was a result of the power of modern weapons, which made it too dangerous to fight a battle on open ground. For over three years, Allied and German soldiers attacked each other from their trenches, often gaining only a few metres of ground at a time. The numbers of dead were horrific. For example, in 1916, on the first *day* of the Battle of the Somme, 21,000 British soldiers perished and 40,000 more were wounded.

The Western Front was only one of the battle zones of World War I. The Russians attacked the Central Powers along the Eastern

△ *Although tanks were used during the First Battle of the Somme in 1916, the first time they played a crucial role was at Cambrai on November 20, 1917. They were originally called "land ships" but because they looked rather like large, mobile water tanks, they were nicknamed "tanks".*

Front, which ran the length of the Russian border with Germany and Austria–Hungary. In 1914, the Ottoman Empire (Turkey) joined the Central Powers. Italy joined the war in 1915 on the side of the Allies and attacked Austria–Hungary along the northern Italian border. There was even war in Africa and the Pacific, as Germany's colonies were attacked by Allied forces.

GAS MASKS

Poison gas was first used by the Germans in the Second Battle of Ypres, in 1915. The gas rolled in a wall of yellow–green smoke across the Allied trenches, suffocating the soldiers who breathed in its deadly fumes. In Britain, an appeal went out for volunteers to make half a million gas masks to help the soldiers in the trenches withstand these attacks. Later in 1915, the Allies also started to use gas. However, it was a difficult weapon to control, especially if the wind changed direction once the gas was released.

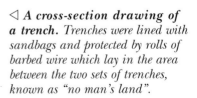

◁ *A cross-section drawing of a trench. Trenches were lined with sandbags and protected by rolls of barbed wire which lay in the area between the two sets of trenches, known as "no man's land".*

The Armistice

1918 President Woodrow Wilson sets out war aims in "The Fourteen Points". Germany launches final attacks against Allies. Allies begin final attack against Germans (August). Bulgaria surrenders (September 29th). Ottoman Empire (Turkey) signs armistice (October). Austria–Hungary signs an armistice (November 3rd). Germany signs an armistice ending World War I (November 11th).

△ German troops going "over the top". This was the dangerous moment when troops advanced into the area between the trenches, known as "no man's land".

1919 Paris Peace Conference. Peace settlement agreed and agreement to set up a League of Nations (January). Treaty of Versailles signed by Germany (June).

1920 Treaty of Trianon signed by Hungary. Treaty of Sèvres signed by Ottoman Empire (August).

At the start of World War I, the USA had declared itself to be a neutral country. However, the sinking of the British ship the *Lusitania* in 1915 and other similar attacks against civilians drew American support for the Allies. The USA declared war on Germany in 1917.

In 1918, the Germans launched a series of attacks to try finally to crush the Allies before the Americans arrived in force. In July and August, at the Second Battle of the Marne, the Allies and Germans fought over the same ground, east of Paris, as in 1914. But by this time American soldiers helped the Allies to push the Germans back. By September and October it became clear that Germany was on the point of collapse. The British naval blockade had led to severe food shortages and the German people were starving. There were riots and demands for peace. On November 11, 1918, the Germans accepted the Allies' peace terms and the war ended.

The announcement of peace was greeted with euphoria in London, as large crowds gathered outside Buckingham Palace. But it was impossible to forget the terrible cost of the war – over 900,000 soldiers from the British Empire had died, and the death toll for all the countries involved in World War I was over 8.5 million. People hoped that this was the "war to end all wars".

◁ In January 1919, the Allied war leaders, President Woodrow Wilson (centre), Georges Clemenceau (far left) and David Lloyd George (right) met in Paris to formally end the war.

In January 1919, members of the Allied countries met in Paris to agree a peace settlement. The US president, Woodrow Wilson, had already drawn up a plan for peace, known as the 'Fourteen Points'. Although France and Britain refused to accept many of these points, they did agree to set up an organization called the League of Nations. The aim of this League was to prevent another similar worldwide conflict by settling international disputes by diplomacy and agreement. It was later replaced by the United Nations, in 1946.

In June 1919, the agreements made in Paris were accepted by Germany in the Treaty of Versailles. All the other Central Powers signed separate treaties. Under the Treaty of Versailles, Germany was forced to accept responsibility for starting the war and to pay reparations (compensation for war damages) to the Allied countries. Germany also lost territory to various European countries. The ending of World War I completely redrew the map of Europe, as boundaries changed and new countries emerged out of the old empires.

△ *Armistice celebrations* in London in 1918. *Huge crowds assembled outside Buckingham Palace and sang and cheered as King George V and Queen Mary appeared on the balcony with their family.*

△ *The peace settlement* agreed by the Allies *was presented to the Germans at the Palace of Versailles, near Paris. Under threat of invasion, the Germans agreed to sign the document in June, 1919.*

▽ *By the end of World War I the trenches* had claimed 947,000 British casualties. Many vowed that this was a war to end all wars.

1905 Sinn Fein, meaning "Ourselves Alone", founded by Arthur Griffiths with policy of non-cooperation with British.

1912 Third Irish Home Rule Bill introduced in parliament. Ulster Volunteers formed to fight against Home Rule.

1913 Home Rule bill rejected by House of Lords. Irish nationalists form Irish Nationalist Volunteers (later Irish Republican Army, or IRA).

1916 Easter Rising by Irish nationalists put down by British troops. Execution of leaders sparks off anti-British feeling.

1917 Eamon de Valera becomes leader of Sinn Fein.

1918 Seventy-three Sinn Fein MPs elected.

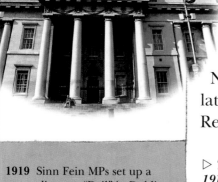

▽ **The Custom House in Dublin.** *In 1921, it was burned down by the IRA to destroy the public tax records stored there.*

Anglo-Irish Relations

At the beginning of the 20th century, the issue of Irish independence from Britain was still unresolved. After two defeats in the 1880s and '90s, a third Home Rule bill was introduced in the British parliament in 1912, but its passage was interrupted by World War I.

Not all Irish people supported Home Rule. It was backed by Irish Catholics who believed that Ireland should have its own parliament in Dublin. Irish Protestants, who were in the majority in the province of Ulster, were opposed to Home Rule. In 1912 and 1913, both sides formed armed organizations: those against Home Rule set up the Ulster Volunteers and the nationalists formed the Irish Nationalist Volunteers, later the Irish Republican Army (IRA).

△ **Michael Collins (1890–1922)** *took part in the Easter Rising in 1916. He was one of the 73 Sinn Fein MPs elected in 1918, and he was leader of the IRA during the troubles of 1920–1. He signed the Anglo-Irish Treaty believing it was the best deal for Ireland at the time. The following year he was assassinated.*

1919 Sinn Fein MPs set up a parliament "Dail" in Dublin. Clashes between British troops and IRA.

1920 "Bloody Sunday": IRA gunmen kill 14 in Dublin.

1921 Signing of Anglo-Irish Treaty. Civil war breaks out.

1923 Republicans accept the treaty.

1932 Southern Ireland renamed Eire.

1949 Ireland Act recognizes Eire as an independent republic and confirms Northern Ireland as part of United Kingdom. Republic of Ireland leaves Commonwealth.

▷ **The Easter Rising in 1916** *was led by Patrick Pearse and involved about 1,600 nationalists. They believed that Ireland would only become a republic if force was used. Pearse took over the Post Office as his headquarters, and barricades were set up in the Dublin streets with British soldiers on one side and republicans on the other.*

BLACK AND TANS

The British soldiers sent to Ireland to help the Royal Irish Constabulary in 1920–1 were known as the "black and tans" because of the colour of their uniform. They were hated by the Irish because of their ruthless attacks in revenge for IRA actions.

The start of war in 1914 prevented a crisis over the Home Rule issue, but people on both sides continued to campaign. In 1916, protestors belonging to various nationalist movements seized buildings in Dublin and proclaimed Ireland a republic. The British government responded by sending troops and bombarding the rebels until they surrendered. Most Irish people disapproved of the rebels' actions. But when the British arrested and imprisoned suspects without trial, and then executed 15 of the republican leaders, public opinion quickly changed. The rebels of the "Easter Rising" were seen as heroes. In 1918, the republican movement, Sinn Fein, won 73 seats in the general election. However, Sinn Fein's MPs refused to go to Westminster. Instead, they declared Ireland a republic and set up a parliament, called the Dáil Eirann, in Dublin.

This started three years of fighting between the Royal Irish Constabulary, backed by British troops, and the IRA. In July 1921 British Prime Minister Lloyd George proposed a compromise in which the 26 counties of southern Ireland would become a dominion within the British Empire, known as the Irish Free State. The Dáil approved the Anglo-Irish Treaty in 1921. This led to more civil war, between the Republicans who wanted independence, and the Free-Staters who supported the treaty. A ceasefire was called in 1923 when the Republicans, under their leader Eamon de Valera, decided to accept the treaty.

△ *This map shows Ireland after 1923.*
Three of the nine counties of Ulster became part of the Irish Free State. The other six remained part of the United Kingdom.

1921 Miners' strike (April–June).

1924 First Labour government takes office. Succeeded by Conservative government in November.

1925 Britain returns to gold standard (April). Mine owners propose a cut in miners' wages and longer working hours. Commission set up to look into mining industry under Herbert Samuel.

1926 Samuel report rejected by both sides (March). Miners refuse wage cuts. TUC calls general strike (May 3–12). Miners start to return to work (November).

1927 Trade Disputes Act makes general strike illegal.

△ *The mines were dangerous places – thousands of miners were killed each year. Many more suffered from severe health problems as a result of their work. Even before the general strike in 1926 there was a long history of miners' strikes about pay and working conditions.*

1929 New York stock exchange crashes (October). Start of Great Depression.

1931 Formation of National Government. Britain comes off gold standard (September).

1931–2 Almost three million people (22 percent of workforce) unemployed.

1936 Jarrow Crusade.

Strike and Depression

On May 3, 1926, the Trades Union Congress (TUC) called a general strike in support of the miners. Over two and a half million men and women, including transport workers, gas and electricity workers, and printers joined the one million miners who were already locked out of work. The strike lasted for nine days.

The immediate cause of the strike was the mine owners' demands that workers should accept lower pay and longer working hours. There were problems in the British mining industry. Foreign mines produced coal more efficiently and cheaply than British suppliers. Demand for coal was declining because of a new fuel – oil. To make matters worse, the government returned Britain to the gold standard. This was a way of fixing the value of the pound to a set amount of gold. But the effect was to make British exports more expensive – and therefore even less competitive abroad.

To try to avert a strike, the government commissioned a report on the mining industry.

▽ *Strikers on a protest march during the general strike. The government said that the strike was an attempt by the unions, led by the TUC, to take over the running of the country. The government printed its views in a newspaper called the "British Gazette".*

Despite the government's attempts, the country was still brought to a standstill by the general strike. Troops were ordered to do the strikers' work. After nine days, the TUC called off the strike leaving the miners to fight on alone. Eventually, the miners were forced to accept their employers' demands.

Even though the strikers were back at work, the problems of British industry remained. Britain was still paying off massive debts from World War I. In 1929 there was a financial crisis in the USA, and many banks, businesses and individuals were ruined. Americans no longer had enough money to buy goods from abroad and, as demand fell, more people lost their jobs. In 1931–2, the number of unemployed people in Britain reached almost three million.

The regions hardest hit by the Depression of the 1930s were the industrial areas in the north of England, south Wales, Scotland and Northern Ireland. In some towns, over half the workforce was out of work. Despite "dole" money paid to the unemployed, people suffered severe hardships. The 1920s and '30s saw many protest marches to London to draw attention to the plight of the hungry unemployed.

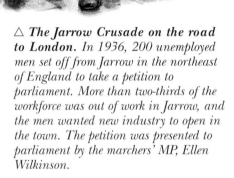

△ **The Jarrow Crusade on the road to London.** *In 1936, 200 unemployed men set off from Jarrow in the northeast of England to take a petition to parliament. More than two-thirds of the workforce was out of work in Jarrow, and the men wanted new industry to open in the town. The petition was presented to parliament by the marchers' MP, Ellen Wilkinson.*

▽ **During the Depression,** *soup kitchens were set up in many towns and cities to feed the hungry. Britain was not the only country hit by the Depression. Millions of people in the USA lost their jobs and were forced to rely on government hand-outs and charity for survival.*

1903 Emmeline Pankhurst and her daughters Christabel and Sylvia found Women's Social and Political Union (WSPU).

1905 Christabel Pankhurst and Annie Kenney become first suffragettes to be sent to prison.

1908 About 500,000 women attend suffrage demonstration in London.

△ *Emmeline Pankhurst is arrested during a suffragette demonstration. The slogan of the WSPU was "Deeds not Words", and the suffragettes' tactics included actions such as disrupting public meetings and damaging property.*

1909 Over 100 suffragettes arrested while trying to meet prime minister.

1911 Suffragette riots in West End of London.

1913 Emily Davison throws herself under the King's horse at the Derby. She dies from her injuries.

1918 Vote given to women over 30, if they are ratepayers or wives of ratepayers.

1928 Vote given to all women over 21.

Votes for Women

The Reform Acts of the 19th century had given the vote to an increasing number of men, but not to women. From the 1860s onwards, women began to campaign peacefully to be allowed to vote. These women were known as "suffragists" from the word "suffrage", which means a vote.

In 1903, Emmeline Pankhurst and her daughters Christabel and Sylvia decided that peaceful means were not sufficient. They set up the Women's Social and Political Union (WSPU), aiming to use militant action to get publicity. Their campaign started in 1905 when Christabel and another member of the WSPU, Annie Kenney, shouted suffrage slogans at a meeting where the foreign secretary was speaking. They were arrested and imprisoned. The militant campaigners of the WSPU became known as "suffragettes".

The suffragettes continued their campaign until the outbreak of war in 1914. They were often arrested and badly treated by the police. In prison, some suffragettes went on hunger strike and were forcibly fed. If they became too ill to stay in prison they were released, but were re-arrested once they had recovered. During World War I, the suffragettes stopped their violent actions and engaged in war work. Women took men's places in factories and mines. In 1918, they also got the vote.

▽ *Many women campaigned peacefully for the vote and disapproved of the violent methods of the WSPU. Women were eventually given the vote in two stages, in 1918 and 1928.*

Abdication

"I have found it impossible to carry on the heavy burden of responsibility and to discharge the duties of king as I would wish to do without the help and support of the woman I love."

With these words, King Edward VIII became the only British monarch ever to abdicate (resign) from the throne voluntarily. In the early 1930s he had met and fallen in love with an American called Wallis Simpson. Mrs Simpson had been married twice and divorced once. When her divorce to her second husband came through, the King was determined to marry her. However, the King was the head of the Church of England, which opposed divorce. George V died in January 1936 and was succeeded by the Prince of Wales as Edward VIII.

△ **Edward VIII with his brothers.** *After his abdication, Edward spent his life in exile, often unhappily and with regret. He was never crowned and his brother, the Duke of York, succeeded him as George VI.*

The prime minister, Stanley Baldwin, advised the new king that he could not marry Mrs Simpson and remain on the throne. On December 10, 1936, Edward made his choice and abdicated.

His place was taken by his brother, who became King George VI. Edward became Duke of Windsor and he married Mrs Simpson in 1937. The Duke and Duchess of Windsor spent the rest of their lives in exile abroad, living mainly in France.

▷ **"High society"** *encompassed a fashionable and glamorous circle of people. Women particularly had a new freedom, and displayed this in their appearance. Hair was worn bobbed (short) and instead of accentuating curves, clothing was designed to disguise them, creating a boyish appearance. People of society enjoyed a whirl of cocktail parties and foreign holidays and, as Prince of Wales, Edward moved in this world.*

World War II

After the end of World War I, many people hoped that this was the "war to end all wars". But the peace settlements drawn up by the victorious nations in 1919 were the start of a whole new set of problems that led, eventually, to the outbreak of an even more vicious and destructive worldwide war.

△ **Hitler** *at a Nazi rally in Nuremberg in 1938. The rise of fascism affected other countries as well as Germany. Italy was the first to have a fascist government when Benito Mussolini took control in 1922.*

The 1920s and 30s saw the growth in many European countries of a movement called fascism. In Germany, support quickly grew for the fascist Nazi Party, which promised strong leadership and to restore national pride. In 1933 the Nazi Party, under its leader Adolf Hitler, was declared to be the only political party in Germany.

Hitler began to build up the German armed forces and to reclaim the territories lost by Germany after World War I. This was in defiance of the Treaty of Versailles, but the League of Nations was too weak to stop Hitler's aggression. When Hitler tried to occupy part of Czechoslovakia, the Czechs turned to their allies for help. In 1938, Hitler promised the British prime minister, Neville Chamberlain, that was this was the last of his territorial demands. Chamberlain wanted to avoid war at all costs, so he and the French prime minister forced Czechoslovakia to accept Hitler's demands. However, in March 1939 Germany took the

▽ **The Battle of Britain** *was fought between the Royal Air Force (RAF) and the German airforce, the Luftwaffe. The British were helped to victory by an advanced radar system along the south coast of Britain, which gave warning of the approach of German planes.*

1933 Hitler becomes Chancellor of Germany.
1936 Germany occupies Rhineland, defying terms of Treaty of Versailles.
1938 Germany occupies Austria.
1939 Germany occupies much of Czechoslovakia. Germany invades Poland. Britain and France declare war on Germany.

△ *Neville Chamberlain, the British prime minister, waves a copy of the Munich agreement. Chamberlain believed he had negotiated "peace for our time".*

April 9, 1940 Germany invades Denmark and Norway.
May 1940 Germany invades Belgium and the Netherlands. Italy declares war on France. British troops evacuate France.
June 22, 1940 France signs armistice with Germany..
July–September 1940 Battle of Britain.
September–October 1940 "Blitz" in London. German air raids on Coventry.

whole of Czechoslovakia and threatened Poland. Britain guaranteed to aid Poland if its independence was threatened. Hitler invaded Poland on September 1, 1939; France and Britain declared war two days later.

The Germans swept through Poland, Denmark, Norway, Belgium, the Netherlands and France. The Allied forces of Britain and France were trapped by this invasion and had to evacuate from the French port of Dunkerque across the English Channel. Next, Hitler planned his invasion of Britain. First of all he needed to gain control of the skies and to defeat the British airforce. The Battle of Britain began in July 1940.

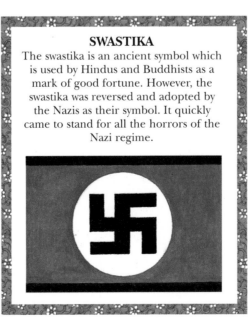

SWASTIKA
The swastika is an ancient symbol which is used by Hindus and Buddhists as a mark of good fortune. However, the swastika was reversed and adopted by the Nazis as their symbol. It quickly came to stand for all the horrors of the Nazi regime.

221

Home Front

The Battle of Britain came to an end in September 1940, when the Germans turned their attention to bombing civilian targets in London and elsewhere. This was the beginning of the "Blitz". The Germans hoped to weaken the morale of the British public and force a surrender.

Starting on September 7, 1940, London was bombed every night for 58 nights. The wail of the air raid sirens would send people running for cover in air raid shelters, or in the deep tunnels of the underground railway. Every day, hundreds of Londoners died in the raids, and thousands more were injured. The Blitz also destroyed cities such as Portsmouth, Coventry and Liverpool. However, British fighters continued to shoot down the German bombers and, by 1941, it was clear

△ *The American B-17 bomber* was also known as the "Flying Fortress" because it was so heavily armoured. The Americans joined the Allies in the war against Germany in 1942, and American bombers took part in many raids over Germany.

1941 Lend-Lease Act signed by US President Roosevelt.
May 1941 German invasion of USSR begins.
June 1941 Germany invades Greece and Yugoslavia.
December 1941 Royal Navy sinks German battleship the *Bismarck*. Britain and United States agree Atlantic Charter pledging world freedom. Japanese attack US fleet in Pearl Harbor. Allies declare war on Japan. Germany and Italy declare war on USA.

△ *Women ambulance drivers.* In 1941, all unmarried women between 20 and 30 years old were conscripted and given the choice between serving in the armed forces or working in key industries such as munitions.

1942 "United Nations" declare they will not make separate peace with Axis.
May 30, 1942 Allied bombing of Cologne.
August 1942 Battle for Stalingrad begins.
1943 Roosevelt and Churchill agree to accept only unconditional surrender of Axis. German troops surrender in Stalingrad. Allies invade Sicily. Italy surrenders to Allies.

◁ *Women workers in a munitions (arms) factory.* During the war, women took the place of men who had been called up in all sort of jobs – for example on the railways, in shipyards and in aircraft factories.

that the Germans could not control the skies.
The invasion of Britain was postponed indefinitely.

Later in the war, Allied bombers made massive
bombing attacks on German cities. The first raid was on
Cologne in May 1942 when 900 Allied bombers battered
the city. By the end of the war many German cities were
reduced to rubble and thousands of civilians killed by
Allied bombing.

Unlike World War I, which was mainly fought by
soldiers, World War II involved the whole civilian
population. Many children were evacuated from cities, and
away from the Blitz, to live in safer country areas. Some
were even sent abroad. Food rationing was introduced on
January 8, 1940. People were also encouraged to grow their
own fruit and vegetables. Clothes were rationed from 1941.

Throughout the war, Britain depended for its survival
on supplies brought across the Atlantic Ocean from North
America. German submarines (U-boats) were a constant
threat. The Allies organized convoys of cargo ships,
escorted and protected by naval ships. Radar and sonar
were also used to detect submarines. By the middle of
1943 many U-boats had been detected and destroyed.

△ **War bonds** *were sold by
the government as a way of
borrowing money from people
to pay for the war, which was
massively expensive. The USA
also gave aid to countries
fighting the Nazis. By the end
of the war, Britain was left
with huge debts.*

▷ **The scene
after an air
raid.** *Both British
and German
civilians suffered
terribly during
bombing raids.
Towards the end
of the war, Allied
bombing raids
destroyed many
German cities. In
1945, over
80,000 civilians
were killed in one
night in Dresden.*

1940–1 Italian and British forces fight in North Africa.

1941 Germans send tank units to North Africa.

December 1941 Japanese attack US fleet in Pearl Harbor. Allies declare war on Japan.

April 1942 Singapore falls to Japanese. US bombers attack Tokyo in Doolittle Raid.

△ *A British soldier (or "Tommy") fighting in the North African desert campaign of 1940–2.*

May 1942 Allies check threat to Australia at Battle of the Coral Sea.

June 1942 Allies defeat Japanese fleet at Battle of Midway.

October–November 1942 Battle of El Alamein in North Africa.

1943 Axis forces in North Africa surrender to Allies. Allied forces begin slowly to drive Japanese forces from Pacific.

War in Africa

On June 10, 1940 Italy joined its Axis ally Germany and declared war on Britain and France. Italy's fascist leader, Benito Mussolini, immediately ordered an invasion of North Africa where he expected to overrun the small Allied forces very quickly.

The main priority for the Allies in North Africa was to retain control over Egypt and the Suez Canal, in order to keep open supply routes to Asia and the oilfields of the Middle East. From the summer of 1940 the fighting swept across North Africa, but by February 1941 the Allies had the upper hand. Hitler sent reinforcements to help the Italians.

The reinforcements were tank units trained for desert warfare, and were under the leadership of General Rommel. Rommel was a clever commander, nicknamed "Desert Fox". The Battle of El Alamein in October 1942 marked a turning-point for the Allies who, commanded by Field-Marshal Montgomery, broke through the Axis defences and forced the Axis troops to retreat. Soon after this victory, Allied troops landed in Algeria and Morocco and moved towards Tunisia. The Axis surrendered in North Africa in May 1943. North Africa provided a base from which the Allies could take control of southern Europe. They invaded Sicily in July 1943 and Italy surrendered in September.

▽ *Under the leadership of Field-Marshal Montgomery, the British tank force, known as the "Desert Rats", fought a tough war against the German "Africa Korps".*

War in the Pacific

Japan joined the two Axis powers, Germany and Italy, in 1940. The Japanese wanted an empire in Southeast Asia, but to do so they had to destroy the American Pacific fleet. On December 7, 1941, Japanese aircraft attacked Pearl Harbor, Hawaii, where the fleet was at anchor.

The attack was unexpected and it inflicted great damage on the American fleet. It also brought the USA into the war – the USA and the Allies declared war on Japan the following day. The Japanese quickly took control of much of Southeast Asia. In Malaysia they forced British troops to retreat to the island of Singapore. On February 15, 1942, Singapore surrendered to the Japanese and 85,000 soldiers were taken prisoner – Britain's worst military defeat.

The Japanese also advanced towards Australia and the Hawaiian Islands. In June 1942, the Americans halted the Japanese advance at the Battle of Midway. This was the first major Allied victory against the Japanese. Between 1942 and 1945 the Allies continued the slow process of driving the Japanese out of their newly captured territories.

△ *The atomic bomb at Nagasaki killed over 40,000 people. It was the second atomic bomb to be dropped on Japan by the Americans, the first one being dropped on Hiroshima. It brought World War II to an end, but at a terrible human cost.*

▽ **An American warship** *is attacked in the Pacific by a Japanese warplane. A British supply ship (in background) is caught up in the conflict.*

▽ **The war in the Pacific** *began with the Japanese bombing of Pearl Harbor. Japan quickly occupied all the areas coloured orange on the map.*

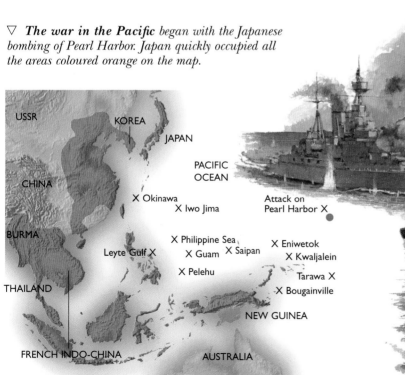

USSR

KOREA

JAPAN

CHINA

PACIFIC
OCEAN

BURMA

X Okinawa

X Iwo Jima

Attack on
Pearl Harbor X

X Philippine Sea

Leyte Gulf X   X Guam   X Saipan

X Eniwetok

X Kwaljalein

X Pelehu

Tarawa X

X Bougainville

THAILAND

NEW GUINEA

FRENCH INDO-CHINA

AUSTRALIA

The End of the War

June 6, 1944 Allied troops make D-day landings in Normandy.

July 20, 1944 Failure of plot to assassinate Hitler.

August 25, 1944 Allied troops and Free French liberate Paris. Battle of the Bulge in Belgium – last German attack against Allies.

△ *Hirohito was emperor of Japan from 1926 until 1989. On August 15, 1945, he made a radio broadcast to announce Japan's acceptance of Allied peace terms.*

1945 Soviet troops enter Warsaw, capital of Poland. Final assault on Germany by Allied troops. Yalta Conference – Roosevelt, Churchill and Stalin agree to divide Germany into four zones after war. Soviet troops surround Berlin. Hitler commits suicide.

May 7, 1945 Germany surrenders to Allies. V-E Day.

August 1945 Americans drop atomic bomb on Hiroshima and Nagasaki, Japan.

September 2, 1945 Japan surrenders. V-J Day.

October 1945 United Nations formed.

Ever since the evacuation of Allied troops from Dunkerque in 1940, Allied leaders were waiting to return to France. By summer 1944, the time was right and thousands of troops were on standby in southern England.

The Germans knew that the Allies would attack somewhere along the north coast of France but they weren't sure where. The most obvious place was near Calais, where the English Channel is narrowest. In fact, the Allies made their landing further west on the beaches of Normandy. D-day was originally planned for June 5, 1944, but bad weather postponed the landings for a day. On June 6th, Allied troops waded ashore.

Under the overall command of the American general, Eisenhower, the Allied troops advanced rapidly. By August 25th, they had reached Paris. Meanwhile Soviet troops were advancing across eastern Europe and Allied forces had landed in southern France and were moving northwards. It soon became clear that victory was in sight in Europe.

In April 1945, as Soviet troops surrounded Berlin, Adolf Hitler committed suicide. The Germans finally

▽ *During the D-Day invasion on June 6, 1944, over 156,000 American, British and Canadian troops landed on the beaches of Normandy. This was the largest sea-borne attack ever mounted. The Germans prepared for an invasion by putting mines and barbed wire along the beaches to slow down the advancing troops.*

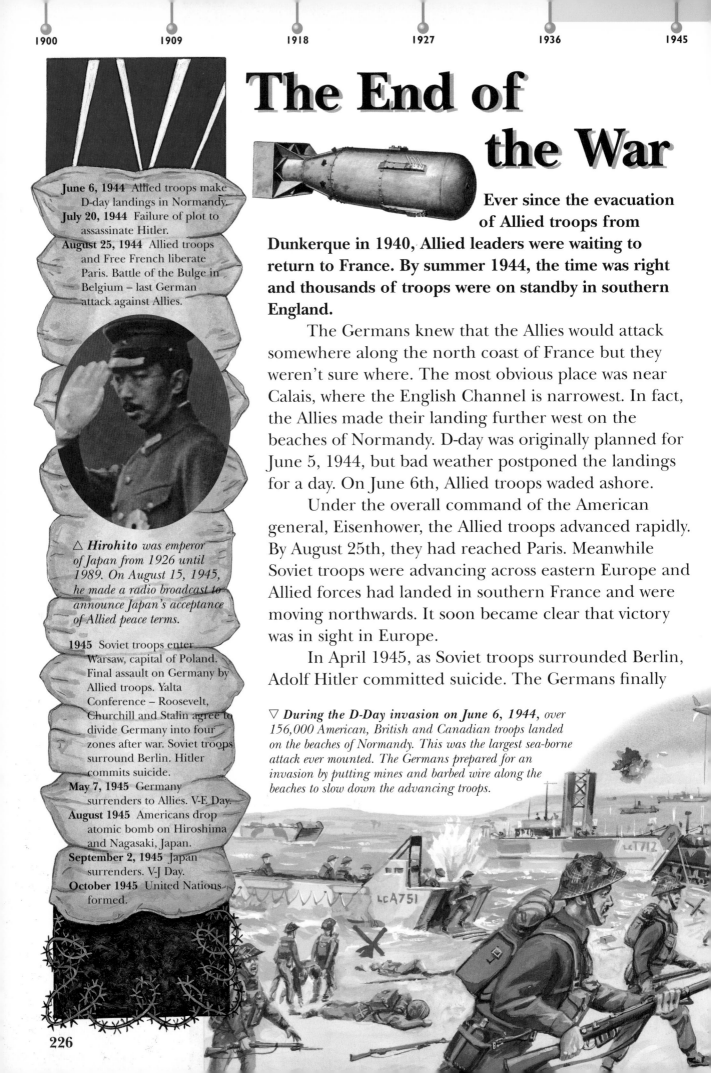

△ **Celebrations on V-E Day,**
May 8, 1945. *People hung out flags, and huge crowds gathered in the streets of London and other towns and cities throughout the United Kingdom.*

▷ **The trial of Nazi war criminals** *was held in Nuremberg, Germany, between 1945 and 1949. The trials were organized by the USA, USSR, Britain and France. The Nazi leaders were charged with crimes against peace, crimes against humanity and specific war crimes, and several were sentenced to death.*

surrendered on May 7th, and the Allies declared May 8th V-E (Victory in Europe) Day. However, in the midst of the rejoicing, the horrors of the Nazi concentration camps were revealed on April 15, 1945, when Allied troops reached Belsen concentration camp in Germany. During the war the Nazis had imprisoned and killed millions of Jews. The starving camp survivors were terrible proof of Nazi brutality.

In the Far East the war was not yet over. Japan seemed determined to fight on, despite defeat looking certain. The American president, Harry S. Truman, decided to use a secret weapon developed by American and British scientists during the war. This was the atomic bomb. President Truman wanted to end the war without losing the lives of thousands more Allied troops. On August 6, 1945, an atomic bomb was dropped on the Japanese city of Hiroshima. Another was dropped on Nagasaki three days later. The Japanese surrendered on September 2nd, V-J (Victory over Japan) Day.

WINSTON CHURCHILL
Before World War II Winston Churchill argued strongly against Chamberlain's attempts to make peace with Hitler. He was prime minister throughout the war, and his own courage and faith in an Allied victory were an inspiration to the British people. Churchill's "trademark" was the V-sign for victory.

227

Independence

After the end of World War II, the British prime minister Clement Attlee insisted that British rule in India must come to an end. This was the beginning of the dismantling of the British Empire, as other colonies in Africa and elsewhere also began to demand their independence.

The campaign for independence in India had started early in the 20th century. In order to ensure Indian loyalty during World War I, the British had promised more self-government to Indians. In 1919, the first Government of India Act made some reforms but still retained most of the power for British officials. In 1920, Gandhi became leader of the Indian National Congress (INC) and started a campaign of non-cooperation against British rule.

By the end of World War II, it was clear that Britain could ignore the demands of Indian nationalists no longer. However, although a large majority of India's population were Hindus, there was also a substantial number of Muslims who did not want to live under Hindu rule. Under their leader, Mohammed Ali Jinnah, the Muslims demanded the creation of a separate state, called Pakistan. On August 14, 1947, two regions in northeast and northwest India became the Muslim state of Pakistan. The following day, India became independent. Millions of Hindus and Muslims found that they now lived in the "wrong" country. As they tried to move, violence exploded between them and hundreds of thousands of people died in the unrest.

Britain's other colonies were soon demanding independence. In 1952, a group called Mau Mau started a violent campaign against the British in Kenya.

◁ *Jawaharlal Nehru (1889–1964)* **(left)** *and Mohammed Ali Jinnah (1867–1948)* **(right)**. *Nehru took part in the struggle against British rule and became the first prime minister of India in 1947. Jinnah was leader of the Muslim League from 1935 and became governor-general of Pakistan in 1947.*

△ **Ghanaian chiefs** *wait for the first session of parliament to begin. Ghana, formerly known as the Gold Coast, became independent from Britain in 1957. It became a republic in 1960, under its leader Kwame Nkrumah.*

It took four years for British forces to defeat the badly equipped Mau Mau and showed the British government the need to speed up the process of independence. In 1957, the Gold Coast was the first African colony to receive independence as Ghana. Kenya became independent in 1963.

THE STRUGGLE FOR INDEPENDENCE

While many countries fought hard for their independence from Britain, others prefer to stay under the protection of the British government. In 1995 Bermuda voted to remain a British colony and, 13 years earlier, under the leadership of Margaret Thatcher, Britain went to war to recapture the Falkland Islands in the South Atlantic, from Argentina.

▽ **Mohandas Karamchand Gandhi (1869–1948)** *was known to the Indian people as Mahatma, meaning "Great Soul". He led a campaign of non-violent resistance against British rule. He was killed by an assassin who disagreed with his tolerance of all religions.*

1919 Massacre at Amritsar. First Government of India Act.
1920–2 Gandhi, leader of Indian National Congress leads policy of non-cooperation.
1930 Gandhi leads Salt March.
1935 Second Government of India Act passed.
1947 India and Pakistan become independent.
1948 Ceylon (Sri Lanka) and Burma (Myanmar) become independent.
1952 Start of Mau Mau rebellion in Kenya.
1957 Gold Coast becomes independent as Ghana.
1960 Cyprus, Nigeria and Somalia become independent.
1961 Tanganyika, Sierra Leone and Cameroon become independent.
1962 Uganda becomes independent.
1963 Zanzibar and Kenya become independent.

Social Change

1956 John Osborne's play *Look Back in Anger* performed at Royal Court Theatre.

1957 Homicide Act abolishes death penalty except for specific offences. First atomic bomb exploded by Britain in Pacific Ocean.

1958 Formation of Campaign for Nuclear Disarmament (CND).

1959 Obscene Publications Act and failed attempt to prosecute publishers of D.H. Lawrence's *Lady Chatterley's Lover*.

1963 *Please Please Me* becomes Beatles' first number one hit. Robbins Report on higher education.

1965 Death penalty abolished.

△ *The human impact upon the globe first became a real concern during the 1960s. The book that helped environmental issues to hit the headlines was Rachel Carson's "Silent Spring", published in 1962.*

1967 Abortion Act makes termination of pregnancies legal.

1969 Divorce Reform Act. Voting age reduced from 21 to 18 years.

1975 Equal Opportunities Act makes discrimination against women illegal.

1981 Riots in Brixton, London.

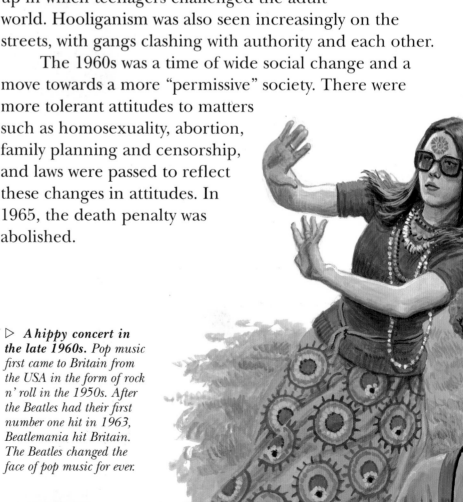

In July 1957, a few months after becoming prime minister, Harold Macmillan told an audience at a meeting: "Let's be frank about it, most of our people have never had it so good. Go around the country... and you will see a state of prosperity such as we have never had in my lifetime...".

After the difficulties of the post-war years, more families than ever before could afford goods such as cars, fridges, washing machines and television sets. This affluence extended to young people, too. After the war there was a sudden increase in the birthrate and by the late 1950s and 60s the "baby boomers" had reached their teens. For the first time a separate youth culture grew up in which teenagers challenged the adult world. Hooliganism was also seen increasingly on the streets, with gangs clashing with authority and each other.

The 1960s was a time of wide social change and a move towards a more "permissive" society. There were more tolerant attitudes to matters such as homosexuality, abortion, family planning and censorship, and laws were passed to reflect these changes in attitudes. In 1965, the death penalty was abolished.

▷ *A hippy concert in the late 1960s. Pop music first came to Britain from the USA in the form of rock n' roll in the 1950s. After the Beatles had their first number one hit in 1963, Beatlemania hit Britain. The Beatles changed the face of pop music for ever.*

◁ *A woman at work. The 1960s and 70s saw the rise of the women's liberation movement in Britain, inspired by writers such as Germaine Greer who published her book "The Female Eunuch" in 1970. In the same year, the Equal Pay Act made it illegal to pay men and women different rates for the same work. The Act came into effect in 1975.*

FAMILIES ON HOLIDAY

During the 1960s and 70s, laws were passed to give people more holiday. By the 1970s, most people could take three or four weeks off a year. Amusement parks, such as Alton Towers, became popular. As airfares became cheaper, more people chose to go abroad for their holidays.

It was also a time of increasing concern about the development of nuclear weapons. Britain had exploded its first atomic bomb in 1957, and this event was swiftly followed by the formation of the Campaign for Nuclear Disarmament (CND). The protestors demanded that Britain should take the lead by giving up its nuclear weapons, even if other countries kept theirs.

The education system changed during the 1970s. Children used to take an exam at the age of 11 to determine if they would go to a grammar or secondary modern school. Comprehensive schools were introduced, in which children of all abilities were taught together.

The EU

After the end of World War II, many people in Europe believed that the best way to recover from the ravages of the war and to prevent future conflict was increased and stronger cooperation between European nations.

In 1951, several European countries set up the European Coal and Steel Community (ECSC). The nations in this organization agreed to trade coal and steel without charging each other customs duties. In 1957, this idea was extended by the creation of the European Economic Community (EEC). The six countries that signed up to the EEC agreed to trade all goods in a single market. Britain did not join either the ECSC or the EEC.

In the 1950s, British politicians still believed that Britain had a wider role to play in the world. There were strong ties with the remaining countries in the British Empire and the Commonwealth nations. Britain also felt a close link, often referred to as the "special relationship", with the USA.

By 1961, the situation had changed enough for Britain to open negotiations to join the EEC. It was becoming clear that the EEC was an economic success. But Britain's application to join the EEC was rejected by French leader General de Gaulle. He was suspicious of Britain's "special relationship" with the USA, and of its trade links with Commonwealth countries. The same thing happened

1951 Treaty of Paris establishes European Coal and Steel Community.

1957 Treaty of Rome establishes European Economic Community (EEC).

1958 EEC comes into operation with six member states.

1960 Britain sets up European Free Trade Association (EFTA) as rival to EEC.

1961 Britain opens negotiations to join EEC.

1963 Britain's application to join EEC rejected by French leader General de Gaulle.

1967 France rejects Britain's second application to join EEC.

1973 Britain, Denmark and Ireland become members of EEC (January 1st).

1975 Referendum in Britain. Majority vote for staying in EEC.

△ *The Channel Tunnel* *was built between 1987 and 1991 to link Britain and France. It is a powerful symbol of Britain's links with mainland Europe.*

1993 EEC becomes European Community (EC). Establishment of European Union (EU).

1995 Austria, Finland and Sweden join EU.

▷ *The areas marked in red* show the countries that were members of the EEC by the late 1980s. Britain joined in 1973.

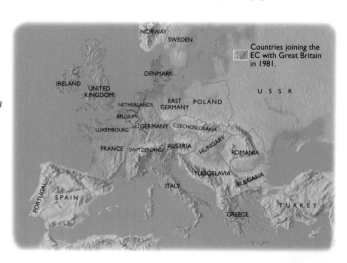

Countries joining the EC with Great Britain in 1981.

in 1967 when Britain applied for a second time. It was not until 1973, after de Gaulle had retired (in 1969) that Britain was finally admitted to the EEC. Even then, many people in Britain were unsure about membership of the EEC. In 1975, the Labour government held a referendum to find out whether Britain should remain a member of the EEC. Over 26 million people voted, and the result was two to one in favour of staying in.

In November 1993, the EEC became the EC (European Community) forming the basis for the European Union (EU). The EU is working towards even greater political and economic union between European countries. Some people think that Britain should be part of this move towards an even more integrated Europe. Others believe that Britain should be free to make its own political decisions, and would like to limit the power of the EU.

△ *The Euro* came into existence as a working currency on January 1, 1999. By 2002 it will have replaced the traditional currencies of many EU members.

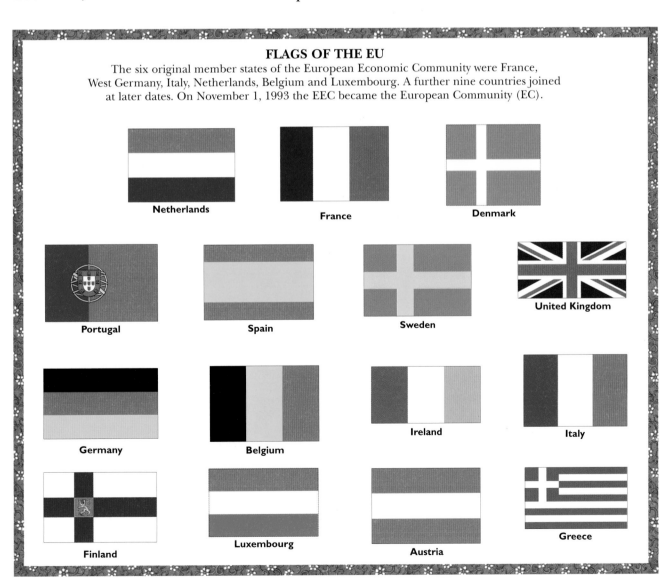

FLAGS OF THE EU

The six original member states of the European Economic Community were France, West Germany, Italy, Netherlands, Belgium and Luxembourg. A further nine countries joined at later dates. On November 1, 1993 the EEC became the European Community (EC).

Netherlands

France

Denmark

Portugal

Spain

Sweden

United Kingdom

Germany

Belgium

Ireland

Italy

Finland

Luxembourg

Austria

Greece

	500,000–5000 BC	5000BC–AD 0	AD 0–300	300–600	600–800
POLITICS	c.230,000 BC Neanderthal peoples arrive, ousting original hominid settlers c.30,000 BC Advanced Homo sapiens ousts Neanderthal species c.12,000 BC Human groups begin to return to Britain as Ice Age ends	c.2500 BC Beaker people migrate to Britain from Europe c.700 BC Celtic peoples begin to settle in Britain 55 BC Roman army led by Julius Caesar lands in southern England	43 Full-scale Roman invasion under Emperor Claudius 60 Revolt of the Iceni under Boudicca 296 Britain divided into four Roman provinces	367 Hadrian's Wall overrun by Picts and Scots 408 Saxon invasion begins; most Roman troops withdrawn 577 Decisive Saxon victory over Celts at Dyrham	736 Ethelbald declare himself first king of Britain 757-96 Offa unites an rules Mercia 789 First Viking raid on Britain
EXPLORATION	c.500,000 BC First human settlers arrive in Britain c.10,000 BC Settlers reach northwest coast of England c.7000 BC First settlements in Scotland and Ireland	c.4000 BC Orkney, Shetland and other remote islands colonized	84 Roman troops under Agricola penetrate Scottish Highlands c.150 First detailed world map shows Britain and Ireland	c.555 St Brendan sails from West of Ireland and claims to have reached America	c.726 Inc, King of We is one of many to dangerous pilgrim to Rome
TECHNOLOGY	c.450,000 BC Use of fire and flint hand-axes developed c.7000 BC Hunters begin to use bows and arrows	c.4500 BC New Stone Age begins; farming techniques established in Britain c.2150 BC Bronze Age begins c.750 BC Iron Age begins	c.120 Road-building programme begins 122 Romans start construction of Hadrian's Wall 160 Iron smelting flourishes in Sussex	c.300 Pottery industry flourishes in central England c.325 Large iron foundry established in Silchester, Hampshire	685 Completion of lar new monastery at Jarrow, Tyne and ' c.690 Development of new and better weapons, includin double-edged swo iron and steel 735 Bede states that t Earth is round
ARTS	c.500,000 BC First human settlers arrive in Britain c.10,000 BC Settlers reach northwest coast of England c.7000 BC First settlements in Scotland and Ireland	c.30 BC White Horse carved on chalk downs at Uffington,Oxfordshire	c.85 Lavish villas constructed, including Fishbourne in Sussex c.150 Romans redesign cities with grand civic buildings such as bath houses and fora	c.350 Silver treasure buried at Mildenhall, Suffolk c.590 Golden age of Anglo-Saxon jewellery-making begins	c.624 Ship burial of K Redwald with trea at Sutton Hoo, East Anglia c.670 The monk Caed writes first Christia poems in Anglo-Sa c.725 Anglo-Saxon po *Beowulf* written
RELIGION	c.24,000 BC Elaborate cave burial rituals at Paviland, South Wales	c.3700 BC Ritual burials in long barrows and chambered tombs common c.3000 BC Stone circles erected throughout British Isles c.70 BC Power of Druid priests grows	60 Romans destroy Druid stronghold on Anglesey c.200 Christianity reaches northern Britain	325 Christianity becomes the official religion of the Roman Empire 450 St Patrick begins the conversion of Ireland 597 St Augustine sent from Rome to convert the English	c.600 Death of St Davi Welsh missionary 664 Synod of Whitby affirms Roman Christian calendar 731 Bede completes History of the English Church
DAILY LIFE	c.23,000 BC Last Ice Age begins c.8500 BC Beginning of thaw; ice retreats again c.6500 BC Hunters burn patches of growing woodland to attract herds of game	c.4000 BC Farming settlements in most parts of Britain c.1500 BC Village communities develop, especially in southern England c.550 BC Hillforts built to protect scarce farmland	90-98 Roman colonies built at Lincoln and Gloucester 150 Bigger area of farmland brings bigger crops c.190 Six-hour working day introduced for all but slaves	c.370 Beginning of new villa-building boom, especially in southern England c.425 Economy collapses following end of Roman rule and Saxon attacks c.570 Anglo-Saxons now settled in small "states" ruled by kings	c.695 Southampton established as trading port c.710 Beginnings of fe system,with kings rewarding bands of retainers c.750 London now Britain's largest tov and major port

800–1000	1000–1100	1100–1200	1200–1300	1300–1350
Danish Great Army lands in Kent Alfred defeats the Danes at Edington Irish victory over Norse invaders at Tara	1042 Edward the Confessor becomes king of England 1066 Norman conquest of England led by William 1087 William I succeeded by William II	1100 Death of William I; Henry I becomes king 1139-53 Civil War in England during reign of Stephen 1154 Henry of Anjou invades England and becomes King Henry II	1215 King John signs Magna Carta 1272 Death of Henry III: Edward I becomes king 1282-83 Edward conquers Wales	1314 Robert the Bruce defeats English at Bannockburn 1337 Beginning of Hundred Years' War with France 1346-47 English successes at Crécy and Calais
Ohthere arrives at Alfred's court after exploring Lapland	1030 New map of Europe, including Britain, produced in Kent	1170 Prince Madoc of Wales alleged to have established a colony in North America	1280 New "Mappa Mundi", or world map, drawn for Hereford Cathedral	1304–11 Nearly 40,000 sacks of wool exported to Europe each year. Network of trading routes established with Near East
Vikings establish base at Dublin and dominate Irish Sea shipping	c.1000 Mint for gold coins founded at Bristol 1067 Programme of castle-building in England and Wales begins 1097 Completion of White Tower (later part of the Tower of London)	1100 Westminster Hall completed 1110 "Exchequer" cloth devised to calculate royal accounts	1222 Widespread introduction of windmills to East Anglia 1290 Completion of massive castle-building programme in Wales	c.1350 Introduction of plate armour
Completion of the beautifully illuminated *Book of Kells* in Ireland Alfred orders the making of gold and crystal jewels for his bishops Collection of many Anglo-Saxon poems, including *The Wanderer* and *The Seafarer*	c.1050 Irish legends and sagas written down in Latin and Gaelic 1077 Bayeux Tapestry completed	c.1133 Durham Cathedral completed 1136 Geoffrey of Monmouth writes History of the *Kings of Britain* 1176 First Eisteddfod of poetry and music held in Dyfed	c.1200 New stained glass windows in rebuilt Canterbury Cathedral c.1201 First troubadours arrive at English courts 1250 Matthew Parris produces illuminated *Chronicles*	c.1325 A collection of poems and prayers, the *Book of Kildare*, completed in Ireland 1330 The illuminated *St Omer Psalter* completed in East Anglia
Vikings ravage monastery on Iona for third time Monks flee Lindisfarne to escape Vikings Alfric publishes *Lives of the Saints*	1059-65 Rebuilding of Westminster Abbey 1070 First Norman appointed as Archbishop of Canterbury 1083 Founding of new priory on Lindisfarne	c.1128 First Cistercian monastery founded in Surrey 1170 Murder of Thomas Becket 1190-92 Richard I on Crusade to Holy Land	1221 Franciscan and Dominican friars arrive in England 1245 Work begins on rebuilding Westminster Abbey	1326 London mob murders the bishop of Exeter 1338 Inspections by bishops reveal low moral standards in many monasteries
Anglo-Saxon Chronicle begun Norse establish settlements, and many Norse words enter the language Tithes introduced	1013 England divided into shires 1067-69 Normans savagely put down rebellions in northern England 1086 Domesday survey carried out	1117 First leper hospital founded in London 1121 First royal Scottish burgh established at Berwick to encourage trade 1170 Population of London exceeds 30,000	1200 Links with France make greater variety of food available in England 1288 New "piepowder" courts set up to try offenders at local fairs 1290 Jews expelled from England	1315-16 Widespread famine in England and Wales 1327 Rising wool exports bring prosperity to Scotland 1348 First outbreak of Black Death in Britain

	1350–1400	1400–1450	1450–1500	1500–1550	1550–1600
POLITICS	1381 The Peasants' Revolt in southeast England 1388 Major Scots victory over English at Otterburn 1399 Richard II deposed and replaced by Henry IV	1400-10 Revolt of Owain Glyndwr in Wales 1415 English defeat French at Agincourt 1449-50 French recapture Normandy	1453 English rule in France ends with defeat in Gascony 1455 Wars of the Roses begin in England 1485 Henry Tudor seizes power after defeating Richard III at Bosworth	1509 Henry VIII becomes king of England 1536 Union of England and Wales 1542 English victory over invading Scots at Solway Moss	1558 Death of Mary; Elizabeth I becomes queen 1587 Execution of Mary Queen of Scots 1588 Defeat of the Spanish Armada
EXPLORATION	1399 Richard de Clare's expedition to Ireland cut short by rebellion at home	1419–20 English conquest of Normandy	1481 Bristol merchants sponsor exploration of the Atlantic Ocean westwards 1497 John Cabot crosses Atlantic to Newfoundland	1508–09 Cabot sails into Hudson Bay 1527 Cabot explores South American rivers	1553–54 Willoughby and Chancellor search for Northwest Passage 1576 Frobisher explores Baffin Bay and Hudson Strait 1581 Drake completes circumnavigation of the world
TECHNOLOGY	1352 First weight-driven striking clock installed at Windsor 1367 King David II orders new fortifications at Edinburgh castle	1410 Stone bridge built across the Clyde at Glasgow	c.1450 Invention of the astrolabe for studying the stars 1457 Giant siege gun, "Mons Meg", manuafactured in Edinburgh 1478 Caxton produces first printed book in England	1502 Coalmining begins in Bradford area 1507 Italian alchemist fails in attempt to fly from battlements of Stirling Castle, Scotland 1545 Henry's flagship, the *Mary Rose*, sinks at Portsmouth	1564 Horse-drawn coach introduced from the Netherlands 1571 First Irish book, *A Gaelic Alphabet and Catechism*, printed in Ireland 1571 Theodolite for measuring angles invented by Digges
ARTS	c.1370 English poem *Piers Plowman* written 1392 English poet Geoffrey Chaucer begins *The Canterbury Tales* c.1396 Religious painting, called the *Wilton Diptych*, commissioned by Richard II	1412 Cloisters of Gloucester Cathedral completed 1430 English poet John Lydgate writes *Pageant of Knowledge* 1446 Building begins of King's College Chapel, Cambridge	1469 Thomas Malory completed his *Morte d'Arthur*, an account of King Arthur c.1480 Scots poet Robert Henryson writes *The Testament of Cresseid* 1495 Morality play *Everyman* first performed in England	1516 Thomas More writes *Utopia* 1516 Wolsey builds Hampton Court Palace 1527 German painter Hans Holbein begins work in London	1552 Cranmer completes *Second Book of Common Prayer* 1553 Mary restores Catholic rule, and Protestants Ridley and Latimer burned at the stake 1565 Founding of Puritan movement in Cambridge
RELIGION	1373 Mystic Julian of Norwich cured after visions of God 1384 Death of heretic John Wycliffe, leader of the Lollards	1401 Death penalty introduced for heretics 1407 Archbishop of Canterbury leads campaign against Lollards	1472 Scotland's first archbishop is appointed	1526 Bishops order the burning of Tyndale's English translation of the New Testament 1533 Henry declares himself head of the Church, beginning English Reformation 1549 *First Book of Common Prayer* compiled	1575 Publication of collection of Sacred Songs by Thomas Tallis and William Byrd c.1588–1613 Writing career of William Shakespeare 1597 Completion of Hardwick Hall, Derbyshire
DAILY LIFE	c.1351 Peasants' wages rise as plague makes labour scarce 1360 Major outbreak of Black Death in Ireland 1363 Football banned on holidays in England, to encourage people to practise archery	1407 Bethlehem Hospital (Bedlam) in London becomes first institution for the insane 1424 King James imposes first tax in Scotland for 50 years 1443 Riots by tradesmen in Norwich	1479 Severe outbreak of plague in England c.1480 Extravagant fashions at English court c.1490 Wool trade brings great prosperity to East Anglia	1505 Royal College of Surgeons founded in Edinburgh 1518 Landowners enclose common lands for grazing sheep 1536 Beginning of dissolution of the monasteries	1557 Third successive year of bad harvest causes famine 1557 Protestant settlers "planted" in Laois and Offaly, Ireland 1572 New Poor Law provides parish relief for the needy

1600–25	1625–50	1650–75	1675–1700	1700–25
ames VI of Scotland ›ecomes James I, first tuart king of England ›nd Ireland Gunpowder Plot to ›low up Parliament ails and conspirators re executed Protestation of Iouse of Commons tating right of MPs to ree speech	1625 Death of James I. Charles succeeds as Charles I 1642 Civil War breaks out in England between supporters of King Charles and Parliamentarians 1649 Execution of King Charles I. England becomes a republic under Cromwell	1651 Defeat of Royalist troops at Worcester. Charles II escapes to France 1652 Act of Settlement – 6 Irish counties are cleared of Catholic landholders and settled by English Protestants 1660 Restoration of monarchy, King Charles II takes throne	1685 Death of Charles II. Succeeded by his brother as James II 1688 "Glorious Revolution" 1689 Parliament declares abdication of James II. William and Mary take over throne jointly James lands in Ireland and is defeated at Battle of the Boyne (1690)	1701 English Parliament passes Act of Settlement ensuring Protestant succession to throne 1702 Death of William. Anne succeeds to the throne 1707 Act of Union 1714 Death of Queen Anne. The Elector of Hanover is proclaimed George I 1715 Jacobite rebellion fails
Colony of Virginia ounded "Plantation of Ulster" Protestant settlers move ›n to land taken from ‹rish Catholics	1629 Massachusetts Bay Company obtains charter from Charles I 1630 About 1000 Puritans settle in Massachusetts under Governor John Winthrop	1661 Bombay becomes British trading post, ceded by Portugal 1663 Royal African Company set up to trade in slaves, ivory and gold	1686 East India Company base established at Calcutta, India 1691 Plymouth Colony is annexed to Massachusetts Bay	1708 Rescue of Alexander Selkirk, the model for Robinson Crusoe from an island off the coast of Chile
British trading station ›pens in Surat, India	1645 Meetings of the "Invisible College" – group of scientists who met in London and Oxford	1666 Isaac Newton (1642–1727) discovers nature of white light by passing light through prism 1668 Newton builds first reflecting telescope 1669 Newton invents calculus	1675 Royal Observatory opens in Greenwich 1687 Publication of Newton's *Mathematical Principles of Natural Philosophy* 1698 Thomas Savery develops steam pump 1699–1703 First Eddystone lighthouse designed by Henry Winstanley	1701 Introduction of Jethro Tull's horse-drawn seed drill 1705 Thomas Newcomen develops steam-powered pumping engine for use in mines 1709 Abraham Darby develops coke-fired blast furnace
Death of Shakespeare	1634 John Milton writes *Comus* 1642–60 Theatres shut down in England	1653 Izaak Walton writes *The Compleat Angler* 1659 Samuel Pepys begins his diaries 1660 Royal Society is founded 1667 Milton writes *Paradise Lost*	1680 Henry Purcell is organist at Westminster Abbey 1689 Publication of *Essay Concerning Human Understanding* by John Locke 1689 First production of Purcell's *Dido and Aeneas*	1715 G. F. Handel writes Water Music 1719 Daniel Defoe writes Robinson Crusoe
Publication of the Authorized Version of the Bible, known as the King James Bible	1637 Riot in Edinburgh after Charles tries to force Scots to use a new Anglican prayerbook 1639–40 Bishops' Wars fought between Charles and the Scots	1645 Presbyterianism is made official religion in England 1648 George Fox founds the Society of Friends (Quakers)	1675 Rebuilding of St Paul's Cathedral begins 1678 John Bunyan writes *The Pilgrim's Progress*	1710 Building of St Paul's Cathedral completed
James I issues Book of Sports which permits a variety of sports. It provokes objections from Puritans Publication of the *Corante*, the first English newspaper	1634 Opening of Covent Garden Market, London	1650 Tea first drunk in England 1652 First coffee house opens in London 1665 Great Plague causes thousands of deaths 1666 Great Fire of London (3–6 September)	1692 Lloyd's Coffee House, London, becomes insurance office 1694 Bank of England set up 1695 Window tax enforced in England	1720 Collapse of South Sea company leaves thousands of people financially ruined

	1725–50	1750–75	1775–1800	1800–25	1825–50
POLITICS	1721 Robert Walpole becomes Britain's first prime minister 1727 Death of George I. He is succeeded by Prince of Wales as George II 1745–6 Jacobite rebellion led by Bonnie Prince Charlie. British army defeats Jacobites at Battle of Culloden	1756–63 Seven Years' War 1760 Death of George II. He is succeeded by his grandson (son of Frederick Louis) as George III 1773 Boston Tea Party (16 December) 1775–83 American War of Independence	1776 American Declaration of Independence 1783 Treaty of Versailles. Britain recognises United States 1788 Illness of king provokes "Regency Crisis" 1789 Start of French Revolution 1793 France declares war on Britain	1800 Act of Union establishes the United Kingdom of Great Britain and Ireland 1805 Nelson defeats French–Spanish fleet at the Battle of Trafalgar (21 October) 1815 Wellington defeats the French at the Battle of Waterloo (18 June) 1820 George III dies. George IV succeeds	1830 George IV dies. William IV succee[d] 1834 Slavery abolishe[d] British Empire 1837 Death of Willia[m] succeeded by Victo[ria] 1846 Repeal of Corn [Laws] Free trade in corn established 1848 Feargus O'Conn[or] presents third Cha[rtist] petition. It is rejec[ted] by parliament
EXPLORATION	1740 George Anson begins round-the-world voyage	1768–71 First voyage of Captain Cook on *Endeavour*. Scientific voyage to Pacific Ocean 1772–5 Second voyage on ships *Resolution* and *Adventure* to cirumnavigate and investigate the Antarctic	1776 Third voyage on ships *Resolution* and *Discovery* to look for northwest passage around Canada and Alaska 1779 Cook is killed in Hawaii 1780 *Resolution* and *Discovery* return to Britain	1812 William Moorcroft explores Tibet	1831 James Clark Ros[s] reaches North Magnetic Pole 1833 East India Comp[any] becomes administ[rative] agent in India for British governmen[t]
TECHNOLOGY	1731 Publication of *The New Horse Houghing Husbandry* by Jethro Tull 1733 John Kay develops flying shuttle	1757 Sankey Brook Navigation completed 1761 Bridgewater Canal from Worsley to Manchester opened. 1764 "Spinning Jenny" developed 1769 Richard Arkwright patents water-frame (water-powered spinning machine); James Watt patents improved steam engine	1779 First iron bridge built across river Severn 1782 James Watt develops rotary steam engine 1784 Henry Cort develops puddling iron 1784 Edmund Cartwright invents power loom 1796 Edward Jenner proves vaccination theory	1804 Richard Trevithick's steam locomotive 1815 Invention of Davy safety lamp for use in mines by Sir Humphry Davy 1825 Opening of Stockton to Darlington railway	1829 Success of Georg[e] Stephenson's *Rock[et]* Rainhill steam tria[l] 1830 Opening of Live[rpool] and Manchester ra[ilway] 1835 Cooke and Wheatstone take out patent on electric telegraph 1843 Launch of Great Britain, first iron-h[ulled] steamship driven b[y] screw propeller
ARTS	1726 Jonathan Swift writes *Gulliver's Travels* 1728 *The Beggar's Opera* written by Pepusch and John Gay 1737 Start of censorship of plays in England 1747 Samuel Johnson starts work on his dictionary	1759 Opening of British Museum 1768 Royal Academy of Arts is founded	1776 Adam Smith writes *Wealth of Nations* 1789 William Blake writes *Songs of Innocence*	1811–18 Publication of Jane Austen's six great novels. 1813 Founding of Philharmonic Society of London. 1822 Royal Academy of Music founded in London.	1830 William Cobbett writes *Rural Rides* 1835 Charles Dickens [writes] *Sketches by Boz* 1838 National Gallery opens.
RELIGION	1739 John Wesley begins his life as an open-air preacher 1744 First Methodist conference held at Foundry Chapel, London	1756 John Wesley publishes *Twelve Reasons against a Separation from the Church*	1795 Separation of Methodist and Anglican churches	1801 Church Missionary Society founded 1804 British and Foreign Bible Society formed in London 1807 Clapham Sect formed to campaign on social issues	1827 John Nelson Dar[by] founds Plymouth Brethren 1829 Catholic Emancipation Act [–] Catholics allowed t[o sit] in parliament
DAILY LIFE	1725 Guy's Hospital founded 1732 Completion of first Covent Garden Theatre 1744 First official cricket match in Britain	1751–72 Over 380 turnpike Acts passed through Parliament 1752 Britain adopts Gregorian calendar and "loses" ll days 1773 Stock Exchange founded	1779 Derby horse race at Epsom runs for the first time 1782–1820 First period of Highland Clearances 1799 Combination Act prevents "combinations" of workers	1807 Britain ends slave trade 1811 Beginning of Luddite disturbances 1813 Elizabeth Fry begins prison reform 1819 "Peterloo Massacre" in Manchester 1824 Repeal of Combination Act	1840 Introduction of Rowland Hill's Penny Post 1840-54 Second perio[d] Highland Clearanc[es] 1844 "Ragged Schools" [set] up for poorest chil[dren] 1845–9 Failure of pota[to] crop in Ireland is followed by famine 1848 Public Health Ac[t] set up boards of he[alth] 1854–6 Crimean War

1850–75	1875–1900	1900–25	1925–50	1950–90s
Prince Albert dies (14 December) Second Reform Act gives vote to about one in three working men	1877 Queen Victoria is proclaimed Empress of India 1879–1902 Boer Wars in South Africa 1885 Third Reform Act 1885 First Home Rule Bill defeated in House of Commons	1901 Death of Queen Victoria. Succeeded by Edward VII 1909 Lloyd George's "People's Budget" rejected by House of Lords 1910 Death of King Edward VII. Succeeded by George V 1914–18 World War I 1916 Easter Uprising in Dublin	1926 General strike 1929 New York Stock Exchange crash and start of Great Depression 1939–45 World War II 1945 Labour wins general election 1948 *Empire Windrush* arrives with 492 Jamaican immigrants on board	1952 Death of George VI. He is succeeded by Elizabeth II 1973 Britain becomes a member of EEC 1979 Margaret Thatcher becomes Britain's first woman prime minister 1997 Labour win the general election 1998 Northern Ireland peace agreement
–6 David Livingstone explores the Zambesi river John Speke and Richard Burton reach Lake Tanganyika Henry Stanley sets out to look for Livingstone	1876–7 Henry Morton Stanley explores Lake Tanganyika	1907–9 Expedition in Antarctica of Ernest Shackleton 1910–2 Robert Falcon Scott's attempt to reach to South Pole ends in disaster, with death of all five members of the expedition	1933 Wilfred Thesiger crosses Danakil in Ethiopia	1953 Edmund Hillary and Norgay Tenzing become first people to climb Mount Everest. Vivien Fuchs makes first crossing of Antarctica 1981–2 Ranulph Fiennes' Transglobe expedition circumnavigates world around the poles
Over 6000 miles of railway track open Underwater cable laid across English Channel Henry Bessemer's new method of making steel Launch of *Great Eastern*, first ship with double iron hull *Great Eastern* used to lay underwater cable across Atlantic Ocean	1880 Over 15,000 miles of railway track open 1876 Alexander Bell sends first voice message along a telegraph line 1878 Joseph Swan makes successful light bulb	1917 Ernest Rutherford splits the atom 1920 First public broadcasting service opens in Britain	1926 John Logie Baird invents television 1928 Alexander Fleming discovers penicillin 1937 Frank Whittle builds first jet engine	1957 First atomic bomb exploded by Britain in the Pacific 1969 US astronaut Neil Armstrong becomes first man on the Moon 1978 Louise Brown first test-tube baby born 1984 First Apple Macintosh computer goes on sale 1994 Completion of the Channel Tunnel
Charles Darwin writes *Origin of Species* George Eliot writes *The Mill on the Floss* Lewis Carroll writes *Alice in Wonderland*	1883 Royal College of Music founded in London 1883 Robert Louis Stevenson writes *Treasure Island* 1895 Beginning of Promenade Concerts in London	1909 Vaughan Williams composes *Fantasy on a Theme by Tallis* 1913 D. H. Lawrence writes *Sons and Lovers* 1914 Charlie Chaplin creates film character *The Tramp*	1926 A A Milne writes *Winnie the Pooh* 1935 T.S. Eliot writes *Murder in the Cathedral*	1956 Bill Haley's hit "Rock Around the Clock". 1963 "Please Please Me" becomes Beatles' first number 1 hit 1985 "Live Aid" rock concert raises money for famine relief 1998 Museum of Pop Music opens in Sheffield
Bishop Wilberforce attacks Darwin's theory of evolution William Booth founds Salvation Army	1890 James Frazer writes *The Golden Bough: A Study in magic and Religion* 1895 Construction of Catholic cathedral at Westminster begins	1917 Balfour Declaration: Britain backs homeland for Jews in Palestine 1920 Disestablishment of Anglican Church in Wales	1929 Presbyterian churches in Scotland unite	1968–9 Civil Rights marches in Northern Ireland 1970 Completion of New English Bible 1982 Pope John Paul II visits Britain 1994 First women priests ordained in the Church of England 1995 Opening of Hindu temple in Neasden
Factory Act establishes standard working day Great Exhibition held in Crystal Palace, Hyde Park, London First Trades Union Congress (TUC) in Manchester Education Act sets up School Boards and aims to "cover the country with good schools"	1875 Public Health Act sets up authorities to oversee housing, sanitation etc 1880 Education Act makes school compulsory for children aged 5–10 1887 Queen Victoria celebrates her Diamond Jubilee	1906 Education Act to provide free school meals for poor 1907 Education Act to provide medical inspections in schools 1908 Coal Mines Act fixes working day to 8 hours 1912 Sinking of the *Titanic* 1918 Vote given to women over 30 if they are ratepayers or wives of ratepayers	1928 Vote given to all women over 21 1931–2 Almost 3 million people (22 percent of workforce) unemployed 1936 Jarrow Crusade 1940 "Blitz" in London 1948 Start of National Health Service	1951 Festival of Britain 1958 Formation of Campaign for Nuclear Disarmament (CND) 1967 Abortion Act makes termination of pregnancies legal 1969 Divorce Reform Act 1975 Equal Opportunities Act introduced 1981 Social Democratic Party (SDP) founded

KINGS AND QUEENS

Boudicca (Iceni tribe leader) led
  revolt against Romans in AD 60

King Arthur thought to have
  defeated Saxons in AD 500

Ethelbald of Mercia proclaims
  himself king of all Saxon
  kingdoms 736

Offa is first proper English king
  757–796

The Viking King Canute rules
  England 1016–1035

Edward "the Confessor" 1035–1066
Harold 1066 (killed at Battle
  of Hastings)

William "the Conqueror"
  (William I) 1066–1087

William II (William Rufus)
  1087–1100

Henry I 1100–1135

David I (Scotland) 1124–1153

Stephen 1135–1154

Malcolm IV (Scotland) 1153–1165

The Plantagenets

Henry II 1154–1189

William I (Scotland) 1165–1214

Richard I 1189–1199

John 1199–1216

Alexander II (Scotland) 1214–1249
  (Britain ruled by council
  1216–1232)

Henry III 1216–1272

Llywelyn I "the Great" (Wales)
  1219–1240

Llywelyn II "the Last" (Wales)
  1240–1283

Alexander III (Scotland)
  1249–1306

Edward I 1272–1307

Prince Edward (son of Edward I)
  crowned Prince of Wales 1301

Robert Bruce (Scotland)
  1306–1329

Edward II 1307–1327

Edward III 1327–1377

Richard II 1377–1399

Henry IV 1399–1413

Owain Glyn Dwr pronounced
  Prince of Wales 1400

Henry V 1413–1422

House of Lancaster

Henry VI 1422–1453 (declared
  insane and York is appointed
  protector) –1455 King recovers
  –1461 deposed

House of York

Edward of York 1461–1470

House of Lancaster

Henry reinstated 1470–1471

House of York

Edward V 1471–1483

Richard III (Richard of
  Gloucester) 1483–1485

The Tudors

Henry VII (Henry Tudor)
  1485–1509

Henry VIII 1509–1547

Edward VI 1547–1553

Jane Grey 1553 (nine days)

Mary 1553–1558

Elizabeth I 1558–1603

House of Hanover

George I 1714–27

George II 1727–60

George III 1760–1820

George IV (Prince Regent
 1811–20) 1820–30

William IV 1830–7

Victoria 1837–1901

House of Saxe-Coburg-Gotha (Windsor after 1917)

Edward VII 1901–10

George V 1910–36

Edward VIII 1936 (abdicated)

George VI 1936–52

Elizabeth II 1952–

House of Stuart

James I (James VI of Scotland)
 1603–1625

Charles I 1625–1649 (executed)

Republicans rule 1649–1660

Charles II (The restoration)
 1660–1685

James II 1685–1688

William of Orange and Mary
 (Glorious revolution) 1688–1702

Anne 1702–1714

BATTLES IN BRITISH HISTORY

500 BC Many hillforts are constructed, and civil wars begin to break out

55 BC First attempted invasion of Britain by Julius Caesar

AD 43 Successful Roman invasion of Britain under Claudius (advance throughout country continued for next 20 years)

367 Roman Britain is raided by Picts, Scots, Saxons and Irish

408 Saxon invasion of Britain

500 Celtic Briton victory over Anglo-Saxons at Mount Badon, led by King Arthur

789 First of the major Viking raids

793 Sacking of the monastery at Lindisfarne

878 Defeat of Danes at Edington in Wiltshire

1066 Battle of Stamford Bridge

1066 Battle of Hastings

1096 The First Crusade; Jerusalem retaken

1139 Civil War

1147 Second Crusade

1189–91 Third Crusade

1202–54 Four more crusades

1264 Civil War

1271 Eighth crusade

1314 Battle of Bannockburn

1337–1453 Hundred Years War (England and France)

1346 Battle of Crécy

1356 Battle of Poitiers

1381 Peasants' Revolt

1415 Battle of Agincourt (England–France)

1455 Civil war (War of the Roses) begins

1485 Battle of Bosworth Field

1513 Battle of Flodden
(England–Scotland)

1534 The Reformation

1536 England united with Wales

1585 War between England
and Spain

1588 Defeat of Spanish Armada
(invasion averted)

1594 Start of Nine Years' War
between England and Ireland

1603 Irish starved into surrender
and war ends

1624–30 War with Spain

1626–9 War with France

1642–6, 1648 Civil Wars

1690 Battle of the Boyne

1701–13 War of the
Spanish Succession

1704 Battle of Blenheim

1715 and 1745 Jacobite Rebellions

1740–8 War of the
Austrian Succession

1746 Battle of Culloden

1756–63 Seven Years' War

1775–83 War of American
Independence

1793–1815 Wars with France

1805 Battle of Trafalgar

1815 Battle of Waterloo

1839–42 First
Opium War

1845–6, 1848–1849
Sikh wars

1854–5 Crimean War

1856–60 Second Opium War

1857–8 Indian Mutiny/
First War of Independence

1878–9 Zulu War

1880–1 First South African War

1899–1902 Boer War

1914–18 World War I

1916 Battle of the Somme, Battle
of Jutland

1916–21 Anglo-Irish conflict

1917 Battle of Passchendaele

1939–45 World War II

1940 Battle of Britain

1942 Battle of El Alamein

1944 D-day invasion

1952–60 Mau Mau revolt

1956 Suez Crisis

1969–98 Northern Ireland

1982 Falklands War

1990 Gulf War

Index

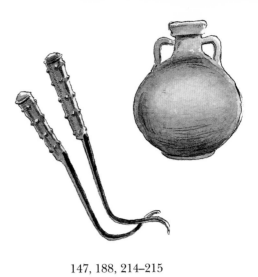

SEMPER EADEM

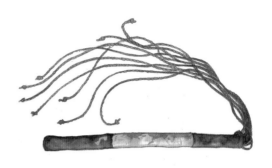

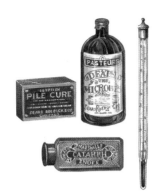

Acknowledgements

The publishers wish to thank the following artists who have contributed to this book:

Richard Hook, Vanessa Card, Peter Sarson, Mike White, James Field,
Mike Taylor, Stephen Sweet, Alison Winfield, Mel Pickering, Stephan Chabluk,
Theodore Rowland-Entwistle, Mike Lacey, Sue Stitt, Roger Kent, Roger Payne,
Martin Sanders, Rob Sheffield, David Ashby, Chris Forsey, Simon Girling Associates,
Linden Artists and Temple Rogers Agency.

The publishers wish to thank the following for supplying photographs for this book:

Page 22 (CL) ET Archive; 25 (TR) ET Archive; 27 (CR) English Heritage; 36 (CL)
English Heritage; 41 (TR) Corbis (BR) English Heritage; 43 (BR) ET Archive; 44 (BL)
ET Archive; 46 (BL) ET Archive; 48 (TL) Corbis; 56 (CL) ET Archive; 59 (TR) ET
Archive; 60 (BR) ET Archive; 66 (BL) Corbis; 70 (TR) English Heritage; 73 (TR) ET
Archive; 75 (CR) ET Archive; 79 (TR) ET Archive; 81 (TR) Corbis; 83 (TR) ET
Archive; 85 (TR) ET Archive; 87 (BR) ET Archive; 87 (TR) ET Archive; 99 (CR) AKG
London; 102 (BL) AKG London; 105 (BR) AKG London; 107 (BR) AKG London;
109 (TR) AKG London; 90 (BL) AKG London; 124 (BL) AKG London;
128 (BL) AKG London; 130 (BL) ET Archive; 136 (TL) ET Archive; 139 (BR) ET
Archive; 141 (BR) ET Archive; 145 (TR) AKG London; 147 (TR) ET Archive; 160
(BL) ET Archive; 175 (TR) AKG London, (TFR) AKG London; 177 (BR) AKG
London; 186 (CL) AKG London.

All other photographs from Miles Kelly Archives.